CIVICS AND THE
CONSTITUTION

AN AMERICAN VIEW OF LAW, LIBERTY, & GOVERNMENT

MICHAEL A. PEROUTKA,
JAKE MACAULAY & RICKI PEPIN

First printing: June 2019
Second printing: February 2021

ISBN: 978-1-68344-168-7
ISBN: 978-1-61458-713-2 (digital)

Cover Design: Diana Bogardus
Book Design: Terry White

Unless otherwise noted, Scripture quotations are from the King James Version of the Bible.

Printed in the United States of America

Please visit our website for other great titles:
www.masterbooks.com

For information regarding author interviews, please contact the publicity department at (870) 438-5288.

Publishers' Note:
This course is modified from The Institute of the Constitution's course on the U.S. Constitution. The course originally had 12 lectures instead of the current 15; therefore, the video may sometimes reference lectures, page numbers, etc. that are different from what is written in the book. Please follow the book references rather than the video references.

Disclaimer:
This course was developed by Institute on the Constitution as an educational outreach. We are not providing legal advice nor practicing law through this forum.

Note from Authors:

Dear Friends,

Welcome to this course developed by the Institute on the Constitution! As one of the founders of the Institute, I want to commend you for your interest in constitutional government and for your love and respect of America.

As you work through this course, you should know that you are taking part in the noble experiment in self-government that our Founders envisioned. It is essential that all Americans have a foundational understanding of the proper role and limits of civil government in these United States of America, and that this understanding be passed on to our children and to their children. Liberty under law is our heritage and it is the blessing we earnestly seek to preserve for posterity.

For God, the Family, and the Republic,

Michael A. Peroutka

A Dedication

This course of study is dedicated to the memory of Georgia State Representative Bobby Franklin, whose faithful Christian witness and tireless commitment to The American View of Law, Liberty, and Government, inspire us to persevere and to plow our row in Our Master's field. For more information, please visit TheAmericanView.com and see the Profiles in Courage page.

Unless otherwise noted, all images are from istock.com, Library of Congress (LOC-image), and Wikimedia Commons. Other photos are public domain (PD-US) and (PD-Art).

ABOUT THE AUTHORS

Michael Anthony Peroutka, Esquire, is a lifelong student of American history and jurisprudence and cofounder of the Institute on the Constitution. In 2004, he was the Constitution Party's candidate for President of the United States. In 2014, Michael was elected to serve on the County Council for Anne Arundel County, Maryland. Having authored hundreds of commentaries on law and liberty for WCBM radio in Maryland and hosted a radio series on the American View of law and government for WNAV in Annapolis and WAVA in Washington, D.C., he has also appeared on ABC, CNN, C-SPAN, and FOX News.

Pastor David P. Whitney serves as Senior Instructor at Institute on the Constitution. In that capacity, he has authored courses of instruction on the Constitutions of the State of Maryland and the Commonwealth of Virginia and has made numerous radio appearances as an expert in American constitutional law and history. David graduated from Rutgers University as a Henry Rutgers Honors Scholar with Honors in History. He received his master's degree from Denver Seminary and serves as pastor of Cornerstone Evangelical Free Church in Pasadena, Maryland.

Jake MacAulay serves as the Chief Executive Officer of the Institute on the Constitution. An ordained minister and former syndicated talk show host, Jake has been instrumental in educating tens of thousands of constitutionalists across America. An energetic and entertaining presenter, Jake has been seen on Yahoo News, Fox News, The Blaze, AP, CBS, NBC, and The Weekly Standard.

Ricki Pepin is a former employee of the FBI, a published author and international lecturer. Her primary passion is teaching citizens how to work together to restore America's foundations. To that end, she has been leading courses on the U.S. Constitution as the head of the Ohio state chapter of the Institute on the Constitution.

Our Mission

Institute on the Constitution (IOTC) is a non-profit 501(c)3 corporation headquartered in Pasadena, Maryland.

Our desire is to help Americans understand their own history and to learn and fully appreciate their own heritage by reacquainting them with the worldview and vision of America's Founders.

We want to encourage individuals, families, churches, legislatures, and civic and other organizations to become conversant with the foundational principles on which American civil government and proper jurisprudence rest.

Our Challenge

Alexis de Tocqueville, a French aristocrat who toured America during the 1830s and who wrote extensively of his observation of American culture, after noting American ignorance about European affairs, wrote the following:

But if you question him [the average American]

respecting his own country, the cloud which dimmed his

intelligence will immediately disperse; his language will

become as clear and as precise as his thoughts. He will

inform you what his rights are, and by what means he

exercises them…The American learns to know

the laws by participating in the act of legislation; and he

takes a lesson in the forms of government from governing.

The great work of society is ever going on beneath his eyes,

and, as it were, under his hands.

Clearly, major changes have occurred in America since the time of Tocqueville's observations, and we suffer the results of our current ignorance of our history by living in a culture that gradually acquiesces to increasing infringements on rights and liberties that our founders considered God-given and unalienable.

The Vision

What to do? Let us, first of all, thank God for the freedoms that He has allowed us to retain and let us begin to recover the lost tools of self-government by learning about our place in His history. Let us learn the history of our own country, and the plan that our Founders fashioned for its preservation. The purpose of that plan was set forth in the Declaration of Independence in 1776, and the structure of that plan took the form of an agreement between the sovereign states known as the United States Constitution.

We need to study these profound documents and the historical context in which they were written and adopted. We need, furthermore, to understand the religious and philosophical worldview of the drafters of the Constitution and the clear intent of the States in ratifying a document that set forth the limited nature of the powers being vested in the Federal government. We need to understand the Founders' intent in adopting a Bill of Rights that acted as a check on the power of Congress and the executive authority from infringing the rights of the people from whom their authority was derived.

Regrettably, but perhaps not surprisingly, the public schools have failed to properly teach American history and government. There seems to be a systematic and organized attempt to disconnect the youth of America from their heritage so that, at the present, although but a few generations from our Founders, school children have very little concept of basic principles that their forefathers fought and died to defend.

The materials you hold in your hand are designed to help you appreciate the worldview and political theory on which American law and justice are founded. We hope that they will also empower you to articulate and defend the American view of law, liberty, and government and to pass on the "blessings of liberty" to your children and grandchildren.

TABLE OF CONTENTS

Quick Start Guide

1. Read the opening quotes, general objective, and specific objectives of the lecture.

2. Watch the lecture video.

3. Review the lecture video notes.

4. Read the lecture's related topic information.

5. Review the notes or the lecture video. (Optional)

6. Complete the lecture review worksheet. (Teacher Guide)

7. Complete any additional worksheets for the lecture. (Teacher Guide - Optional)

8. Complete the lecture quiz. (Teacher Guide)

9. For additional information and videos on matters pertaining to the Constitution and related news, please visit: theamericanview.com.

10. If you are interested in looking up words from *Webster's 1828 Dictionary*, it can be found at: http://webstersdictionary1828.com.

Note: Chapters 15, 16, and 17 do not have an associated video lecture. Students will read the lecture (including historical documents) in this student book and complete the assignments in the Teacher Guide. Video Lecture 15 is associated with Chapter 18 in the book.

About this course:

This course is based on a system of learning known as the Principle Approach — the method of education used by our Founding Fathers. This system enables students to begin to think and reason for themselves from a biblical worldview. Unlike our current education system that teaches students what to think, the Principle Approach uses definitions from *Noah Webster's 1828 Dictionary*, seven biblical principles, and leading questions to help students search out the truth in any subject.

The Principle Approach method is known as the Four R's:

- **Research** – using the Bible, *Webster's 1828 Dictionary,* and other primary sources, such as the Founders' original writings, so as to better define terms.

- **Reason** – using leading questions to identify truth or former misconceptions.

- **Relate** – connecting this truth to history, a current event or any subject before us.

- **Record** – writing or applying the knowledge; i.e. contacting Congressmen or speaking to others with constitutional or principled arguments rather than opinions.

Traditionally, schools who use this approach have been successful. The students from these schools have consistently maintained their biblical worldview through the years. They are becoming citizens who can consistently think and reason from a biblical perspective, absolutely an essential element in restoring America to its biblical foundations of limited, constitutional government.

Using the Principle Approach

It was this process of learning that led to the very documents and form of government that we are studying in this Constitution course. It is for this reason that we have incorporated this approach into the development of the materials in this course. You will learn how to think, not be told what to think!

Webster's 1828 Dictionary Definitions

Noah Webster was a master of 27 languages and dedicated years of his life to compiling the first American dictionary. His mastery of languages combined with his strong Christian underpinnings are two main reasons for using this specific dictionary, but the third and greatest reason is to overcome modern revisionist definitions of words and terms. Words matter and their meaning shouldn't change, but unfortunately over time, people use words in ways that alter their meaning in popular culture. Therefore, it is vital that you understand the context of the word in the historical time and place and how it was used. When you are assessing a document like the Declaration of Independence or the U.S. Constitution, words matter a lot and it is vital you review it with the definitions of the time to know what the Founding Fathers really meant and how important these words were for them to be included in these and other historical documents with their original meaning. This is why *Webster's 1828 Dictionary* definitions are key to this course. The following example will dramatically demonstrate this phenomenon:

- Right – conformity to standards or prevailing conditions[1] *(Harcourt Brace Dictionary, 1968)*

- Right – according to the will of God[2] *(Webster's 1828 Dictionary)*

The modern dictionary declares that "right" is determined by the circumstances in which we find ourselves — no absolute standard — whereas *Webster's 1828 Dictionary* establishes an absolute truth.

---

1 *Harcourt Brace Intermediate Dictionary*, (New York: Harcourt, Brace & World, 1968), p. 631.
2 Definition for the word as an adverb – see definition 2. http://webstersdictionary1828.com/Dictionary/right

Seven Biblical Principles

The Seven Biblical Principles are listed below and are emphasized throughout the course.

1. God's Sovereignty

2. Man's Individuality

3. Government – as related to Self, Family, Church, and Civil realms

4. Property or Stewardship

5. Christian Character

6. Sowing and Reaping or Education

7. Unity and Union or Covenant

Leading Questions

The purpose of leading ideas or questions is to guide the student to the biblical or constitutional root of any issue, policy or law. Using the Four R's (Research, Reason, Relate, Record) to answer these questions, students are taken through a process of thinking that teaches them a biblical worldview. Examples of some leading questions are as follows:

1. What is the foundation of all law?

2. What is the purpose of law?

3. Does this policy, action, law, or idea adhere to the principles of our U.S. Constitution?

Answers to these basic research questions are built upon by asking more leading questions to teach the student biblical reasoning, and ultimately relating that reasoning to the question before them. The questions used in this course, including in the teacher guide, are done with this method, so it is important that you understand this concept. (See the example of Figure 1, pages 11-12.)

The teacher guide for this course contains your daily schedule for this semester course, as well as worksheets and quizzes for you to complete after each lecture and lesson.

VIDEO LECTURES

This course also includes 15 video lectures led by Michael Anthony Peroutka, founder of IOTC and former Presidential Candidate, along with Jake MacAulay, ordained minister, former syndicated talk show host and current President of the IOTC. Students can watch the lessons as they follow along and add to the video notes included in their student book.

Figure 1 - The Principle Approach In Action

PRESS RELEASE STATEMENT - 1973:

The Supreme Court decision of Roe v. Wade made abortion the law of the land, legal in all 50 states.

 RESEARCH:

Leading Question #1: What is the foundation of all Law?

Answer #1 – The Laws of Nature and of Nature's God.

Source(s) #1 – Declaration of Independence, U.S. Constitution, *Webster's 1828 Dictionary*

Leading Question #2: What are the Laws of Nature and of Nature's God?

Answer #1 – The Laws of Nature's God is the Moral Law contained in the Ten Commandments as written by the finger of God.

Source(s) #1 – *Webster's 1828 Dictionary*

Answer #2 – The Law of Nature is a rule of conduct arising out of the natural relations of human beings established by the Creator, and existing prior to any positive [written] precept. Thus, it is a law of nature that one man should not injure another, and murder and fraud would be crimes, independent of any [written] prohibition from the supreme power.

Source(s) #2 – *Webster's 1828 Dictionary*

 REASON

In other words, the Laws of Nature and of Nature's God come from God and the Bible. The first is written, the other is intuitively and instinctively known to man, written in his heart by God, his Creator. Both are derived from the principle of God's Sovereignty as the Supreme Ruler of the universe.

O'Halloran, Thomas J, photographer. "Right to Life" demonstration, at White House and Capitol Crowd with banner, Abortion is murder. , 1978. Photograph. https://www.loc.gov/item/2016646416/.

 RELATE

Leading Question #3: Does this court opinion adhere to the principles of our U.S. Constitution? Can abortion, the taking of an innocent life (murder), be legalized by a court decision?

 RECORD

Answer #3 – Clearly and simply, NO! In order for man's law to be valid, it must conform to God's law. The Supreme Court (man) does not have the authority to overrule the Supreme Being (God's) law. In addition, the U.S. Constitution declares only Congress can make law (Article I, Section 1) that cannot contradict the "Laws of Nature and of Nature's God" to be legitimate. Lastly, the purpose of law is to protect life, not take it.

CONCLUSION – Roe v. Wade is not law at all, much less the "law of the land." No Supreme Court decision is the "law of the land" as only Congress can make law.

A. **Restoring not Revolutionary!** The mission of this course is not a *revolutionary* one. Rather, it addresses the need to restore a constitutional system.

Too many citizens of this country seem to be ignorant of:

1. Our form of government.[1]

2. Our American history and heritage.

In today's America, most "Americans" know very little about America, what it means to be American, or what beliefs and values define America.

The result is we don't have the basic tools we need to do our duty as citizens. You may have concerns or be dissatisfied with Economy-Bailouts-Wars-Health Care-Property Rights-Right to Self Defense or generally believe something is broken in America.

Are we lost at sea? Can we uncover and recover the foundational principles of American thinking and believing?

B. **Can we restore lawful government?** Yes. Thankfully, the documents are still here, and some oral history remains (it is fading away), but there is much evidence that some spark is still in the people's hearts.

Our belief is that fundamentally we have lost our way because we don't think like Americans anymore.

But we can recover this view, and it is essential to the future of our country.

---

1   https://www.theamericanview.com/what-is-a-republic-anyway/

CHAPTER ONE
AN AMERICAN VIEW OF LAW, LIBERTY, AND GOVERNMENT

GENERAL OBJECTIVES

You should understand that there is a specific view of Law and Government which is distinctively American in nature. This is called "The American View," and it is based on a biblical worldview.

SPECIFIC OBJECTIVES

☆ Understand the presuppositions upon which "The American View" is based and be able to identify these presuppositions in the text of the Declaration of Independence.

☆ Understand the relevance of God and His Word to Law and Government by articulating the biblical purpose of government.

☆ Distinguish The American/Biblical View from other views of law and government.

☆ Appreciate the basic principles of law, including Blackstone's definitions of The Law of Nature, Revealed Law, and Municipal Law.

☆ Understand the definition of "Constitution."

☆ Appreciate the importance of the study of history to the restoration and maintenance of lawful government.

"Anyone who desires to be ignorant and free, desires what never was and never will be."[1]
–Thomas Jefferson

"My people are destroyed for lack of knowledge."
–Hosea 4:6

---

1 "Will We Be Ignorant or Free?" https://www.theamericanview.com/will-we-be-free/

▶ **Lecture One:** An American View of Law, Liberty, and Government; follow along with the notes in the following section.

A. **PRESUPPOSITIONS:** These are the things which are accepted as true before any argument can commence.

General Presupposition	that truth exists and is absolute, objective and unchanging.
	...We hold these truths to be self-evident...
Specific Presuppositions	contained in The Declaration of Independence.
1. There is a GOD	*...that all men are created equal*
2. Our rights come from Him	*...that they are endowed by their Creator with certain unalienable rights; that among these are life, liberty, and the pursuit of happiness;*
3. Purpose of civil government is to protect God-given rights	*...that to secure these rights governments are instituted among men...*
4. All civil government is derived through the consent of the people	*...deriving their just powers from the consent of the governed;*
5. Whenever any government becomes destructive of this purpose the people have a right and a duty to "alter or abolish" it.	*...that whenever any form of government becomes destructive of these ends, it is the right of the people to alter or abolish it...*

This is the *American View of Law and Government,* which is based on a biblical worldview, and is an application of the Bible and God's law to civil government and the body politic.

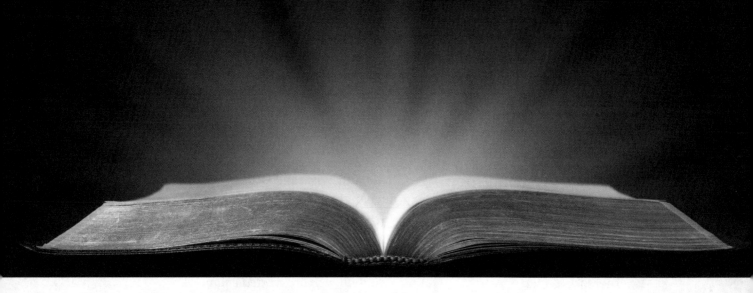

B. THE RELEVANCE OF GOD AND HIS WORD TO LAW AND GOVERNMENT

1. God exists.

2. He knows what is happening on earth.

3. He has moral convictions about what is happening on earth.

4. He communicates those convictions to us.

5. He communicates those convictions through the Bible.

6. Much of the Bible addresses law and government.

7. If we ignore what the Bible says about law and government, we are not preaching the whole counsel of God. (Acts 20:27)

8. Church leaders throughout history have addressed issues of civil government: Augustine, Aquinas, Luther, Calvin, Rutherford, our own Pilgrim and Puritan forbearers.

9. The refusal of many modern Christians to address issues of law and government is a modern heresy.

C. THE FUNCTIONS OF CIVIL GOVERNMENT: it is given the power of the sword (force) in order to:

1. Restrain the exercise of sin (Romans 13:3-4): "For rulers are not a terror to good works, but to the evil. Wilt thou then not be afraid of the power? do that which is good, and thou shalt have praise of the same: For he is the minister of God to thee for good. But if thou do that which is evil, be afraid; for he beareth not the sword in vain: for he is the minister of God, a revenger to [execute] wrath upon him that doeth evil."

2. Enforce God's standard of right and wrong. (Romans 13:3-4)

3. Maintain order so Christians and others can practice right living (1 Timothy 2:2): "For kings, and [for] all that are in authority; that we may lead a quiet and peaceable life in all godliness and honesty."

COMPARISON OF AMERICAN AND ALTERNATE VIEWS OF GOVERNMENT

There are other views of government and its purpose that are not biblical: Socialist View, Marxist View, Communist View. We can compare the views by contrasting their various attributes:

A. ELEMENTS OF BIBLICAL VS PAGAN

Biblical View of Government	Pagan View of Government
State is Divinely Ordained	State is Divine
State Authority is Limited	State Authority is Unlimited
Leads to Patriotism	Leads to State Worship
Results in Republic	Results in Tyranny

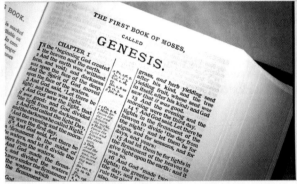 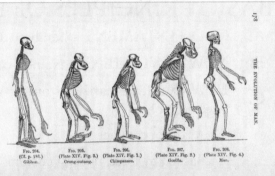

Based on Creation	Based on Evolution

B. AMERICA WAS FOUNDED ON THE BIBLICAL VIEW, but the Pagan View is in operation today, which is creating unrest and lawlessness. Some examples:

1. Unconstitutional wars

2. Lawlessness in our cities with a bloated welfare system

3. The murder of 60 million unborn babies in the United States

C. HISTORICAL FACTORS contributing to American cultural disconnect and dissension

1. Revolution in American thought – American institutions promote anti-American values and ideas. This topic will be explored in greater depth later in this study.

2. False understanding of Separation of Church and State[1]

3. U.S. Supreme Court case Engel v. Vitale, 370 U.S. 421 (1962)[2]

4. Many attribute it to the failure of American churches. No longer independent.[3]

---

1 For additional information, see IOTC's DVD "Separation of Church & State: The Truth and The Lie" by Michael Peroutka's June 2016 video.
2 https://www.law.cornell.edu/supremecourt/text/370/421
3 For additional information, see IOTC's DVD "Why Churches Must Not Incorporate or Become 501C3 Organizations" by Pastor David Whitney.

"...when Christ said, 'Render unto Caesar the things that are Caesar's and unto God the things that are God's,' He gave to the State a legitimacy it had never before enjoyed, and set bounds to it that had never yet been acknowledged. And He not only delivered the precept, but He also forged the instrument to execute it. To limit the power of the State ceased to be the hope of patient, ineffectual philosophers and became the perpetual charge of a universal Church." — Lord Acton in a speech delivered February 26, 1877[4]

BASIC PRINCIPLES OF LAW

A. **OLD TESTAMENT** – Torah: to direct, to point out, to lead.

B. **NEW TESTAMENT** – Nomos: commandment or assignment from higher authority.

C. **LAW IS** – (Summarizing from Sir William Blackstone's *Commentaries on the Laws of England*, Volume I)

1. A rule of conduct.

2. Backed by force, not just custom.

3. Based on higher moral authority.[5]

D. **FORMS OF LAW** according to Sir William Blackstone's *Commentaries on the Laws of England*.

"Man, considered as a creature, must necessarily be subject to the laws of his Creator… it is necessary that he should, in all points, conform to his Maker's will. This will of his Maker is called the law of nature… This law of nature, dictated by God himself, is… superior in obligation to any other. It is binding over all the globe, in all countries, and at all times; **no human laws are of any validity if contrary to this**." [emphasis added][6]

1. Law of Nature – revealed by God through human reason and conscience (Romans 2:14-15): "For when the Gentiles, which have not the law, do by nature the things contained in the law, these, having not the law, are a law unto themselves: Which shew the work of the law written in their hearts, their conscience also bearing witness, and [their] thoughts the mean while accusing or else excusing one another."

2. Revealed Law – which is found only in Scripture (e.g. Ten Commandments, Leviticus, Deuteronomy, etc.)

3. Municipal Law – man-made, enacted by civil government, valid only if it conforms to Law of Nature and Revealed Law.

E. **NOT REVOLUTIONARY** … but restorative.

---

4 Himmelfarb, Gertrude. 2015. "Lord Acton And The Idea Of Liberty." Acton Institute. https://acton.org/pub/commentary/2015/11/10/lord-acton-and-idea-liberty

5 Blackstone, William. *Commentaries on the Laws of England. Book the First.* Third Edition. (Oxford: Clarendon Press, 1768).

6 Ibid, pp. 39-41.

16

WHAT IS A CONSTITUTION?

A. ***BLACK'S LAW DICTIONARY*, 4TH EDITION:**

"The organic and fundamental law of a nation or state, which may be written or unwritten, establishing the character and conception of its government, laying the basic principles to which its internal life is to be conformed, organizing the government, and regulating, distributing, and limiting the functions of its different departments, and prescribing the extent and manner of the exercise of sovereign powers."[7]

1. Every organization has one.

2. Can be written or unwritten.

3. More general, basic, and foundational than statutory law.

B. **NATURE OF THE U.S. CONSTITUTION:**

1. Document of omission. Limits government, not the people.

2. Tenth Amendment as STOP sign!

"The powers not delegated to the United States by the Constitution, nor prohibited by it to the States, are reserved to the States respectively, or to the people."

---

7   Black, Henry Campbell. *Black's Law Dictionary*. Fourth Edition. (St. Paul: West Publishing Company, 1968), p. 384.

THE ROLE OF HISTORY

A. **"Mall directory"** illustration – Professor Chris Schlect said, "History is like a mall map that gives contextual meaning to the little red arrow that says, 'You are here.'"

B. History shows **God's Sovereign** and providential plan for the United States.

C. History helps us appreciate our constitutional **heritage.**

D. History shows us how various forms of government have **worked** or not worked.

E. History helps us understand the **meaning and intent** of those who drafted the Constitution.

F. History shows how the Constitution has been **interpreted and applied** since it was written and adopted.

G. History alerts us to **dangers** facing our constitutional republic today.

topic

SHOULD CHRISTIANS BE INVOLVED IN POLITICS? ©Ricki Pepin 2016

A politician's response:

Today, a very little publicized historical fact is that President James A. Garfield was a Christian Minister. He said:

"Now, more than ever before, the people are responsible for the character of their Congress. If that body be ignorant, reckless, and corrupt, it is because the people tolerate ignorance, recklessness and corruption. If it be intelligent, brave and pure, it is because the people demand these high qualities to represent them in the national legislature…If the next centennial does not find us a great nation…it will be because those who represent the enterprise, the culture and the morality of the nation do not aid in controlling the political forces."

A theologian's response:

Charles Finney was arguably the greatest preacher during the Second Great Awakening, a time of incredible spiritual revival during America's founding period. He said:

"The time has come that Christians must vote for honest men and take consistent ground in politics…God cannot sustain this free and blessed country which we love and pray for unless the Church will take right ground…God will bless or curse this nation according to the course Christians take [in politics]."[8]

Politics: the science of government; that part of ethics which consists in the regulation and government of a nation or state for the preservation of its safety, peace and prosperity… also for the protection of its citizens in their rights, with the preservation and improvement of their morals.[9]

8   Finney, C.. *Lectures on Revivals of Religion.* (New York: Fleming H. Revell Company, 1968), p. 281. https://archive.org/details/lecturesonreviva00finn/page/280
9   http://webstersdictionary1828.com/Dictionary/politics

	Who is better equipped to "preserve and improve morals," Christians with a biblical worldview or non-Christians?
	Therefore, who should be involved in politics?

Edward Everett Hale	John Quincy Adams	John Adams	George Washington
I am only one, but I am one. I can't do everything, but I can do something. What I can do, that I ought to do. And what I ought to do, by the grace of God, I shall do.[10]	*Duty is ours. Results are God's.*[11]	*Statesmen may plan and speculate for liberty, but it is religion and morality alone which can establish the principles upon which freedom can securely stand.*	*No people can be bound to acknowledge and adore the Invisible Hand [the Almighty Being] which conducts the affairs of men more than those of the United States.*[12]

topic

THE FOUNDATIONS AND PURPOSE OF AMERICAN GOVERNMENT & LAW IN THE WORDS OF THE FOUNDERS

Read the excerpts from the following historical documents:

Mayflower Compact – "Having undertaken [this voyage] for the glory of God, and advancement of the Christian Faith…"[13]

Note: This was a government document, not a church document, declaring the purpose for which America was founded.

Declaration of Independence – "We hold these truths to be self-evident, that all men are created equal…"[14]

Note: This statement presupposes a God who created men. It is made in a foundational government document, not a church document.

Declaration of Independence – "…that [men] are endowed by their Creator with certain unalienable Rights, that among these are Life, Liberty and the pursuit of Happiness. That to secure these rights, Governments are instituted among Men…"[15]

Note: The Founder's declaration of the purpose of government – protection of God-given rights, not provision of goods and/or services.

Declaration of Independence – "When…it becomes necessary to dissolve the political bands which have connected them with another, and the assume among the powers of the earth, [in other words to rule or govern themselves] the separate and equal station to which the Laws of Nature and Nature's God entitle them…"[16]

10 Popularly attributed to Edward Everett Hale. Another variant attributed to him is: I am only one, but still I am one. I cannot do everything, but still I can do something; and because I cannot do everything, I will not refuse to do something I can do. https://en.wikiquote.org/wiki/Edward_Everett_Hale

11 Ricki Pepin, "Overcoming the World - 'Duty is ours - Results are God's.'" October 13, 2016. The American View. https://www.theamericanview.com/overcoming-the-world-duty-is-ours-results-are-gods/

12 First Inaugural Address of President George Washington, 1789. https://www.bartleby.com/124/pres13.html

13 Bowman, G. *The Mayflower compact and its signers: with facsimiles and a list of the Mayflower passengers.* (Boston, MA: Massachusetts Society of Mayflower Descendants, 1920), p. 6.

14 The Library of Congress holds a number of artifacts related to this historic document, including the "original Rough draught" showing edits from the initial text to the final text. http://www.loc.gov/exhibits/treasures/tr00.html#obj1

15 Ibid.

16 You can read a transcription of the full text of the Declaration of Independence at the National Archives website. https://www.archives.gov/founding-docs/declaration-transcript

Laws of Nature's God	Laws of Nature
...the moral law...contained in the...10 Commandments written by the finger of God." [17]	"A rule of conduct arising out of the natural relations of human beings established by the Creator, and existing prior to any positive [written] precept. Thus, it is a law of nature that one man should not injure another, and murder and fraud would be crimes independent of any [written] prohibition from the supreme power." [18]

Paraphrase and simplified: The Laws of Nature are intuitively and instinctively known to man. They do not have to be written out. They are in your God-given conscience.

The Laws of Nature and Nature's God, according to the Founders, are the foundation for all law in America. All Laws, Executive Orders or Supreme Court decisions are valid only if they conform to the Laws of Nature and Nature's God. Any laws, orders or rulings made outside the boundaries of the Laws of Nature and Nature's God are not real, legitimate, enforceable or legally binding. Check it out with the words of the Founders:

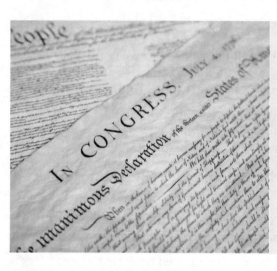

Declaration of Independence

Grievance #13 – "He [the king] has combined with others to subject us to a jurisdiction foreign to our constitution, and unacknowledged by our laws; giving his Assent to their Acts of pretended legislation…

Grievance #19 – "…for transporting us beyond Seas to be tried for pretended offenses." [19]

Question: What does "pretend" mean? – The Founders declared any laws outside the Laws of Nature and Nature's God to be "pretend": not real but make-believe; not legal or enforceable.

LECTURE ONE

OPTIONAL READING ASSIGNMENTS	1.	*The Law* by Frederic Bastiat (text in Student Manual; pages 239-269). French Statesman article written in 1850, beautifully stating republican government principles and comparing them to the woes of Socialism. Optional weekly assignments will be given until it is finished.
		Lecture One: Start at "The Law" and read to "The Complete Perversion of the Law" (pages 251-252).
	2.	"How Tyranny Came to America" (pages 241-250 in the back of this book).

17 Note the dictionary definition 8 for "law". http://webstersdictionary1828.com/Dictionary/Law
18 Note the dictionary definition 3 (and 17) for "law". http://webstersdictionary1828.com/Dictionary/Law
19 https://www.archives.gov/founding-docs/declaration-transcript

LECTURE REVIEWS

1. Complete Lecture One Review Worksheet.

2. Complete the worksheet questions on "How Tyranny Came to America" (optional).

3. Complete Lecture One Quiz, including True & False Questions.

GOING DEEPER: SUPPLEMENTAL READING & VIDEO OPTIONS

 Found at www.theamericanview.com/constitution-course-supplemental-assignments which can also be found at the bottom of TheAmericanView.com under Resources.

"Separation of Church & State: The Truth and The Lie" (DVD) by Michael A. Peroutka. This video gives the student a grounding in understanding the four God-ordained governments and the essential boundaries God has placed on each of those four governments.

CHAPTER TWO
AMERICA'S BEGINNINGS:
DISCOVERY, PURPOSE, & THE FOUNDERS' FAITH

GENERAL OBJECTIVES

You should understand the value of primary sources in learning history, both the good and the bad. Learn the critical connection between the Framers' biblical worldview and the political theory and principles of the American form of government.

SPECIFIC OBJECTIVES

✯ *Connect historical details from primary sources concerning Islam and Columbus as they relate to America's founding.*

✯ *Understand that the Pilgrims' purpose in founding what would become America was to advance the Christian faith.*

✯ *Understand why the colonies were successful in developing stable, productive, just and prosperous communities and enunciate the basic elements of what is sometimes referred to as Puritan Political Theory.*

✯ *Understand the concept of Deism and be able to articulate an opinion as to whether the frequent accusation that the Framers were Deists is true and relevant. Combine this accusation with the overwhelming evidence of a Christian majority among the delegates to the Constitutional Convention.*

✯ *Identify selected quotations of the Framers demonstrating the authority they quoted and the connection between their biblical worldview and their political opinions and decisions.*

"It was the Lord who put into my mind (I could feel His hand upon me) to sail to the Indies... There is no question that the inspiration was from the Holy Spirit because He comforted me with rays of marvelous illumination from the Holy Scriptures."[1]
                    –Christopher Columbus

"When the righteous are in authority, the people rejoice: but when the wicked beareth rule, the people mourn."
                    –Proverbs 29:2

---

1   Christopher Columbus in *The Book of Prophecies* (Circa 1502), *Columbus & Cortez, Conquerors for Christ* (Green Forest, AR: New Leaf Press, 1992), p. 90.

Lecture Two: America's Beginnings:
Discovery, Purpose & the Founders' Faith; follow along with the notes in the following section.

THE PLAN OF GOD

A.   To bring the gospel to the Western Hemisphere

B.   Too many citizens of this country seem to be ignorant of:

    1.   The well-being of the people of America

    2.   Being an example and model for the rest of the world

C.   The United States of America

    1.   Is not the Kingdom of God

    2.   But is the best the world has to offer

    3.   Built upon a biblical foundation

THE AGE OF DISCOVERY (1492-1620)

A.   Others such as Vikings pre-dated Columbus (around 1000 A.D.), but their presence faded.

B.   Columbus brought together the Eastern and Western hemispheres.

C.   It is a myth that Columbus came to America for the sole purpose of getting rich - "For the execution of the journey to the Indies I did not make use of intelligence, mathematics, or maps. It is simply the fulfillment of what Isaiah prophesied… The fact that the gospel must still be preached to so many lands in such a short time - this is what convinces me."[2]

D.   Conditions in Europe

    1.   Belief that the return of Christ was near

    2.   Belief that the gospel should be spread to Asia/Africa

    3.   Barrier – Islam, who controlled trade routes since 600 A.D.

    4.   Crusades – Muslims controlled the Holy Land

    5.   Rise of Ottoman Turks (Muslims), leading to the fall of Constantinople in 1453 A.D.

    6.   Moors (Muslims) driven out of Spain in 1492 A.D., allowing King Ferdinand and Queen Isabella to fund Columbus' journey.

---

2. Columbus, Christopher. *Book of Prophecies*, Introduction. English translation. c. 1502.

E. Columbus' journey

1.	Goal – Bring gospel to Asia
2.	Obstacle – Islamic Empire
3.	Method – Reach Asia by sailing West from Spain, going around the Muslim-controlled trade routes.
4.	Despite his mistakes and sins, his heart was for the gospel
5.	His Journal, October 11, 1492:

"I, in order that they might develop a very kindly disposition towards us, because I knew that they were a people who could better be freed and converted to our Holy Faith by love than by force, gave to some of them red caps and to others glass beads, which they hung on their necks, and many other things of slight value, in which they took much pleasure. They remained so much our (friends) that it was a marvel… I believe that they would easily be made Christians, because it seemed to me that they belonged to no religion."[3]

F. Pilgrims – The families who founded America (1608-1620)

1.	Religious freedom was not the primary reason they came to America.
2.	They came as families (not male explorers only). Why? To establish a Christian nation under the God of the universe, not an earthly ruler.
3.	The Mayflower Compact united God and government – "…Having undertaken [this voyage to America] for the glory of God and the advancement of the Christian faith…"
4.	This principle of self-government under God set the foundation for liberty and prosperity upon biblical principles.

3 From the journal of Christopher Columbus, Thursday, 11 October, 1492. https://sourcebooks.fordham.edu/source/columbus1.asp

THE POSITIVE EFFECT OF A BIBLICAL WORLDVIEW ON AMERICAN POLITICAL THEORY, ECONOMY AND CULTURE

A. Why did the 13 colonies succeed in establishing a system of freedom and stability, justice, and prosperity, while others (even in the Western Hemisphere) failed to do so?

We can cite five principle reasons:

1. The Colonial Charters and later the United States Constitution gratefully acknowledged God and sought to enforce His standard thus providing a unique balance of liberty and stability.

2. The free enterprise system – based on a realistic (biblical) view of human nature – gives incentive to produce.

3. The theology of the priesthood of all believers.

   a. Led to widespread literacy.

   b. Implied concept of equality.

   c. Provided practical experience in church government.

4. The biblical work ethic helped make free enterprise work.

5. The Fixed Standard of God's Eternal Law (Bible) – loyalty to fixed standard of Oath to Constitution, rather than loyalty to faction.

B. Modern secularist theorists enjoy no such fixed standard. Such loyalty is to faction rather than principle.

PURITAN POLITICAL THEORY

A. Government ordained by God – Rule of Law

B. Government limited by God – Doctrine of Rights

1. Rev. John Cotton, Puritan preacher:

"Let all the world learn to give to mortall men no greater power than they are content they shall use, for use it they will: and unless they be better taught of God, they will use it ever and anon ... for whatever transcendent power is given, will certainly over-run those that give it, and those that receive it: there is a straine in a mans heart that will sometime or other runne out to excess, unless the Lord restrain it, but it is not good to venture it:

It is necessary therefore, that all power that is on earth be limited, Church-power or other... It is counted a matter of danger to the State to limit Prerogatives; but is a further danger, not to have them limited: A Prince himselfe cannot tell where he will confine himselfe, nor can the people tell.

...It is therefore fit for every man to be studious of the bounds which the Lord hath set: and for the People, in whom fundamentally all power lyes, to give as much power as God in His word gives to men: And it is meet that Magistrates in the commonwealth, and so Officers in Churches should desire to know the utmost bounds of their own power, and it is safe for both: All intrenchment upon the bounds which God hath not given, they are not enlargments but burdens and snares: They will certainly lead the spirit of a man out of his way sooner or later. It is wholesome and safe to be dealt withall as God deales with the vast Sea; Hitherto shalt thou come, but there shalt thou stay thou proud waves: and therefore if they be but banks of simple sand, they will be good enough to check the vast roaring Sea."[4]

2. Richard L. Bushman:

"Puritans were not content to let abject submission totally define their relationship to authority. Even more than persons living in a permissive atmosphere, they felt the need. This inward impulse was expressed in Puritan political philosophy as **the doctrine of rights and the rule of law**..." [emphasis added] Angered by the slightest hint of oppression, Puritans jealously defended their rights against attacks from any source. Thus his awe of the rulers did not reduce the Puritan to slavish servitude, for the general respect for power led to stress on the limits of government."[5]

C. Liberty of Conscience – Government has jurisdiction over actions, but conscience is between man and God. Therefore, what are referred to as "hate crimes," are not punishable by civil government.

THE FRAMERS OF THE CONSTITUTION: CHRISTIANS OR DEISTS?

A. Deism is the belief in an "absentee God."

B. God created the universe.

1. God established absolute, unchanging laws (physical laws, moral laws) to govern the universe.

2. God retreated from the universe and is no longer involved with His creation.

3. Deists are similar to Christians in view of God's law. Declaration of "Laws of Nature and of Nature's God."

---

4 From Reverend Cotton's "Limitation of Government" (1646); http://academic.brooklyn.cuny.edu/english/melani/english2/puritan_excerpts.html
5 From *Puritan to Yankee: Character and the Social Order in Connecticut 1690 – 1765* (Cambridge: Harvard University Press, 1967-1980), pp. 20-21.

C. In 18th century America, Deists were a very small minority.

D. Church affiliations of Constitutional Convention delegates (55 total):

- 28 Episcopalians
- 8 Presbyterians
- 7 Congregationalists
- 2 Dutch Reformed
- 2 Lutherans
- 2 Methodists
- 2 Roman Catholics
- 1 unknown
- 3 Deists (?) *Evidence doesn't support that they were.*[6]

E. 34% of quotations in Framers' writings came from the Bible. - (American Political Science Review, 1984: Dr. Donald Lutz and Dr. Charles Heineman [sic] researched 15,000 writings, letters, diaries, sermons and other works that were written by various leading Americans from 1760-1805 as quoted in *Christianity and the Constitution* by John Eidsmoe.[7])

F. Bible was chief source of Framers' education, illustrated by their creation of *The New England Primer* as a school book (reprinted by Institute on the Constitution).

THE FRAMERS' OWN STATEMENTS ABOUT CHRISTIANITY

A. Ben Franklin: Constitutional Convention, June 28, 1787

"In the beginning of the contest with Britain, when we were sensible of danger, we had daily prayers in this room for the divine protection. Our prayers, Sir, were heard, and they were graciously answered. I have lived, Sir, a long time; and the longer I live, the more convincing proofs I see of this truth, *that God governs in the affairs of men* [emphasis added]. And if a sparrow cannot fall to the ground without his notice, is it probable that an empire can rise without his aid? We have been assured, Sir, in the sacred writings that 'except the Lord build the house, they labor in Vain that build it.' I firmly believe this; and I also believe that, without his concurring aid, we shall succeed in this political building no better than the builders of Babel...."[8]

---

6 Dr. M.E. Bradford, A Worthy Company (Plymouth Rock Foundation, 1982).

7 There are some that believe this study has flaws, including Dr. Joel McDurmon from American Vision. To read more, visit: www.americanvision.org/9760/christian-american-friends-please-stop-citing-lutz-study/#sthash.AiZisvD2.dpuf

8 Franklin, B. and Sparks, J., Editor. *The Works of Benjamin Franklin; Containing Several Political and Historical Tracts Not Included in Any Former Edition, and Many Letters, Official and Private, Not Hitherto Published; with Notes and a Life of the Author, Volume 5.* (Milwaukie, Wisconsin: Tappan, Whittemore, and Mason, 1837), p.154.

B. Thomas Jefferson: 2nd Inaugural Address, 1805

"I shall need ... the favor of that Being in whose hands we are, who led our forefathers, as Israel of old, from their native land, and planted them in a country flowing with all the necessaries and comforts of life; who has covered our infancy with His providence, and our riper years with His wisdom and power; and to whose goodness I ask you to join with me in supplications, that He will so enlighten the minds of your servants, guide their councils, and prosper their measures, that whatsoever they do shall result in your good, and shall secure to you the peace, friendship, and approbation of all nations."[9]

C. George Washington: Speech to Delaware Chiefs, May 12, 1779

"You will do well to wish to learn our ways of life, and above all, the religion of Jesus Christ. These will make you a greater and happier people than you are." In a Letter to 13 Governors, 8 June 1783, he refers to Jesus Christ as "the Divine Author of our blessed Religion."[10]

D. Alexander Hamilton: Urged formation of the "Christian Constitutional Society" to preserve values essential to this nation; on his deathbed, July 11, 1804

"I have a tender reliance on the mercy of the Almighty, through the merits of the Lord Jesus Christ."[11]

E. John Jay: First Chief Justice, U.S. Supreme Court; Founder and President of the American Bible Society. His description of a gathering of French Atheists:

"They spoke freely and contemptuously of religion. I took no part in the conversation. In the course of it, one of them asked me if I believed in Christ. I answered that I did, and that I thanked God that I did. Nothing further passed between me and them or any of them on that subject."12

9   https://www.bartleby.com/124/pres17.html
10 "Address to the Delaware Nation, 12 May 1779"; https://founders.archives.gov/documents/Washington/03-20-02-0388; Sparks, Jared. The Writings of George Washington, Vol. XII. (Boston: American Stationers' Company, 1837), p. 404.
11 The Complete Works of John M. Mason, Volume 4; Ebenezer Mason, editor. (New York: Charles Scribner, 1852), p. 525
12 William, Jay. The Life of John Jay: With Selections from His Correspondence and Miscellaneous Papers, Vol. II. (New York: J & J Harper, 1833), pp. 346-347.

F. Roger Sherman: Connecticut Puritan, author of Great Compromise by which Congress has two houses, Elder in Church pastored by Jonathan Edwards, Jr.

"(The) threatenings of the law against impenitent sinners... are (as important) as the promises of the Gospel."[13] In the words of John Adams, Sherman was "an old Puritan, as honest as an angel and as firm in the cause of American independence as Mount Atlas."[14]

G. Patrick Henry: Last Will and Testament

"This is all the inheritance I can give to my dear family. The religion of Christ can give them one which will make them rich indeed."[15]

CONCLUSION

A. An overwhelming majority of Framers believed basic doctrines of Christianity and were active in Christian churches.

B. Even those who did not believe the basic doctrines of Christianity nonetheless believed the basic values of Christianity were true and were good for society.

BIBLICAL PRINCIPLES: BASIS FOR AMERICA'S LAWS		
Principle	**Legal Document**	**Bible Source**
Sovereign authority of God, not sovereignty of the state or sovereignty of man	Mayflower Compact, Declaration, Constitution, currency, oaths, all 50 state constitutions, Pledge of Allegiance	Ex. 18:16, 20:3, Dt. 10:20, 2 Chron. 7:14, Ps. 83:18, 91:2, Isa. 9:6-7, Dan. 4:32, Jn. 19:11, Acts 5:29, Rom. 13:1, Col. 1:15-20, 1 Tim. 6:15
Existence of objective moral values, fixed standards, absolute truth, sanctity of life	Declration ("unalienable" rights – life, etc., "self-evident" truths)	Ex. 20:1-17, Dt. 30:19, Ps. 119:142-152, Pr. 14:34, Isa. 5:20-21, Jn. 10:10, Rom. 2:15
Ruler of law rather than authority of man	Declaration, Constitution	Ex. 18-24, Dt. 17:20, Isa. 8:19-20, Mat. 5:17-18
All men are sinners	Constitutional checks and balances, separation of powers	Gen. 8:21, Jer. 17:9, Mk. 7:20-23, Rom. 3:23, 1 Jn. 1:8
All men created equal	Declaration	Acts 10:34, 17:26, Gal. 3:28

13 Bradford, Melvin Eustace. *Founding Fathers: Brief Lives of the Framers of the United States Constitution*. (University of Kansas Press, 1982), p 28.
14 https://history.army.mil/books/RevWar/ss/sherman.htm
15 Morgan, George. *The True Patrick Henry*. (Philadelphia: J.B. Lippincott Company, 1907), p. 457.

Principle	Legal Document	Bible Source
Judicial, legislative, and executive branches	Constitution	Isa. 33:22
Religious freedom	First Amendment	1 Tim. 2:1-2
Church protected from state control (and taxation), but church to influence the state	First Amendment	Dt. 17:18-20, 1 Kgs. 3:28, Ezra 7:24, Neh. 8:2, 1 Sam. 7:15-10:27, 15:10-31, Mat. 14:3-4, Lk. 3:7-14
Republic – Electing leaders	Constitution (Art. IV, Sec. 4)	Ex. 18:21, Dt. 1:13, Jud. 8:22, 9:6
Importance of governing self and family as first level of governance	First, Second, Ninth, and Tenth Amendments	Mat. 18:15-18, Gal. 5:16-26, 1 Cor. 6:1-11, 1 Tim. 3:1-5, Tit. 2:1-8, 1 Tim. 5:8
Establish justice	Declaration	Ex. 23:1-9, Lev. 19:15, Dt. 1:17
Fair trial with witnesses	Sixth Amendment	Ex. 20:16, Dt. 19:15, Pr. 24:28
Private property rights	Fifth Amendment	Ex. 20:15, 17, Jer. 32:9-15
Biblical liberty, free enterprise	Declaration	Lev. 25:10, Jn. 8:36, 2 Cor. 3:17
Creation not evolution	Declaration	Gen. 1:1
Biblical capitalism not Darwinian capitalism (service and fair play over strict survival of the fittest)	Anti-trust laws	Ex. 20:17, Mat. 20:26, 25:14-30, 2 Thes. 3:6-15, 1 Pet. 2:16
Importance of the traditional family	State marriage laws, few reasons for divorce	Ex. 20:12, 14, Mat. 19:1-12, Mk. 10:2-12, Rom. 1:18-2:16
Religious education encouraged	Northwest Ordinance	Dt. 6:4-7, Pr. 22:6, Mat. 18:6, Eph. 6:4
Servanthood not political power	Concept of public servant	Ex. 18:21, Rom. 13:4, Php. 2:7
Sabbath day holy	"Blue laws"	Ex. 20:8
Restitution	Restitution laws	Lev. 6:1-5, Num. 5:5-7, Mat. 5:23-26
Uniform immigration laws	Constitution (Art. I, Sec. 8)	Lev. 19:34
President natural born citizen	Constitution (Art. II, Sec. 1)	Dt. 17:15

Principle	Legal Document	Bible Source
Witnesses and capital punishment	Constitution (Art. III, Sec. 3)	Dt. 17:6
Provision Against Attainder[16]	Constitution (Art. III, Sec. 3)	Ex. 18:20
Instructions for Judge		2 Chr. 19:6-7, Ezra 7:25

LECTURE TWO

OPTIONAL READING ASSIGNMENTS

1. Continue reading *The Law* by Frederic Bastiat. Start at "A Fatal Tendency of Mankind" and read to "The Results of Legal Plunder" on pages 253-254.

LECTURE REVIEWS

1. Complete Lecture Two Review Worksheet.

2. Complete Property Ownership, Lecture Two Worksheet 2.

3. Complete Lecture Two Quiz, including True & False Questions.

GOING DEEPER: SUPPLEMENTAL READING & VIDEO OPTIONS

Found at www.theamericanview.com/constitution-course-supplemental-assignments which can also be found at the bottom of theamericanview.com under Resources.

What is a Republic Anyway? by Scott T. Whiteman, Esq. which will be accessible by visiting the homework section of the IOTC website. This article will give you the seven distinctives which are essential for a Republic to exist. These are drawn from our Founders, primarily from the *Federalist Papers*.

---

16 Defined by *Webster's 1828 Dictionary* as 8: 1. Literally a staining, corruption, or rendering impure; a corruption of blood. Hence,

2. The judgment of death, or sentence of a competent tribunal upon a person convicted of treason or felony, which judgment attaints, taints or corrupts his blood, so that he can no longer inherit lands. The consequences of this judgment are, forfeiture of lands, tenements and hereditaments, loss of reputation, and disqualification to be a witness in any court of law....

CHAPTER THREE

THE PHILOSOPHICAL WORLDVIEW OF THE CONSTITUTION

GENERAL OBJECTIVES

You should be able to identify the principles of American political theory and their historic sources. Also you should be able to identify the major problem facing the Framers of the Constitution and their formula for addressing this problem.

SPECIFIC OBJECTIVES

☆ *Know the main contributions to American political theory of Baron Charles Montesquieu, William Blackstone and John Locke.*

☆ *Enunciate the underlying principles of American Political Theory including the following concepts:*

The Laws of Nature and Nature's God

Natural Rights

Equality

Government by Consent of the Governed

The Sinfulness of Human Nature

☆ *Articulate the main problem facing the Framers of the Constitution*

☆ *Articulate the Framers' formula for addressing the problem*

"John Calvin was the virtual founder of America."[1]
    –Leopold von Ranke
    (Modern School of History)

"For when the Gentiles, which have not the law, do by nature the things contained in the law, these, having not the law, are a law unto themselves: Which shew the work of the law written in their hearts, their conscience also bearing witness, and their thoughts the mean while accusing or else excusing one another."
                    –Romans 2:14-15

---

1   "Celebrating John Calvin's Legacy - not so much Charles Darwin's." John Eidsmoe. July 12, 2009. Foundation for Moral Law. https://web.archive.org/web/20101220232953/http://morallaw.org/blog/?p=872

MAJOR INFLUENCES ON THE FRAMERS

A. The Bible.

B. Baron Charles Montesquieu: (France, 1689-1755)

  1. Roman Catholic

  2. Main work: *The Spirit of the Laws* (1748)

  3. Main contributions to Framers' thought:

   a. God is the Author of all law.

   • Physical Laws.

   • Moral Laws.

   b. Because of man's sinful nature, man departs from God's laws.

   c. Civil government is necessary to keep men within the confines of God's law.

   d. Sinfulness of human nature causes government to become despotic.

   e. To keep government moderate, it is best to separate government power into three branches: legislative, executive, judicial (Isaiah 33:22).

   f. Christianity makes government more humane.

Montesquieu compared Christianity to Islam and declared Christianity superior partly because of the better government it promotes:

The Christian religion, which ordains that men should love each other, would, without a doubt, have every nation blest with the best civil, the best political laws; because these next to this religion, are the greatest good that men can give and receive ... *A moderate Government is most agreeable to the Christian Religion, and a despotic Government to the Mahommedan* ... The Christian religion is a stranger to mere despotic power. The mildness so frequently recommended in the gospel is incompatible with the despotic rage with which a prince punishes his subjects, and exercises himself in cruelty.... While the Mahommedan princes incessantly give or receive death, the religion of the Christian renders their princes less timid, and consequently less cruel. The prince confides in his subjects, and the subjects in the prince. How admirable the religion which, while it only seems to have in view the felicity of the other life, continues the happiness of this![2]

---
2 Montesquieu, Baron. *The Spirit of Laws, Vol. II*; translated by Thomas Nugent. (New York: The Cooperative Publication Society, 1900), pp. 27, 29.

C. Sir William Blackstone: (England, 1723-1780)

1. Anglican (Church of England or Episcopal).

2. Main work: *Commentaries on the Laws of England* (1765).

3. Main contributions to Framers' view:

   a. Better understanding of English common law.

   b. Judicial Restraint: Judges do not "make" law; they discover and apply law.

   c. Three categories of Law:

Law of Nature: "...when He Created man, and endued him with free will to conduct himself in all parts of life, He laid down certain immutable laws of human nature, whereby that free will is in some degree regulated and restrained, and gave him also the faculty of reason to discover the purport of those laws."[3]

Revealed Law: "The doctrines thus delivered we call the revealed or divine law, and they are to be found only in the Holy Scriptures." (i.e. the Ten Commandments)[4]

Municipal Law, that which is adopted by civil government, must conform to the higher law of God (i.e. applying the Laws of Nature and Nature's God to human institutions): "Upon these two foundations, the law of nature and the law of revelation, depend all human laws: that is to say, no human law should be suffered to contradict these."[5]

The Proper Understanding of Precedent

"For it is an established rule to abide by former precedents, where the same points come again in litigation; as well to keep the scale of justice even and steady, and not liable to waver with every new judge's opinion; as also because the law in that case being solemnly declared and determined, what before was uncertain, and perhaps indifferent, is now become a permanent rule, which it is not in the breast of any subsequent judge to alter or vary from, according to his private sentiments: he being sworn to determine, not according to his own private judgment, but according to the known laws and customs of the land; not delegated to pronounce a new law, but to maintain and expound the old one.

Yet this rule admits of exception, where the former determination is most evidently contrary to reason; much more if it be contrary to the divine law [emphasis added]. But even in such cases the subsequent judges do not pretend to make a new law, but to vindicate the old one from misrepresentation. For if it be found that the former decision is manifestly absurd or unjust, it is declared, not that such a sentence was bad law, but that it was not law; that is, that it is not the established custom of the realm, as has been erroneously determined."[6]

---

3 *Blackstone's Commentaries Vol. I*, pp. 39-40.
4 Ibid, p. 42.
5 Ibid.
6 Ibid, pp. 69-70.

D. John Locke: (England, 1632-1704)

    1. Raised in Puritan family, basically Christian though not entirely orthodox.

    2. Main works: *First Treatise on Civil Government, Second Treatise on Civil Government, Essay Concerning Human Understanding of St. Paul's Epistles, by Consulting St. Paul Himself, On the Reasonableness of the Christian Faith.*

    3. Main contributions to Framers' view:

        a. Government is established by covenant or contract of the people, ultimately based upon "that Paction which God made with Noah after the Deluge."[7] Genesis 9:6: "Whoso sheddeth man's blood, by man shall his blood be shed: for in the image of God made he man."

        b. God has ordained the Law of Nature to which all human law must be subordinate.

        c. This Law of Nature: Our God-given natural rights, chiefly: life, liberty and property.

E. Thinkers on international law: Grotius (Holland), Pufendorf (Germany), Vattel (Switzerland). They stressed that international law must be based upon revealed law and law of nature.

F. Roman thinkers: Virgil, Cicero, Seneca, Marcus Aurelius. They stressed the virtue and discipline of the old Roman republic against the later excesses of the Empire.

G. Non-Christian sources often cited negatively by the Framers: Plato, Voltaire, Jean-Jacques Rousseau, Thomas Hobbes, David Hume.

THE LAWS OF NATURE AND OF NATURE'S GOD

A. Sources of this concept:

    1. The Bible.

    2. Founding Father Noah Webster defined these terms as:

        a. Written law – the 10 Commandments and other revealed law

        b. Unwritten law – your God-given conscience

        c. In other words, there exists a higher law than the law of man by which man's law must be judged.

B. Natural law is predicated upon the existence of absolute truth. (See discussion of presuppositions of American government in Lecture One.)

---

7 *Locke on Civil Government*. (London: George Routledge and Sons, Ltd.), p. 296.

C. False view of natural law: That which exists in nature, i.e. Thomas Hobbes, an English philosopher who aligned his thinking with Roman philosophers like Cicero who believed there was no need to look outside ourselves for an expounder or interpreter of natural law.

D. But Nature is fallen – Romans 8:20, 22 - "For the creature was made subject to vanity… For we know that the whole creation groaneth and travaileth in pain together until now."

E. Natural law limits governmental authority.

NATURAL RIGHTS

A. Rooted in view of natural law.

B. Source of natural rights – God.

C. Based on man being created in image of God, possessing human dignity.

D. Based on negative commands of Scripture: "Thou shalt not kill." Exodus 20:13, etc.

E. Exists as a limit on governmental authority.

F. Consists of:

1. Life (basis for exercising other rights).

2. Liberty – defined by Noah Webster as "…the power of acting as one sees fit without any restraint…**except from the laws of nature.**"[8] [emphasis added] The Laws of Nature (and Nature's God) are the revealed law in the Bible, including the 10 Commandments and your God-given conscience. Therefore:

   a. Liberty is not the freedom to do as you please.

   b. True liberty is the freedom to choose to do what is right according to the will of God.

3. Property – Do not steal (Exodus 20:15):

   a. Not just material gain.

   b. Property was viewed as means of productivity.

   c. Property was viewed as an extension of the person.

4. Pursuit of happiness:

   a. Includes property, but more.

   b. Equated with pursuit of virtue, the only basis for genuine lasting happiness.

---

8 http://webstersdictionary1828.com/Dictionary/liberty

Each State recognized and understood these rights; i.e. Maryland's Declaration Rights Article 36: "That as it is the duty of every man to worship God in such manner as he thinks most acceptable to Him, all persons are equally entitled to protection in their religious liberty;

G. wherefore, no person ought by any law to be molested in his person or estate, on account of his religious persuasion, or profession, or for his religious practice, unless, under the color of religion, he shall disturb the good order, peace or safety of the State, or shall infringe the laws of morality, or injure others in their natural, civil or religious rights."[9]

EQUALITY

A. Based not on outcomes, but on being created in God's image.

B. Acts 10:34: "God is no respecter of persons."

C. Galatians 3:28: "There is neither Jew nor Greek, there is neither bond nor free, there is neither male nor female: for ye are all one in Christ Jesus."

D. Old Testament law prohibited partiality in judging; prophets condemned judges for partiality.

GOVERNMENT BY CONSENT OF THE GOVERNED

A. This is a clearly established principle in God's Law:

1.	Judges 8:22: "Then the men of Israel said unto Gideon, Rule thou over us, both thou, and thy son, and thy son's son also: for thou hast delivered us from the hand of Midian."
2.	Judges 9:6: "And all the men of Shechem gathered together, and all the house of Millo, and went, and made Abimelech king, by the plain of the pillar that [was] in Shechem."
3.	2 Samuel 16:18: "And Hushai said unto Absalom, Nay; but whom the LORD, and this people, and all the men of Israel, choose, his will I be, and with him will I abide."
4.	2 Kings 14:21: "And all the people of Judah took Azariah, which [was] sixteen years old, and made him king instead of his father Amaziah."

B. God is the Source of all authority – not just power, but legal authority; i.e. according to the Laws of Nature and Nature's God.

1.	Romans 13:1: "Let every soul be subject unto the higher powers. For there is no power but of God: the powers that be are ordained of God."
2.	Daniel 6:1-10 – Daniel obeyed a pagan king UNTIL he commanded Daniel to worship him rather than God.
3.	Clearly recognized by colonial charters.

C. God delegated authority to civil government through the people.

---

9 https://codes.findlaw.com/md/maryland-constitution-of-1867/md-const-declaration-of-rights-art-36.html

D. John Locke's theory of social contract.

SINFULNESS OF HUMAN NATURE

A. Framers believed man was sinful, self-interested, corruptible, as Bible describes him.

"If men were angels, no government would be necessary. If angels were to govern men, neither external or internal controls on government would be necessary. In framing a government which is to be administered by men over men, the great difficulty lies in this: you must first enable the government to control the governed; and in the next place oblige it to control itself."[10]

— James Madison

"Till the millennium comes, in spite of all our boasted light and purification, hypocrisy and treachery will continue to be the most successful commodities in the political market."[11]

— Alexander Hamilton

B. They, therefore, believed a government is needed to curb man's sinful nature.

C. However, they also knew rulers and government officials have the same nature as the rest of us.

D. For that reason they feared government power.
"All power tends to corrupt and absolute power corrupts absolutely." – Lord Acton[12]

1.	For that reason God has limited government power.
2.	Limited Government has eroded – Modern politicians have largely abandoned the American View of a limited government. An example of this is when two Congressman expressed their views on the role of government, views that are totally incompatible to those found in the Constitution.

  a. Representative Jane Harman (D) California: "The public role in health care and the private role in health care are also reinforcing values. And if we want to achieve what the Constitution requires, which is the protection of life, liberty and the pursuit of happiness, we need a robust public role and a robust private role. And that, I think, is what HR3200 achieves."[13]

  b. Representative John Sarbanes (D) Maryland: "Government does a lot of good things."[14]

E. Socialism - the example of a destitute woman. Can collective force be used to do that which is illegal for individual force? Absolutely not!

---

10 James Madison, *The Federalist Papers*, No. 51 ; https://www.congress.gov/resources/display/content The+Federalist+Papers#TheFederalistPapers-51
11 *The Works of Alexander Hamilton: Containing His Correspondence, and His Political and Official Writings, Exclusive of the Federalist, Civil and Military, Volume V*; edited by John Church Hamilton. New York: Charles S. Francis & Company, 1850, p. 543.
12 Lord Acton Quote Archive. Acton Institute. https://acton.org/research/lord-acton-quote-archive
13 House Energy and Commerce Committee, September 2009
14 Congressional Record: Proceedings and Debates of the 104th Congress, First Session, Vol. 141, No. 1 January 4, 1995, p. S12. https://www.congress.gov/crec/1995/01/04/CREC-1995-01-04.pdf S-12 (bottom, middle)

ISSUE AT CONSTITUTIONAL CONVENTION: How to give government enough power to govern effectively, but limit that power so government does not become tyrannical and corrupt, given the fallen nature of man?

A. **Answer**: Don't let any individual or agency become too powerful.

B. **Method**: Framers' Five-Fold Formula:

1.	Limited, delegated powers – Thomas Jefferson said, "Bind men down with the chains of the Constitution."[15] If it is not mentioned, the federal government has no authority in that area, such as marriage, education or health care.
2.	Vertical division of powers – Local, State, Federal
3.	Horizontal separation of powers – Legislative, Executive, Judicial branches as well as the Fourth Branch, the Jury.
4.	Checks and balances.
5.	Reserved individual rights as stated in Ninth and Tenth Amendments.

NEED FOR CIVIC VIRTUE

A. Framers believed freedom was impossible without virtue.

B. Framers believed man did not possess virtue.

C. How to provide virtue – through religious/Christian values, not doctrine. The role of Christianity in government is to help people become better citizens, not saving their soul!

> "Of all the dispositions and habits which lead to political prosperity, Religion and Morality are indispensable supports."[16]
>
> — George Washington (Farewell Address, 1796)

> "Our Constitution was made only for a moral and religious people. It is wholly inadequate for the government of any other."[17]
>
> — John Adams

---

15 While often shortened to this quote, Jefferson wrote this in the first draft of the Kentucky Resolutions, saying, "In questions of power, then, let no more be heard of confidence in man, but bind him down from mischief by the chains of the Constitution." See his document here: https://www.loc.gov/resource/mtj1.021_0771_0780/?sp=9
16 In Chapter 17 of this book you will read Washington's farewell address in its entirety.
17 "From John Adams to Massachusetts Militia, 11 October 1798." https://founders.archives.gov/documents/Adams/99-02-02-3102

topic

CONTRASTING THE UNITED NATIONS (UN) AND USA PHILOSOPHIES
By Ricki Pepin ©2016

Individual Rights – The UN Charter asserts the need to control the individual for the greater good of a global community: "Rights and freedoms may in no case be exercised contrary to the purpose and principles of the UN."[18]	**Individual Rights** – The Declaration of Independence states we are created equal and are endowed by our Creator with unalienable rights. Government is established to protect those rights.
Life – The UN is pro-abortion, having authored numerous policies in their treaties for population control, including mandatory sterilizations and forced abortions up to and through the 9th month of pregnancy.	**Life** – The United States was founded with the basic God-given right to life – pro-life – listed in our Declaration of Independence.
Education – The UN principles can be found throughout our school textbooks. They desire worldwide curriculum and control, and have indeed already formed an international school board called UNESCO. They vehemently oppose homeschools and Christian education, creating policy to eradicate them.	**Education** – The United States was founded upon the principle that government was not to be involved in the private education decisions of families. If the family functions properly, the State has no authority or jurisdiction to intervene.
Environment – The UN declares land use decisions must be for the good of "Mother Earth" with animal and bug rights often overriding people's rights.	**Environment** – Our founders believed in the biblical mandate to take dominion over the earth and subdue it, meaning responsible caretaking and replenishing of the environment and natural resources, as directed by our sovereign God, not Mother Earth.
Property Ownership – The UN Agenda 21/Sustainable Development treaty calls for the elimination of private vehicle, land, or home ownership.	**Property Ownership** – The primary purpose of the government of the United States is to protect the private property rights of individuals, especially property, land, and homes.

---

18 Article XXIX, Section 3. https://www.un.org/en/universal-declaration-human-rights/

Right to Bear Arms – No firearms allowed, or all guns must be registered so as to be easily confiscated at the Government's first desire. Groups like the National Rifle Association (NRA) and Gun Owners of America (GOA) are demonized.	**Right to Bear Arms** – The United States Constitution guarantees the right to bear arms, for the precise purpose of protection against a government that has overstepped its boundaries and will seek to confiscate privately-owned property and goods from the general population.
Military – The UN uses our military to establish a New World Order, getting us involved as a "Global Police Force" wherever they perceive a vital interest.	**Military** – The purpose of the United States military is to protect lives and property of American citizens, not those of the world.

LECTURE THREE

OPTIONAL READING ASSIGNMENTS

1. Continue reading *The Law* by Frederic Bastiat. Start at "The Fate of Non-Conformists" and read to "The Fatal Idea of Legal Plunder" (pages 242-244).

LECTURE REVIEWS

1. Complete Lecture Three Review Worksheet.

2. Complete Lecture Three Quiz, including True & False Questions.

GOING DEEPER: SUPPLEMENTAL READING & VIDEO OPTIONS

 Visit theamericanview.com for interesting articles and videos, including a chart showing major worldviews at https://www.theamericanview.com/the-six-major-world-views/.

Read Declaration of Independence (text in the appendix of this Student Manual) in preparation for Lecture Four where the student will begin to apply The American View of Law and Government.

CHAPTER FOUR
1776 - 1789: FROM INDEPENDENCE TO THE CONSTITUTION

GENERAL OBJECTIVES

It is our intent and our hope that you will appreciate the historical events leading up to and surrounding the adoption of the Constitution and your relationship to the religious and philosophical worldviews of the Framers and the American culture.

SPECIFIC OBJECTIVES

☆ *Articulate the historical events and circumstances which preceded the formal adoption of a Biblical (American) View of civil government among the English Colonies in America.*

☆ *Appreciate the content and context of the Declaration of Independence and its importance as a document of biblical interposition.*

☆ *Learn the relationship between the Declaration of Independence and the Constitution.*

☆ *Understand and articulate the basic outline and purposes of the Articles of Confederation and have and understanding of the perceived limitations of this document.*

☆ *Understand the dynamics and operation of the Constitutional Convention of May-September 1787 and the principle actors and their roles.*

"Proclaim liberty throughout all the land unto all the inhabitants thereof..."
–Leviticus 25:10
(Also inscribed on the Liberty Bell)

"We hold these truths to be self-evident, that all men are created equal, that they are endowed by their Creator with certain unalienable Rights, that among these are Life, Liberty and the pursuit of Happiness.–That to secure these rights, Governments are instituted among Men, deriving their just powers from the consent of the governed..."
–Declaration of Independence, 1776

Lecture Four: 1776 - 1789: From Independence to The Constitution; follow along with the notes in the following section.

FACTORS LEADING TO INDEPENDENCE

A.   Colonists' belief in ancient rights of Englishmen.

B.   English abrogation of colonial charters' autonomy.

C.   Parliament's taxation without representation.

D.   The "Glorious Revolution" (1688) that overthrew the Stuart kings.

E.   English abrogation of feudal vassal/lord relationships.

F.   English rejection of colonists' petitions.

DECLARATION OF INDEPENDENCE

A.   Drafted by congressional committee: Thomas Jefferson, Benjamin Franklin, John Adams, Roger Sherman and Robert Livingston.

B.   Congress voted to declare independence on July 2, 1776 and adopted the Declaration of Independence on July 4, 1776. (Rhode Island had declared independence on May 4, 1776.)

C.   Outline of the Declaration of Independence.

1.   The colonies are entitled to independence by "the Laws of Nature and of Nature's God," but "a decent respect to the opinions of mankind" required the colonies to state their reasons.

2.   Self-evident truths:

a.   All men are created equal.

b.   All men are endowed by Creator with unalienable rights: life, liberty and the pursuit of happiness.

c.   Civil government is instituted to secure these rights.

d.   Civil government derives its just powers from the consent of the governed.

e.   Civil government may be altered or abolished when it violates these principles.

f.   People should abolish civil government only after a "long train of abuses and usurpations."

3. England engaged in a "long train of abuses and usurpations" against the colonies:

    a. Refused to assent to necessary colonial laws.

    b. Dissolved colonial legislatures.

    c. Prevented emigration to colonies.

    d. Made administration of colonial justice impossible by controlling judges and refusing to approve needed laws.

    e. Appointed bureaucrats to harass colonial population.

    f. Keeping standing armies in colonies, not subject to control of colonial government.

    g. Cutting off colonial trade with the rest of the world.

    h. Taxation without representation.

    i. Denial of trial by jury.

    j. Transporting colonists for trial in England (fatiguing into compliance).

    k. Abrogating English common law in Canada, setting example for same in colonies.

    l. Abolishing colonial charters.

    m. Taking colonists captive on high seas.

    n. Incited insurrection and Indian warfare against the colonists.

    o. Conclusion: King "unfit to be the ruler of a free people."

4. Colonists' efforts to resolve grievances peaceably have gone unheeded.

5. Declaration: "That these United Colonies are, and of Right ought to be Free and Independent States...."

6. "Firm reliance on the protection of divine Providence...."

THE RELATIONSHIP BETWEEN THE DECLARATION AND THE CONSTITUTION

Declaration of Independence sets forth the basic ideals of the new nation. In effect, it is the true preamble to the Constitution. Declaration answers the question "Why"; Constitution answers the question "How." Constitution does not abrogate the Declaration nor repeal it in any way. The American View (biblical worldview) shines through the Constitution just as it is transparent in the Declaration.

A. "The rhetoric of a public document, and especially of a state paper which is so fundamental as a constitution, is very important, for such rhetoric contains propositions which are basic to the legal and political order – beliefs which enable one to understand the principles and purposes of that order. Moreover, such rhetoric conveys a public teaching about what its framers and ratifiers consider to be the most important things for the people who are ruled under the authority of that document to believe. Such beliefs, in turn, imply public and private actions which affect the individual, society and civil government. These beliefs and teachings are crucial for the individual, society, and the political order: they mean sickness or health, slavery or liberty, death or life."[1]

B. Often asked question – Where is God in our Constitution?

1. Subscription clause: "In the year of our Lord…"

2. Excepting of Sundays (Article I, Section 7): Honoring the Sabbath.

3. Oath (Article II, Section 1).

4. Biblical principles are found throughout, such as:

   a. The separation of powers, based on Isaiah 33:22: "For the Lord is our Judge [Judicial branch], the Lord is our Lawgiver [Legislative branch], the Lord is our King [Executive branch]."

   b. Reason for this separation – Jeremiah 17:9: "The heart is deceitful above all things and desperately wicked: who can know it?"

ARTICLES OF CONFEDERATION AND PERPETUAL UNION

A. Drafted by congressional committee led by John Dickinson 1776, approved in modified form by Continental Congress 1777, not ratified by all States until 1781.

B. More a compact among States than a true Constitution.

C. Brief outline of Articles of Confederation and Perpetual Union:

1. Name: United States of America.

2. Sovereignty of States: "Each State retains its sovereignty, freedom, and independence, and every power, jurisdiction and right, which is not by this confederation expressly delegated to the United States in Congress assembled."[2]

3. Purpose: "league of friendship"[3] for common defense, security of liberty, and mutual welfare.

4. Rights of citizens while in other states.

---

1 Archie P. Jones, *America's First Covenant: Christian Principles in the Articles of Confederation*, p. 9.
2 Articles of Confederation (1777). Article II.
3 Articles of Confederation (1777). Article III.

5. Structure of Congress.

6. States may not make treaties or maintain standing armies except as necessary for defense.

7. States appoint militia officers (except generals).

8. Costs of war paid out of confederacy treasury.

9. Powers of Congress.

10. Committee of States, or nine States, may act when congress in recess.

11. Canada may join confederacy.

12. Confederation will honor past debts.

13. Unanimous consent of all States required for amendments.

D. Perceived limitations of Articles of Confederation and Perpetual Union:

1. Lacked central power. While this looks attractive today, it virtually made federal operation impossible.

2. No chief executive.

3. No Federal judiciary.

4. No Federal taxing power; only voluntary requisitions (Congress asked States for money; States did not cooperate very well).

5. No Federal enforcement powers.

6. All States must consent to amendments.

EVENTS LEADING TO CONSTITUTIONAL CONVENTION

A. The Articles of Confederation and Perpetual Union held the country together during the war, but after the war many problems surfaced:

1. Combined inflation and recession (inherent in use of Fiat Money).

2. Congress was unable to raise money by requisitions.

3. Domestic disturbances.

4. States treating each other as foreign nations.

5. Border problems among States.

6. Border problems with the English in Canada, and Spanish in the West.

B. During the War, Alexander Hamilton wrote letters urging a stronger central government.

C. After the War, Alexander Hamilton persuaded New York to pass resolution urging a constitutional convention – no other state joined.

D. In 1783: Alexander Hamilton urged Congress to call a convention – no success.

E. In 1785: George Washington wrote letter to the 13 States urging a constitutional convention.

F. In 1786: Congress called a trade conference, but only five States sent representatives.

G. In 1787: Congress called for Constitutional Convention to be held in Philadelphia on May 14th "for the sole and express purpose of revising the Articles of Confederation and Perpetual Union."[4]

H. On May 14, 1787: Delegates from only two States had arrived, Convention did not begin until May 25th.

I. On May 14, 1787: Madison and others prepared "Virginia Resolves" which became the basic agenda for the Convention.

---

4 "Report of Proceedings in Congress; February 21, 1787." http://avalon.law.yale.edu/18th_century/const04.asp

THE CONSTITUTIONAL CONVENTION
MAY 25TH TO SEPTEMBER 17TH 1787

A. Attended by 55 delegates from 12 States (Rhode Island did not send delegates).

B. Delegates were intelligent and well-educated, with vast and varied experience:

    1. 31 lawyers

    2. 19 military veterans

    3. 28 former delegates to the Continental Congress

    4. Two college presidents

    5. Three college professors

    6. Nine foreign born

    7. Several doctors and scientists

C. Delegates agreed on basic values and principles:

    1. The Laws of Nature and of Nature's God.

    2. God-given unalienable rights: life, liberty, property.

    3. Civil government is established by covenant, authorizing only such limited power as the people delegate to it.

    4. All people, rulers included, have a sinful nature.

    5. People need order, but rulers need limits.

D. Procedures established:

    1. President elected (George Washington).

    2. One vote per state, cast as majority of State's delegation desired.

    3. To prevent false rumors, proceedings kept secret until last delegate died (James Madison, 1836).

    4. No delegate could speak more than twice on issue until all others had spoken, then only by permission of convention.

    5. All remarks addressed to President.

E. Most issues resolved by reaching consensus.

F. Three issues required compromise:

1. Representation in Congress: Large States wanted proportionate representation, but small states wanted equal representation. Therefore, Roger Sherman (of Connecticut) suggested bicameral Congress – with a House and Senate.

2. Counting of slaves for voting and taxes:

   a. North wanted to count slaves for taxes, not voting.

   b. South wanted to count slaves for voting, not taxes.

   c. Compromise: For both purposes, the Constitution specifies 3/5 of a number and refers to slaves as persons. It does not say slaves were counted as 3/5 of a person.

   d. This compromise language has been mischaracterized by revisionist historians who claim it demonstrates the Constitution is a pro-slavery document, declaring slaves less than fully human.

   e. Frederick Douglass, born a slave in 1817 and who rose to become an advisor of President Lincoln declared just the opposite: "It [the three-fifths clause] is a downright disability laid upon the slaveholding States; one which deprives those States of two-fifths of the natural basis of representation… Instead of encouraging slavery, the Constitution encourages freedom by giving an increase of 'two-fifths' of political power to free over slave States…"[5]

3. Compromise: Congress may not end slave trade for 20 years (1808).

G. In June, Convention degenerated into discord.

H. June 28th: Franklin's motion for prayer helped restore harmony, and progress resumed.

I. Closing days of Convention:

1. July 26th: Committee on Detail appointed to work out details.

2. August 6th: Committee on Detail presented report; Delegates refined it until September 8th.

3. September 8th: Committee on Style appointed to prepare draft; Gouverneur Morris did most of writing of final draft.

4. September 12th: Committee on Style presented report; Convention considered it and adopted it with a few minor changes on September 15th.

5. September 17th: Signing of Constitution. Majority from each State signed, but three Delegates did not: Elbridge Gerry of Massachusetts, and George Mason and Edmund Randolph of Virginia. Edmund Randolph later supported Constitution, but Luther Martin (Maryland) signed but later opposed Constitution.

---

5 Frederick Douglass, explaining the true meaning of the three/fifths compromise in a speech delivered in Glasgow, Scotland, March 2, 1860.

6. As the delegates signed the Constitution, Ben Franklin spoke. He referred to an etching of a sun on the back of George Washington's chair: "I have often in the course of the session, and the vicissitudes of my hopes and fears as to its issue, looked at that [chair] behind the president without being able to tell whether it was rising or setting. But now at length I have the happiness to know that it is a rising and not a setting sun."[6]

topic

JURISDICTIONAL BOUNDARIES – GOVERNMENT
Definitions, Jurisdictions, Levels and Boundaries

Government – Direction, regulation, control, restraint. (*Webster's 1828 Dictionary*)

There are four distinct jurisdictions – limits within which each government power may be exercised according to *Webster's 1828 Dictionary*:

First

SELF-GOVERNMENT – Men are apt to neglect the government of their temper and passions.

Second

FAMILY GOVERNMENT – The exercise of authority by a parent or householder. Children are often ruined by a neglect of government in parents.

Third

CHURCH GOVERNMENT – The persons or council who direct the ministries and ordinances of the church.

Fourth

CIVIL GOVERNMENT – That form of fundamental rules and principles by which a nation or state is governed; a constitution by which the rights and duties of citizens and public officers are prescribed and defined.

Within the Civil Government there are three levels: Federal, State, and Local. Each of these also have their own distinct jurisdictions – Constitutional limits within which their power to direct, regulate, control or restrain may be exercised. This is described in the Tenth Amendment which states the following: "The powers not delegated to the United States by the Constitution, nor prohibited by it to the states, are reserved to the states respectively, or to the people."

6 BENJAMIN FRANKLIN, debates in the Constitutional Convention, Philadelphia, Pennsylvania, September 17, 1787.—James Madison, *Journal of the Federal Convention*, ed. E. H. Scott, p. 763 (1893). https://www.bartleby.com/73/323.html

Below are the biblically described details and boundaries – jurisdictional realms – of FAMILY, CHURCH, **and** CIVIL government:

Family	Church	Civil
Marriage – Exodus 22:16-17	Public ministry of the Word of God – Timothy 4:1-2	Ministry of justice – Romans 13:1-4
Raising children – Ephesians 6:1-4	Public ministry of worship – 1 Timothy 2	Ministry of military defense – Numbers 31:3
Property ownership – Leviticus 25	Ministry of ordinances (communion, baptisms, etc.) – 1 Corinthians 11	
Business ownership – Leviticus 25	Ministry to those who do not have family – 1 Timothy 5:3-16	
Inheritance – Leviticus 25		
Education – Deuteronomy 6:7-9		
Welfare – 1 Timothy 5:8		

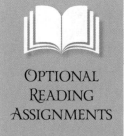

LECTURE FOUR

OPTIONAL READING ASSIGNMENTS

1. *The Law* by Frederic Bastiat. Start at "Perverted Law Causes Conflict" and read to "How to Identify Legal Plunder" (pages 256-257).

2. The U.S. Constitution (included in the appendix of this in Student Manual). In preparation for the three following lectures, which will overview the seven articles of our Constitution.

LECTURE REVIEWS

1. Complete Lecture Four Review Worksheet.

2. Complete Lecture Four Quiz, including True & False Questions.

GOING DEEPER: SUPPLEMENTAL READING & VIDEO OPTIONS

 Read more at: https://www.theamericanview.com/constitution-course-supplemental-assignments/articles-of-confederation-and-perpetual-union/

The Articles of Confederation and Perpetual Union. This will give the student an understanding of the first general government under which the thirteen original States cooperated together.

CHAPTER FIVE
IMMIGRATION:
FROM CONSTITUTIONAL BEGINNINGS TO ANCHOR BABIES

"Let each citizen remember at the moment he is offering his vote that he is not making a present or a compliment to please an individual – or at least that he ought not so to do; but that he is executing one of the most solemn trusts in human society for which he is accountable to God and his country."[1]
– Samuel Adams

"Let every soul be subject unto the higher powers. For there is no power but of God: the powers that be are ordained of God. Whosoever therefore resisteth the power, resisteth the ordinance of God: and they that resist shall receive to themselves damnation."
– Romans 13:1-2

GENERAL OBJECTIVES

How is citizenship defined in the United States and why does it matter? You may be familiar with the basic rights afforded to you as a citizen of this nation, but it is important to realize you have a responsibility to be active in voting, choosing the right representatives that adhere to constitutional principles, and being vigilant about what our leaders choose to support or want to enact as law. As you learn more about the issue of immigration, you will understand how far from the original Founders' intentions we have drifted, and you will begin to understand the ramifications of these unconstitutional decisions. Understanding your role as a citizen is one way to preserve the legacy of freedom you have inherited and will be better informed to support or oppose legislation based on its constitutionality.

SPECIFIC OBJECTIVES

☆ *Examine the drafting of the 14th Amendment in both the House and Senate.*

☆ *Explore the debates which took place in both Houses prior to final approval.*

☆ *Investigate Supreme Court litigation on the citizenship issue as it relates to children of illegal immigrants.*

☆ *Examine both majority and dissenting opinions in terms of how they connected to the meaning assigned the text of the 14th Amendment by those who drafted that language in Congress.*

---

1 Adams, Samuel. *The Writings of Samuel Adams: 1778-1802., Vol. 4.* Edited by Harry Alonzo Cushing. (New York: G.P. Putnam's Sons, 1908), p. 253.

America gains a famous citizen. Albert Einstein receiving from Judge Phillip Forman his certificate of American citizenship. Photo by Al. Aumuller (1940, LOC).

What is a citizen? According to *Webster's 1828 Dictionary*: "in the United States, [it is] a person, native or naturalized, who has the privilege of exercising the elective franchise, or the qualifications which enable him to vote for rulers, and to purchase and hold real estate."[2]

The word "immigration" does not appear in the U.S. Constitution or any of its amendments. "Naturalization" is addressed in both Article I, Section 8 and the 14th Amendment, but both of these are referring to citizenship, not immigration. Therefore, constitutionally, immigration laws are not in the jurisdiction of the Federal government. The rules of immigration were reserved to the States through the Tenth Amendment, which means States could and did make differing determinations regarding the issue of immigration.

In spite of this, Congress passed the "Immigration Act of 1875" – the first federal law regarding immigration. The Founding Fathers would have referred to this as "pretended legislation," as clearly there was no authority for Congress to enact legislation in an area that was unnamed in the Constitution. Piling one wrong on top of another, the U.S. Supreme Court ruled in the following year that immigration regulation was an exclusive Federal responsibility. Congress escalated the active involvement of the federal government by establishing the Immigration Service in 1891, followed by the opening of Ellis Island in 1892 as our nation's first federal immigration station.

A series of legislative action including quotas,[3] adherence to United Nation protocols[4] for

2 http://webstersdictionary1828.com/Dictionary/citizen

3 After World War I (1921 and 1924) Congress enacted quota systems, restricting entry to two percent of the total number of people of each nationality in America as of the 1890 national census to maintain the balance of ethnic groups already in the Americas. Some claimed it favored immigrants from Western Europe, however it also maintained stability so that people of different value systems (those not holding a biblical worldview) would not overwhelm the country and destroy the system designed to secure and protect God-given rights.

4 "The Refugee Act of 1980" was the first time that the U.S. used international standards and definitions for immigration policies with blatant disregard of the impact on the national security and protection of the American people.

refugees, as well as several amnesty programs has led to ever-growing numbers of immigrants – some legal, but many illegally.

Sanctuary cities began in 1979 in Los Angeles to prevent police from inquiring about the immigration status of arrestees. Churches joined the ranks in the 1980s to "provide sanctuary" for people fleeing nations where they were persecuted. Incredibly, this idea morphed into "protecting" illegals who committed other crimes such as rape or murder, shielding them from arrest and deportation.

This lawlessness has become so rampant that Congress proposed legislation in 2015 – Mobilizing Against Sanctuary Cities. The idea was to withhold federal funds for one year from any cities that aided and abetted known criminal illegals.

Why is federal money being sent to cities for the expressed purpose of assisting criminals (illegal immigrants) to break the law? Do we have sanctuary cities for other categories of lawbreakers? The entire idea of "sanctuary cities" is ridiculous, illegal and immoral. Lawbreakers should find no sanctuary.

In 2012, President Barack Obama created the Deferred Action for Childhood Arrivals (DACA) which allowed some protection from deportation of children illegally brought to the United States by their undocumented parents. He did so using an executive branch memorandum – bypassing the legislative process completely. In 2014, President Obama wanted to expand the controversial program and multiple states sued to stop it. Efforts have been made to stop the program, but courts have kept the issue alive. In 2018, it was determined by District Court Judge Andrew Hanen that DACA is likely unconstitutional, but the program remains while moving through in the court system.

In summary, what we have today is an immigration system that is unconstitutional from the ground up, with layer upon layer of unconstitutionality. The constitutional solution is found in Article IV which requires the federal government to protect the States from invasion. In addition, returning immigration authority to the States would certainly cause a sharp decline in illegal immigration. If State Governors could muster the will to do so, they could put the feds on notice that they are in violation of the Constitution and that they will no longer tolerate this and will pass their own immigration laws and enforce them.

Citizenship Rights and Responsibilities

Rights	Responsibilities
Freedom to express yourself.	Support and defend the Constitution.
Freedom to worship as you wish.	Stay informed of the issues affecting your community.
Right to a prompt, fair trial by jury.	Participate in the democratic process.
Right to vote in elections for public officials.	Respect and obey federal, state, and local laws.
Right to apply for federal employment requiring U.S. citizenship.	Respect the rights, beliefs, and opinions of others.
Right to run for elected office.	Participate in your local community.
Freedom to pursue "life, liberty, and the pursuit of happiness."	Pay taxes honestly, and on time, to federal, state, and local authorities.
	Serve on a jury when called upon.
	Defend the country if the need should arise.

▶ **Lecture Five:** Immigration: From Constitutional Beginnings to Anchor Babies; follow along with the notes in the following section.

WHAT MAKES A U.S. CITIZEN?

A. A group of undocumented (also termed illegal alien) parents are currently suing the state of Texas because their babies weren't awarded birth certificates by that State.

    1. Some refer to these children as "anchor babies" – children born in America to parents who are illegally in the country, having bypassed legal immigration channels, and who hope these children will help them to stay in the country despite their illegal status.

B. Mexico's amicus brief against Texas includes:

    1. The argument that "the denial of birth certificates to U.S. citizen children born to immigrant parents not only jeopardizes their dignity and well-being, but could threaten the unique relationship between Mexico and Texas."[5]

    2. The amicus brief claims that denying the children U.S. birth certificates also blocks their claims to Mexican citizenship. A child born to Mexican parents has that right but must show proof of identity. Mexico claims that infringing on that *is a violation of international law.*[6]

---

5 "Mexican Government: Denial of Birth Certificates Harms Children." Julian Aguilar. August 25, 2015. https://www.texastribune.org/2015/08/25/mexican-government-denial-birth-certificates-could/; case information at https://law.justia.com/cases/federal/district-courts/texas/txwdce/1:2015cv00446/753442/82/
6 Ibid.

4. Also, the amicus brief indicates that Mexican children born in the U.S. are eligible for Mexican citizenship. In the 1990s, Mexico changed its citizenship law to permit dual citizenship, and it did so to permit Mexicans residing in the U.S. to exercise dual citizenship and vote in the U.S.[7]

C. The Framers' view of interpreting the Constitution:

1. "If the sense in which the Constitution was accepted and ratified by the Nation … be not the guide in expounding it, there can be no security for a faithful exercise of its powers." – James Madison[8]

2. "The Constitution on which our Union rests, shall be administered by me according to the safe and honest meaning contemplated by the plain understanding of the people of the United States, at the time of its adoption." – Thomas Jefferson[9]

3. In 1823, Thomas Jefferson noted, "On every question of construction, (let us) carry ourselves back to the time when the Constitution was adopted, recollect the spirit manifested in the debates, and instead of trying what meaning may be squeezed out of the text, or invented against it, conform to the probable one in which it was passed."[10]

D. Six critical words from the Constitution are key to this issue:

1. "All persons born or naturalized in the United States, **and subject to the jurisdiction thereof**, are citizens of the United States and of the State wherein they reside."

2. This is known as "the jurisdiction phrase."

E. These issues are connected to the 14th Amendment, which was debated at the time in Congress.

1. The Senate debate before the 14th Amendment's ratification makes clear that the Citizenship Clause's proponents were careful to preclude any automatic grant of citizenship based only on birth within the territory of the United States.

2. They were well aware that a blanket grant of birthright citizenship was not consistent with American tradition and **could lead to a demographic transformation in the event of high immigration**. To prevent it, the senators included the jurisdiction phrase. The floor debate reveals their concerns and their views of how far birthright citizenship should extend.

    a. A primary concern of the Amendment's proponents was the extension of civil rights to recently freed slaves. Senators feared that state legislatures would assert that, not having been born U.S. citizens, emancipation did not make freedmen citizens of their states (hence of the United States; state citizenship was a prerequisite to U.S. citizenship). To forestall any denial of citizenship to freed blacks and to overturn the Dred Scott decision explicitly, the 14th Amendment's proponents introduced the Citizenship Clause.

7   Ibid.
8   "From James Madison to Henry Lee, 25 June 1824." https://founders.archives.gov/documents/Madison/04-03-02-0333
9   "From Thomas Jefferson to Providence Citizens, 27 March 1801." https://founders.archives.gov/documents/Jefferson/01-33-02-0410
10   "From Thomas Jefferson to William Johnson, 12 June 1823." https://founders.archives.gov/documents/Jefferson/98-01-02-3562

b. Introducing the proposed amendment, Senator Jacob Merritt Howard of Michigan stated that he believed the Citizenship Clause was "simply declaratory of what I regard as the law of the land already, that every person born within the limits of the United States, and subject to their jurisdiction, is by virtue of natural and national law, a citizen of the United States."[11] He went on to say specifically whom he considered that natural and national law excluded:

- "This will not, of course, include persons born in the United States who are foreigners, aliens, who belong to the families of ambassadors or foreign ministers accredited...."[12]

- What about Native Americans? As Howard pointed out: "Indians born within the limits of the United States, and who maintain their tribal relations, are not, in the sense of this amendment, born subject to the jurisdiction of the United States. They are regarded, and always have been in our legislation and jurisprudence, as being quasi-foreign nations." [i.e. the Cherokee nation, Sioux nation, Shawnee nation.][13]

- Senator Edgar Cowan of Pennsylvania spoke of citizenship as it related to the Chinese in California who had immigrated in large numbers to work on the railroad. He said, "It is perfectly clear that the mere fact that a man is born in the country has not heretofore entitled him to the right to exercise political power. ...I do not know that there is any danger to many of the States in this Union; but is it proposed that the people of California are to remain quiescent while they are overrun by a flood of immigration...? Are they to be immigrated out of house and home by Chinese? I should think not. It is not supposed that the people of California, in a broad and general sense, have any higher rights than the people of China; but they are in possession of the Country of California, and if another people, of different religion, of different manners, of different traditions, different tastes and sympathies are to come there and have the free right to locate there and settle among them, and if they have an opportunity of pouring in such an immigration as in a short time will double or treble the population of California, I ask, are the people of California powerless to protect themselves? ... As I understand the rights of the States under the Constitution at present, California has the right, if she deems it proper, to forbid the entrance into her territory of any person she chooses who is not a citizen of some one of the United States."[14]

- Senator James Rood Doolittle, (R-WI, 1866) – "[C]itizenship, if conferred, carries with it, as a matter of course, the rights, the responsibilities, the duties, the immunities, the privileges of citizens, for that is the very purpose of this constitutional amendment to extend. ... [I]n the Constitution as [the Founding Fathers] adopted it they excluded the Indians who are not taxed; not enumerate them, indeed, as part of the population upon which they based representation and taxation; much less did they make them citizens of the United States."[15]

---

11 *A Century of Lawmaking for a New Nation: U.S. Congressional Documents and Debates, 1774 - 1875.* Congressional Globe, Senate, 39th Congress, 1st Session. Pg. 2890. http://memory.loc.gov/cgi-bin/ampage?collId=llcg&fileName=073/llcg073.db&recNum=11
12 Ibid.
13 Ibid.
14 Ibid, p. 2890-2891.
15 Ibid, p. 2893.

- Senator Reverdy Johnson of Maryland – "Now, all this amendment provides is, that all persons born in the United States and not subject to some foreign power – for that, no doubt, is the meaning of the committee who have brought the matter before us – shall be considered as citizens of the United States. … I am, however, by no means prepared to say, as I think I have intimated before, that being born within the United States, independent of any new constitutional provision on the subject, creates the relation of citizen to the United States."[16]

- Johnson went on to quote from the Civil Rights Act of 1866, which had just passed. He considered that its wording better expressed what the Citizenship Clause was meant to achieve: "That all persons born in the United States and not subject to any foreign Power, excluding Indians not taxed, are hereby declared to be citizens."[17]

F. Current federal policy is to confer American citizenship automatically on any child (with very narrow exceptions, none applicable to illegal, undocumented aliens) born within the United States. The legal status of the parents is deemed irrelevant.

1. A baby born to foreign parents five minutes after they came over the border illegally is just as American as a baby whose parents are both Americans and U.S. citizens and whose ancestors have been here 350 years.

   a. This new American baby is not the end of the story. The U.S.-born child becomes what some refer to as an "anchor" in American soil that will permit his parents and minor siblings to remain and, later, his grandparents, aunts, uncles, in-laws and all of their children to immigrate legally, not to mention any friends and acquaintances from home who may follow them illegally. All of their children born here will also be considered American citizens.

G. What the 14th Amendment really says:

1. But the actual text of the 14th means anyone who illegally enters the country and gives birth to a baby, both the parents and the baby are still subject to a foreign jurisdiction, that of the country which they left.

2. The birth of a baby does not change the status of the parents, whose status in turn determines that of their offspring.

3. Thus, regarding these children as so-called "anchor babies" are a misinterpretation of the text of the 14th Amendment.

LECTURE FIVE

OPTIONAL READING ASSIGNMENTS

1. Continue reading *The Law* by Fredric Bastiat. Start at "Legal Plunder Has Many Names" and read to "The Seductive Lure of Socialism" (pages 258-259).

2. "The Constitutional Pardon of Joe Arpaio" by Jake MacAulay; this article is found at https://www.theamericanview.com/the-constitutional-pardon-of-joe-arpaio/. We will learn more about Presidential pardons in a later chapter.

---

16 Ibid, p. 2893.
17 Ibid, p. 2894.

LECTURE REVIEWS

1. Complete Lecture Five Review Worksheet.

2. Complete Lecture Five Quiz, including True & False Questions.

GOING DEEPER: SUPPLEMENTAL READING & VIDEO OPTIONS

 Found at www.theamericanview.com/constitution-course-supplemental-assignments which can also be found at the bottom of theamericanview.com under Resources.

"Is The Blue Wave Actually a Crime Wave?" optional video featuring Jake MacAulay: https://www.theamericanview.com/blue-wave-actually-crime-wave/

The U.S. Constitution (text in Appendix on pages 222-231). In preparation for the three following lectures, which will overview the seven articles of our Constitution.

CHAPTER SIX

OVERVIEW OF THE CONSTITUTION:
PREAMBLE AND ARTICLE I

GENERAL OBJECTIVES

It is our intent and hope that you will understand the ratification debates and the ratification process, the purposes set forth in the Preamble, and the content of Article I of the Constitution.

SPECIFIC OBJECTIVES

☆ *Know the general details of the ratification debates including the parties involved, their respective viewpoints and arguments and the eventual result of their debates viewed through the prism and with the benefit of history.*

☆ *Understand the purpose and meaning of the Preamble to the Constitution and its legal and authoritative effect.*

☆ *Understand the provisions of Article I of the Constitution and the relevance of the limits it sets on the authority of Congress.*

"...every word of (the Constitution) decides a question between power and liberty..."[1]

–James Madison

"And Moses came and called for the elders of the people, and laid before their faces all these words which the LORD commanded him."
– Exodus 19:7

---

1 "For the National Gazette, 18 January 1792." https://founders. archives.gov/documents/Madison/01-14-02-0172

Lecture Six: Overview of the Constitution: Preamble and Article I; follow along with the notes in the following section.

THE RATIFICATION DEBATES

A. "Federalism" simply means shared power between Federal and State governments.

B. Constitution supporters called themselves Federalists. Alexander Hamilton, James Madison and John Jay wrote essays called The Federalist Papers. Federalists had two advantages:

   1. Federalism was a popular term.

   2. They were intimately familiar with the Constitution; the Anti-Federalists, such as Patrick Henry and Samuel Adams, had not seen it before September 17th.

   3. Anti-Federalist arguments:

      a. Congress had authorized the Convention only to revise the Articles of Confederation, not to create a new Constitution.

      b. Defects in Articles of Confederation could be corrected by a few amendments.

      c. Lack of Bill of Rights was dangerous. (But inclusion of Bill of Rights was dangerous.)

      d. Republic could succeed only in a small nation; large nations needed to be a loose confederation to remain Republican (i.e. concept of State Sovereignty) (Montesquieu).

      e. Federal government had too much power.

      f. Congress controlled both treasury and military.

      g. Judicial review could be dangerous.

THE CONSTITUTION IS RATIFIED (Nine States Required)

A. Delaware ratified unanimously, December 6, 1787.

B. Pennsylvania ratified 46 - 23, December 12, 1787.

C. New Jersey ratified unanimously, December 18, 1787.

D. Georgia ratified unanimously, January 2, 1788.

E. Connecticut ratified 128 - 40, January 9, 1788.

F. Massachusetts ratified 187 - 168, February 16, 1788.

G. Maryland ratified 63 - 11, April 26, 1788.

H. South Carolina ratified 149 - 73, May 23, 1788.

I. New Hampshire ratified 57 - 46, June 21, 1788.

J. Virginia ratified 87 - 79, June 25, 1788.

K. New York ratified 30 - 27, July 26, 1788.

L. North Carolina ratified 194 - 77, November 21, 1789.

M. Rhode Island ratified 34 - 32, May 29, 1790.

THE PREAMBLE

A. "We the People"

    1. Shows that governmental power is derived from the consent of the governed.

    2. Shows the Framers' view of the covenantal or contractual nature of governmental authority.

B. "In Order to" sets forth the basic purposes for which government is formed:

    1. "Form a more perfect Union" (Ends the disunity that was rampant under the Articles of Confederation.)

    2. "Establish Justice" (The Articles of Confederation had no court system. The Constitution provides for an orderly and fair court system. Recognizes there is such a thing as justice, which implies a fixed absolute standard.)

    3. "Insure domestic Tranquility" (Prevents insurrections such as were threatening under the Articles.)

    4. "Provide for the common defense" (Framers believed in defense and had difficulty providing for the common defense under the system of voluntary requisitions.)

    5. "Promote the general Welfare" (Not specific welfare of individuals, or groups.)

    6. "Secure the Blessings of Liberty to ourselves and our Posterity"

        a. Shows Framers' fundamental concern for liberty.

        b. Shows they intended the Constitution to be a permanent document.

        c. Shows their concern for future generations.

        d. May imply protection of unborn children.

C. "Do ordain and establish this Constitution for the United States of America." (Again, this demonstrates the covenantal and contractual nature of governmental authority.)

D. The Preamble simply states purposes: It grants no powers to the Federal government.

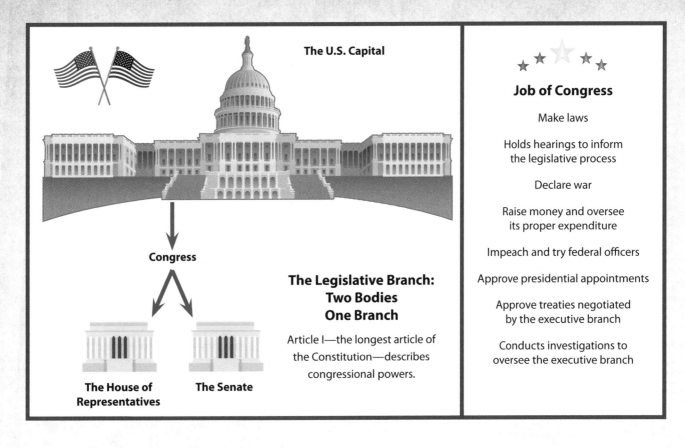

The U.S. Capital

Congress

The Legislative Branch:
Two Bodies
One Branch

Article I—the longest article of
the Constitution—describes
congressional powers.

The House of
Representatives

The Senate

Job of Congress

Make laws

Holds hearings to inform
the legislative process

Declare war

Raise money and oversee
its proper expenditure

Impeach and try federal officers

Approve presidential appointments

Approve treaties negotiated
by the executive branch

Conducts investigations to
oversee the executive branch

E. The Preamble is brief because the Declaration of Independence sets forth the basic ideals of the nation and is the true preamble to the Constitution.

ARTICLE I - LEGISLATIVE BRANCH Section 1 -"All" legislative authority is "vested." Establishes bicameral (two-house) Congress.

A. House of Representatives:

    1. Popularly elected.

    2. Represents people by district.

B. Senate:

    1. Chosen by State legislatures before 1915.

    2. After 1915 (17th Amendment), popularly elected. (This change represented a change away from a constitutional republic and more towards a democracy.)

    3. Represents people by State.

C. Why two houses?

    1. Result of the Great Compromise suggested by Roger Sherman of Connecticut.

    2. Prior to 1915, senators were chosen by state legislatures to represent the sovereign states and to be accountable to the states. This was a check on Federal Power.

3. Partially parallel to English Parliament:

    a. House like the British House of Commons, more popular.

    b. Senate originally like House of Lords, more aristocratic and deliberative.

4. Requiring two Houses to pass a bill before it becomes law, cools hotheaded legislation and provides additional time for reflection – especially since Senators are chosen differently and serve staggered six-year terms.

5. Can a bicameral legislature thwart the majority will? Yes – and the Framers thought it sometimes should because they distrusted popular majorities.

    They created a constitutional republic; not a democracy.

6. Distinctions of a "republic":

    a. Republican government is indirect through representatives; Democracy is more direct.

    b. In a republic, the law is supreme and all men including its leaders are subject to it (objective, fixed standard – Rule of Law).

    c. In a republic, the minority has rights which even the majority may not violate; in a democracy, majority rule is absolute (Subjective, ever-changing standard – Rule of Man).

SECTIONS 2-6:

"... provide for the composition of the House and Senate and establish the authority of each House to determine its own procedures, discipline, etc. Section 6 ensures that Congressmen shall be free to discuss all matters by protecting them from being sued for what they say on the floor of Congress, and also preserves the separation of powers by providing that no Congressman may simultaneously hold another Federal office."

SECTION 7: THE LEGISLATIVE PROCESS

A. Revenue bills originate in House (the people); Senate must concur.

B. Legislation starts in Congress; President only can suggest legislation.

C. Presidential veto:

1. President may veto "the bill" (implies whole bill, not line item veto).

2. Congress may override 2/3 vote in each House.

3. Partially parallel to English Parliament

    a. House like the British House of Commons, more popular.

SECTION 8: 18 SPECIFIC, GRANTED AND ENUMERATED POWERS OF CONGRESS

A. Tax and spend for:

   1. Payment of Debts.

   2. Common Defense.

   3. General Welfare.

        a. Original Intent – "Congress has not unlimited powers to provide for the general welfare, but is restrained to those specifically enumerated…"[2] Thomas Jefferson.

        b. Subsequent court opinion upheld original intent – U.S. v. Butler, 297 U.S. 1 (1936); "General" welfare implies government may not tax and spend for "specific" welfare of individuals, regions, or socioeconomic groups, or to regulate under the guise of taxation. "The power to confer or withhold unlimited benefits is the power to coerce or destroy."[3]

        c. Subsequent court opinion destroying original intent, after President Franklin D. Roosevelt's new Supreme Court Appointments – Steward Machine Co. v. Davis, 301 U.S. 548 (1937): This and subsequent decisions held that Congress may tax some groups and subsidize others, because the subsidized groups will spend more and thus stimulate the general welfare. The distinction between general and specific welfare has been virtually obliterated, and the word "general" has been effectively written out of the Constitution, vastly expanding Federal power.[4]

B. Borrow money.

C. Regulate commerce:

   1. With foreign nations.

   2. With Indian tribes (nations within our nation).

   3. Among the several States:

        a. Carter v. Carter Coal Co., 298 U.S. 238 (1936); Congress cannot regulate intrastate production under guise of regulating interstate commerce.[5]

        b. NLRB v. Jones & Laughlin Steel, 301 U.S. 1(1937); Congress can regulate labor disputes in intrastate steel production when necessary to ensure free flow of steel in intrastate production of any goods which are intended for interstate commerce.[6]

        c. Wickard v. Filburn, 317 U.S. 111(1942); Congress may regulate domestic production of grain intended for consumption by livestock on same farm, because such production could potentially affect interstate commerce.[7]

---

2 "Thomas Jefferson to Albert Gallatin, June 16, 1817." https://www.loc.gov/item/mtjbib022897/

3 "U.S. Reports: United States v. Butler, 297 U.S. 1 (1936)." https://www.loc.gov/item/usrep297001/

4 "U.S. Reports: Steward Machine Co. v. Davis, Collector of Internal Revenue, 301 U.S. 548 (1937)." https://www.loc.gov/item/usrep301548/

5 "U.S. Reports: Carter v. Carter Coal Co., 298 U.S. 238 (1936)." https://www.loc.gov/item/usrep298238/

6 "U.S. Reports: National Labor Relations Board v. Jones & Laughlin Steel Corp., 301 U.S. 1 (1937)." https://www.loc.gov/item/usrep301001/

7 "U.S. Reports: Wickard v. Filburn, 317 U.S. 111 (1942)." https://www.loc.gov/item/usrep317111/

How Congress Passes a Law

House	Senate

Bill Introduction

Bill Introduction
Bill is introduce by a member and assigned to a committee, which usually refers it to a subcommittee.

Bill Introduction
Bill is introduce by a member and assigned to a committee, which usually refers it to a subcommittee.

Committee Action

Subcommittee
Subcommittee performs studies, holds hearings, and makes revisions. If appoved, the bill goes to the full committee.

Subcommittee
Subcommittee performs studies, holds hearings, and makes revisions. If appoved, the bill goes to the full committee.

Committee
Full committee may amend or rewrite the bill, before deciding whether to send it to the House floor, recommending its approval, or to kill it. If approved, the bill is reported to the full House and placed on the calendar.

Committee
Full committee may amend or rewrite the bill, before deciding whether to send it to the Senate floor, recommending its approval, or to kill it. If approved, the bill is reported to the full Senate and placed on the calendar.

Rules Committee
Rules Committee issues a rule governing debate on the House floor and sends the bill to the full House.

Leadership
Senate leaders of both parties schedule Senate debate on the bill.

Floor Action

Full House
Bill is debated by the full House, amendments are offered, and a vote is taken. If the bill passes in a different version from that passed in the Senate, it is sent to a conference committee.

Full Senate
Bill is debated by the full Senate, amendments are offered, and a vote is taken. If the bill passes in a different version from that passed in the House, it is sent to a conference committee.

Conference Action

Conference Committee
Conference committee composed of members of both House and Senate meet to iron out differences between the bills. The compromise bill is returned to both the House and Senate for a vote.

Full House
Full House votes on conference committee version. If it passes, the bill is sent to the president.

Full Senate
Full Senate votes on conference committee version. If it passes, the bill is sent to the president.

Presidential Decision

President
Preident signs or vetoes the bill. Congress may override a veto by a two-thirds vote in both House and Senate.

Law

4. These decisions have effectively obliterated the distinction between interstate and intrastate commerce, thereby vastly expanding Federal power.

D. Make rules for Naturalization and Bankruptcy. (The word "immigration" does not appear in the Constitution. Prior to 1875 rules of immigration were reserved to the States through the Tenth Amendment.)

E. Coin money, regulate money value, fix weights and measures.

F. Punish counterfeiting.

G. Establish post offices and post roads.

H. Establish rules for Copyrights and Patents.

I. Establish Federal courts below Supreme Court.

J. Define and punish piracy and felonies on high seas, and violations of Law of Nations (Framers derived concept of "Law of Nations" from Hugo Grotius, Samuel von Pufendorf, Emer de Vattel and others, who based the concept on the Laws of Nature and of Nature's God.)

K. Declare war. Grant letters of marque and reprisal (authority given to commercial ship captains to seize foreign ships). Make rules concerning captures on land and water.

L. Raise and support armies. ("Armies" is generic term for non-naval forces; broad enough to include Air Force.) Two-year limitation on funding indicates armies were to be temporary; basis of land defense was to be reserve militia, again implying temporary force as needed.

M. Provide and maintain Navy (more permanent force).

N. Rules of discipline for military forces (Uniform Code of Military Justice).

O. Provide for calling militia into Federal service to:

    1. Execute Federal laws.

    2. Suppress insurrections.

    3. Repel invasions.

P. Organize, arm, discipline militia:

    1. Congress controls militia while in Federal service.

    2. States reserve right to appoint militia officers, subject to discipline of Congress.

Q. Control Federal property, specifically limited to:

    1. Post offices and post roads (Section 8, Clause 7)

    2. The seat of government of the United States (Washington, D.C.) (Section 8, Clause 17)

3. Military facilities … erection of forts, magazines, arsenals, dockyards… (Section 8, Clause 17)

R. Do what may be "necessary and proper" to carry out foregoing powers and other powers granted to Congress.

1. Often called "elastic clause," because it expands Federal power.

2. Limited to that which is necessary and proper to carry out other delegated powers.

3. McCulloch v. Maryland, 17 U.S. 316 (1819):[8]

a. "Necessary" means reasonably suited, not absolutely indispensable.

b. "Proper" means not forbidden by other provisions of Constitution.

SECTION 9: LIMITATIONS OF CONGRESSIONAL AUTHORITY

A. Cannot forbid slave trade before 1808.

B. Cannot suspend Habeas Corpus except in emergency. (Habeas Corpus: Writ demanding that government either give legitimate reason for holding a person, or let the person go.)

C. Cannot pass bill of attainder (legislative finding of guilt; that is left to the courts).

D. Cannot pass ex post facto law:

1. Law punishing person for act that was legal when committed.

2. Law raising status of offense (misdemeanor to felony).

3. Law increasing penalty for offense.

4. Law making it easier to convict (rules of evidence).

E. Direct taxes must be in proportion to census.

F. No tax or duty on items exported from one state to another.

G. No preference for local ships or ports over others.

H. No money drawn from Treasury except by appropriation of Congress; regular public accounting.

I. No title of nobility (Concept of equality).

SECTION 10: LIMITATIONS OF STATE AUTHORITY

---

8 "U.S. Reports: McCulloch v. State of Maryland., 17 U.S. (4 Wheat.) 316 (1819)." https://www.loc.gov/item/usrep017316/

A. States may not:

    1.   Enter treaties, alliances, or confederations.

    2.   Grant letters of marque and reprisal (assume jurisdictional authority for issuing their own laws for payment of any loss at sea.)

    3.   Issue money (paper or coin), or make anything but gold and silver coin a tender in payment of debts.

    4.   Pass bills of attainder (See Section 9).

    5.   Pass ex post facto law (See Section 9).

    6.   Pass law impairing obligation of contracts:

        a.   Framers believed the right to make and enforce contracts was a God-given right.

        b.   Home Building & Loans Assn. v. Blaisdell, 290 U.S. 398 (1934)[9]: State moratorium on mortgage foreclosures was reasonable under emergency circumstances.

        c.   Court has effectively written "unreasonably" into this clause, where Framers did not do so. State authority to interfere with private business relations is thus vastly increased.

    7.   Grant titles of nobility (See Section 9).

B. States may not, without consent of Congress:

    1.   Tax imports and exports, except as necessary for inspections.

    2.   Levy duty of tonnage on ships (equal competition).

    3.   Keep troops or ships in peacetime.

    4.   Make agreements or compacts with other States.

    5.   Make war, except when invaded or in imminent danger.

---

9 "U.S. Reports: Home Bldg & L. Assn. v. Blaisdell, 290 U.S. 398 (1934)." https://www.loc.gov/item/usrep290398/

The United States Capitol Building, Washington DC

CONSTITUTIONAL SHERIFF IN ACTION

NOTE: The County Sheriff is the only elected law enforcement position in the nation. It would seem that one of the best ways to get elected to county sheriff these days is to campaign against encroachments by the federal government on basic rights guaranteed by the U.S. Constitution. Sheriff Brad Rogers is a member of the Constitutional Sheriffs and Peace Officers Association (www.cspoa.org) and was afforded an opportunity to act on that promise (see also www.oathkeepers.org).

County Sheriff Intervenes Against Feds In Raw Milk Case

In 2011, Sheriff Rogers of Elkhart County, Indiana stood up for one of his constituents, raw dairy farmer David Hochstetler, who was being subpoenaed to appear before a federal grand jury in Detroit, exploring felony charges in connection with his distribution of raw milk.[10]

Hochstetler had undergone repeated inspections by federal regulators, culminating in this subpoena. His situation prompted Elkhart County Sheriff Brad Rogers to intervene, telling Hochstetler, "I will protect you in Elkhart County. I can't protect you in Detroit. Are you ready for some sparks to fly?" Hochstetler said he was.[11]

Sheriff Rogers advised the feds to watch their step or face arrest by his department, stating the continuous inspections of Hochstetler constituted harassment and were unreasonable. Rogers emailed the Justice Department trial attorney, "This is notice that if there are any further attempts to inspect this farm without a search warrant signed by a trial judge, I will have you removed or arrested for trespassing."[12]

The response from the Justice Department declared that the federal government had precedence based on the Supremacy Clause (U.S. Constitution, Article VI). Rogers responded back by telling him the federal government is supreme IF the issue at hand has to do with the Constitution. [Note: There is no mention of raw milk or any other food product or production in the Constitution. See Article I, Section 8; also Amendments 9 and 10.]

This exchange happened on a Friday. On Tuesday, Mr. Hochstetler received a certified letter from the Department of Justice saying they had withdrawn the subpoena. U.S. Department of Justice attorney had no reply when interviewed regarding this exchange.

This story is about much more than just raw milk. It's about the role of the federal government in the affairs of the States. Sheriffs take an oath to uphold the Constitution, not to enforce arbitrary, unconstitutional mandates or inspections by federal regulators or bureaucrats. It's about the federal government trampling on individual rights.

"The arrogance of thinking federal law trumps everything flies in the face of the Tenth Amendment," Rogers said. "If we think the federal government trumps everything, we're destined for big trouble in the freedoms here in our country."[13]

10 http://www.goshennews.com/news/middlebury-dairy-farmer-sheriff-stand-up-to-fda/article_b07a8430-9897-5504-9820-d943d60149f6.html
11 http://healthimpactnews.com/2012/sheriff-who-challenged-feds-for-amish-raw-dairy-farmer-receives-award-for-meritorious-valor/
12 https://www.davidgumpert.com/hows-this-for-a-change-of-pace-sheriff-who-challenged-feds-for-amish-raw-dairy-farmer-receives-award-for-meritorious-valor-ca-sheriff-vows-to-protect-herdshares
13 https://thebovine.wordpress.com/2011/12/21/local-sheriff-intervenes-against-federal-agents-in-elkhart-county-raw-milk-case/

LECTURE SIX

1. Continue reading *The Law* by Fredric Bastiat. Start at "Enforced Fraternity Destroys Liberty" and read to "Law Is a Negative Concept" (pages 259-261).

LECTURE REVIEWS

1. Complete Lecture Six Review Worksheet.

2. Complete Lecture Six Quiz, including True & False Questions.

GOING DEEPER: SUPPLEMENTAL READING & VIDEO OPTIONS

 Free videos available on news items related to the Constitution at: https://www. theamericanview.com/commentaries/jake-macaulay/

CHAPTER SEVEN
PROPERTY OWNERSHIP PRINCIPLES:
INDIVIDUAL & STATE OWNERSHIP VS. FEDERAL LAND GRABS

GENERAL OBJECTIVES

It is our intent and hope that you will discover constitutional principles regarding ownership of property, particularly the laws regarding Federal vs. State jurisdiction and authority.

By what right or reason is the federal government able to justify owning almost 30% of land in the United States? It may be time to consider how this practice began and why it continues. Also, what recourse do States have that find themselves with the federal government owning most of the land in the state and therefore, it cannot be developed or taxed to benefit residents? It is a classic case of whether rights of the States in the Union supersede those of the federal government and if all States are truly considered to be "equal."

SPECIFIC OBJECTIVES

☆ *Discover what constitutional issues are at stake in this debate.*

☆ *Learn the history of "Enabling Acts" for Admission of new States.*

☆ *Explore the problems with Federal Land "ownership."*

☆ *Determine what solutions there may be for this controversy.*

"Ultimately property rights and personal rights are the same thing."[1]
–Calvin Coolidge

"A grove of giant redwood or sequoias should be kept just as we keep a great and beautiful cathedral."[2]
–Theodore Roosevelt

"She considereth a field, and buyeth it: with the fruit of her hands she planteth a vineyard."
–Proverbs 31:16

1 "Quotations - P." Calvin Coolidge Presidential Foundation. https://www.coolidgefoundation.org/quote/quotations-p/
2 "Theodore Roosevelt Quotes." National Park Service. https://www.nps.gov/thro/learn/historyculture/theodore-roosevelt-quotes.htm

The federal government currently controls over 640 million acres in the United States, including some that take up a majority of areas in some states. Consider these facts – "the federal government owns 28% of all U.S. land," including 53% of land in Oregon with vast national forests, as well as 85% of land in Nevada.[3] What is the basis for the federal government to own this land? What problems exist from their oversight and management? What rights do states with federal lands have?

▶ **Lecture Seven:** Property Ownership Principles: Individual & State Ownership vs. Federal Land Grabs; follow along with the notes in the following section.

U.S. CONSTITUTION Article I, Section 8 states, "Congress shall have Power to lay and collect Taxes, Duties, Imposts and Excises...."

A. Further, Clause 17 notes: "To exercise exclusive Legislation in all Cases whatsoever, over such District (not exceeding ten Miles square) as may, by Cession of particular States and the Acceptance of Congress, become the Seat of the Government of the United States, and to exercise like Authority over all Places purchased by the Consent of the Legislature of the State in which the Same shall be, [5 purposes] for the Erection of Forts, Magazines, Arsenals, Dockyards, and other needful buildings…"

U.S. CONSTITUTION Article IV, Section 3 states:

A. New States may be admitted by the Congress into this Union; but no new States shall be formed or erected within the Jurisdiction of any other State; nor any State be formed by the Junction of two or more States, or Parts of States, without the Consent of the Legislatures of the States concerned as well as of the Congress.

B. The Congress shall have Power to dispose of and make all needful Rules and Regulations respecting the Territory or other Property belonging to the United States; and nothing in this Constitution shall be so construed as to Prejudice any Claims of the United States, or of any particular State.

---

3 Johnson, D. and Rebala, P. (2016). http://time.com/4167983/federal-government-land-oregon/ [Accessed 18 Oct. 2018].

U.S. CONSTITUTION Article IV, Section 4 states:

A. "The United States shall guarantee to every State in this Union a Republican form of Government..."

FEDERAL TEMPORARY LAND OWNERSHIP began when *the original 13 states* ceded title to more than 40% of their "western" lands (237 million acres between the Appalachian Mountains and the Mississippi River) to the central government between 1781 and 1802.

This type of ownership of the federal government of land continued with acquisition from foreign countries via treaties beginning with the Louisiana Purchase (530 million acres) in 1803 and continued via treaties with Great Britain and Spain (76 million acres) in 1817 and 1819, respectively. Other substantial acquisitions (620 million acres), via purchases and treaties occurred between 1846 and 1853. The last major North American land acquisition by the U.S. federal government was the purchase of Alaska, from Russia (378 million acres) in 1867.

REJECTING THE FOUNDERS' INTERPRETATIONS

A. Those who reject the constitutional interpretation of the Founders regarding federal ownership of land claim the "means by which the federal government came to own its lands can affect which laws govern the management of that land."[4]

B. This would mean States which joined the Union formed from those territories acquired in this fashion do not have the same powers which are possessed by those States which came into the Union by other means.

C. Thus you have a two-tiered structure according to those who defend this "Federal Land Grab."

THE EQUAL FOOTING DOCTRINE

A. House of Representatives:

   1. James Madison had included provisions for equality in admittance of the new States in the first draft of the Constitution:

   2. "If admission be consented to, new states shall be admitted on the same terms with the original states."

   3. Madison insisted that **the Western States neither would nor ought to submit to a union which degraded them from an equal rank with the other States.**"[5]

4 http://www.law.umaryland.edu/marshall/crsreports/crsdocuments/RL34267_12032007.pdf
5 Madison, J. and Hunt, G., Editor, *"Journal of the Debates in the Convention which Framed the Constitution"*. (New York: G. P. Putnam's Sons, 1908), p. 274.

B. George Mason stated: "If the Western States are to be admitted to the Union, they must be treated as equals and subject to no degrading discrimination. They will have the same pride and other passions which we have, and will either not unite with or will speedily revolt from the Union, if they are not in all respects placed on an equal footing with their brethren."[6]

C. The doctrine means that "equality of constitutional right and power is the condition of all States of the Union, old and new." Escanaba v. City of Chicago, 107 U.S. 678, 689 (1883).[7]

D. The term comes from state enabling acts that included the phrase that the state was admitted "into the Union on an equal footing with the original States in all respects whatsoever."[8]

E. See any of the 28 enabling acts[9] (9 States were admitted without enabling acts – VT, KY, TN, AK, MI, FL, KS, ID, WY).

THE U.S. SUPREME COURT HAS CLARIFIED WHAT EQUAL FOOTING RIGHTS ARE:

A. In the context of land, the equal footing doctrine has been held to mean, for example, that states have the authority over the beds of navigable waterways.

6   Carson, C. *A Basic History of the United States, Volume 2,* (Wadley, AL: American Textbook Committee, 1995).
7   https://www.law.cornell.edu/supremecourt/text/107/678
8   Ronald Reagan: "Proclamation 5676—Northwest Ordinance Bicentennial Day, 1987," July 8, 1987. Online by Gerhard Peters and John T. Woolley, The American Presidency Project. http://www.presidency.ucsb.edu/ws/?pid=34525
9   This is defined as "a statute empowering a person or body to take certain action, especially to make regulations, rules, or orders." https://en.oxforddictionaries.com/definition/us/enabling_act [Accessed 18 Oct. 2018].

B. The doctrine and some language within the U.S. Supreme Court case of Pollard's Lessee v. Hagan 44 U.S. (3 How.) 21 (1845) provide an argument that the federal government held the lands ceded by the original states only temporarily pending their disposal.

C. It is clear that the equal footing doctrine prohibits permanent federal land ownership.[10] The vast majority of current federal land ownership violates this principle.

D. The federal government has "allowed" some public use of some government-owned land, i.e. livestock grazing and timber industry, only to disallow it later, causing individuals to lose their livelihood.

OHIO ENABLING ACT[11] includes the following:

A. Section 1 "...shall be admitted into the Union upon the same footing with the original States in all respects whatever."[12]

B. Section 7, Third Article – "The one-twentieth part of the net proceeds of the lands lying within the said State sold by Congress, from and after the thirtieth day of June next, (1803 three months after they were admitted to the Union) after deducting all expenses incident to the same, shall be applied to the laying out and making public roads, leading from the navigable waters emptying into the Atlantic, to the Ohio, to the said State…

C. …and through the same such roads to be laid out under authority of Congress, with the consent of the several States through which the road shall pass; Provided always, That the three foregoing propositions herein offered are on the conditions that the convention of the said State shall provide, by an ordinance irrevocable without the consent of the United State, that every and each tract of land sold by Congress from and after the thirtieth day of June next, shall be and remain exempt from any tax laid by order or under authority of the State, whether for State, county, township, or any other purpose whatever, for the term of five years from and after the day of sale."[13] — Approved April 30, 1802

D. These above provisions allowed Congress to continue selling land and creating roads in Ohio after Ohio was admitted into the Union. This means the federal government was still making money off land that now belonged to the State of Ohio, and deciding where roads would be made, making the federal government an authority inside a sovereign state, thereby clearly not granting them the "equal footing" of all previous states.

OHIO CONSTITUTIONAL CONVENTION REPLIED ON NOVEMBER 29, 1802, REGARDING THE "ENABLING ACT":

A. "…do resolve to accept of the said propositions, provided the following additions to and modification of the said propositions shall be agreed to by the Congress … That not less that three percent, of the net proceeds of the lands of the United States lying within the limits of the State of Ohio, sold and to be sold after the thirtieth day of June last, shall be applied in laying out roads within the State…"[14]

10 https://www.law.cornell.edu/supremecourt/text/44/212 (https://www.law.cornell.edu/supremecourt/text/44/212 has additional notes on the issue.)
11 http://www.ohiohistorycentral.org/w/Enabling_Act_of_1802
12 http://www.ohiohistorycentral.org/w/Enabling_Act_of_1802_(Transcript)
13 Ibid.
14 Ibid.

Northwest Ordinance of July 13, 1787:

A. Article IV – "The legislatures of those districts or new States, shall never interfere with the primary disposal of the soil by the United States in Congress assembled, nor with any regulations Congress may find necessary for securing the title in such soil to the bona fide purchasers. No tax shall be imposed on lands the property of the United States…."[15]

B. Article V – "Any of the said States shall have sixty thousand free inhabitants therein, such State shall be admitted, by its delegates, into the Congress of the United States, on an equal footing with the original States in all respects whatever, and shall be at liberty to form a permanent constitution and State government: Provided, the constitution and government so to be formed, shall be republican, and in conformity to the to the principles contained in these articles…."[16]

Which "Authority" came first?

A. Northwest Ordinance – July 13, 1787

B. U.S. Constitution – September 17, 1787

    1. Ratified by nine States as of June 21, 1788

        a. Article VI, Section 2 – "This Constitution and the Laws of the United States which shall be made in Pursuance thereof…shall be the supreme law of the land…"

Louisiana Enabling Act of 1812: Section 3

Old Louisana State Capitol building, Baton Rouge, Louisiana (1849–1862, 1882–1932).

"And provided also, That the said convention shall provide by ordinance, irrevocable without the consent of the United States, that the people inhabiting the said territory do agree and declare that <u>they forever disclaim all right or title to the waste or unappropriated lands</u> lying within the said territory, and that the same shall be and remain at the <u>sole and entire disposition of the United States</u>, and moreover that each and every tract of land sold by Congress shall be and remain exempt from any tax laid … for the term of five years from and after the respective days of the sales thereof…"[17] [NOTE: Each of the underlined passages revoke the original Equal Footing doctrine of Sovereign Statehood as stated in the Ninth and Tenth Amendments, and replace it with "Enabling" doctrine language, inappropriately giving the federal government ownership rights and privileges of use and taxation.]

15 Transcript of Northwest Ordinance (1787); https://www.ourdocuments.gov/doc.php?flash=false&doc=8&page=transcript
16 Ibid.
17 "Enabling Act (Louisiana)." https://en.wikisource.org/wiki/Enabling_Act_(Louisiana)

"Be it enacted by the Senate and House of Representatives of the United States of America in Congress assembled, That, subject to the provisions of this act, and upon issuance of the proclamation required by section 8(c) of this Act, the State of Alaska is hereby declared to be a State of the United States of America, is declared admitted into the Union on an *equal footing* with the other States in all respects whatever, and the constitution formed pursuant to the provisions of the Act of the Territorial Legislature of Alaska entitled."[18] [NOTE: This language seemed to restore the Constitutional State Sovereignty of the Equal Footing Doctrine but was followed by Section 6 below.]

A. An Act to provide for the holding of a constitutional convention to prepare a constitution for the State of Alaska; to submit the constitution to the people for adoption or rejection; to prepare for the admission of Alaska as a State; to make an appropriation; and setting an effective date, approved March 19, 1955 (Chapter 46, Session Laws of Alaska, 1955), and adopted by a vote of the people of Alaska in the election held an April 24, 1956, is hereby found to be republican in form and in conformity with the Constitution of the United States and the principles of the Declaration of Independence, and is hereby accepted, ratified, and confirmed.[19]

B. Alaska Statehood Act – Section 6 – (Selection of public lands, fish and wildlife, public schools, mineral permits, mineral grants, confirmation of grants, internal improvements, submerged lands) (b) *The State of Alaska*, in addition to any other grants made in this section, is *hereby granted and shall be entitled to select, within twenty-five years after the admission of Alaska into the Union, not to exceed one hundred and two million five hundred and fifty thousand acres from the public lands of the United States in Alaska* which are vacant, unappropriated, and unreserved at the time of their selection: Provided, That nothing herein contained shall affect any valid existing claim, location, or entry under the laws of the United States, ... And provided further, That no selection hereunder shall be made in the area north and west of the line described in Section 10 without approval of the President or his designated representative.[20] [NOTE: This language completely strikes down the principles of the Ninth and Tenth Amendments and the Equal Footing Doctrine, declaring Alaska under the ownership of the federal government, and "giving permission" for Alaska to claim 24% of its land over the next 25 years. After Alaska became a state this language kept the federal government in possession of Alaskan land and never conferred Alaska with its rights as a sovereign state.]

18 Alaska Statehood Act. The Alaska State Legislature website. https://www.akleg.gov/basis/get_documents.asp?session=29&docid=29890
19 Ibid.
20 Ibid.

THE MEANING OF THE ADMISSION CLAUSE:

A. (**Article IV, Section 3, Clause 1**) – New States may be admitted by the Congress into this Union; but no new States shall be formed or erected within the Jurisdiction of any other State; nor any State be formed by the Junction of two or more States, or Parts of States, without the Consent of the Legislatures of the States concerned as well as of the Congress.

B. The Congress shall have Power to **dispose** of and make all needful Rules and Regulations **respecting the Territory** or other Property belonging to the United States; and nothing in this Constitution shall be so construed as to Prejudice any Claims of the United States, or of any particular State.

WHAT ARE THE SOLUTIONS TO THE "FEDERAL LAND GRAB"?

Nullification and Interposition

A. **Interposition** – The action of a State while exercising its sovereignty in rejecting a federal mandate that it believes is unconstitutional or overreaching. — *Black's Law Dictionary*[21]

Nullification – The act of making something void; the action of a State in abrogating a federal law on the basis of State sovereignty. — *Black's Law Dictionary*[22]

    1. Utah Legislation approved in the House with a 61-9 vote State Jurisdiction of Federally Managed Lands Joint Resolution.

        a. "Be it resolved, that the Legislature of the state of Utah calls on the United States, through their agent, Congress, to relinquish to the state of Utah all right, title, and jurisdiction in those lands that were committed to the purposes of this state by **terms of its Enabling act** compact with them and that now reside within the state as public lands managed by the Bureau of Land Management that were reserved by Congress after the date of Utah statehood,"[23]

        b. "the federal trust respecting public lands obligates the United States, through their agent, Congress, to extinguish both their governmental jurisdiction and their title on the public lands that are held in trust by the United States for the states in which they are located."[24]

        c. If that is not done, the resolution said, "the state is denied the same complete and independent sovereignty and jurisdiction that was expressly retained by the original states, and its citizens are denied the political right to establish or administer their own republican self-governance as is their right under the Equal Footing Clause."[25]

---

21 Black, Henry Campbell. *Black's Law Dictionary*. Fourth Edition. (St. Paul: West Publishing Company, 1968), p. 953.
22 Black, Henry Campbell. *Black's Law Dictionary*. Fifth Edition. (St. Paul: West Publishing Company, 1979), p. 963.
23 "State Jurisdiction of Federally Managed Lands Joint Resolution." Utah State Legislature Site. https://le.utah.gov/~2011/bills/hbillint/HJR039.htm
24 Ibid.
25 Ibid.

2.	The resolution explains that use of the more than 22 million acres at issue "has been eroded by an oppressive and over-reaching federal management agenda that has adversely impacted the sovereignty and the economies of the state of Utah and local governments."[26]
3.	Now, suddenly, it explains, the Department of Interior has "arbitrarily created a new category of lands, denominated 'Wild Lands,' and has superimposed these mandatory protective management provisions upon BLM operations and planning decisions in violation of the provisions of the Federal Land Policy and Management Act, the provisions of the Administrative Procedures Act, and Presidential Executive Order 13563 concerning openness in policymaking."[27]
4.	Related Montana Legislation – HB - 506 Transfer management of certain federal public lands gives the Federal government 90 days to prove that its claim to Montana land meets the constitutional requirements of Article I, Section 8, Clause 17 or the land will be claimed by the State.[28]

QUESTIONS WE NEED TO ASK OURSELVES ABOUT WHAT IS THE PURPOSE OF GOVERNMENT RELATED TO THIS ISSUE:

A. What business does civil government have owning any land?

B. Does ownership comport with the sole purpose of civil government — to secure and protect the God-given rights of the citizens?

C. Therefore, does government owning land somehow protect the life, liberty or property of those citizens?

OPTIONAL READING ASSIGNMENTS

LECTURE SEVEN

1.	Continue reading *The Law* by Fredric Bastiat. Start at "The Political Approach" and read to "The Influence of Socialist Writers" (pages 261-263).
2.	The topic of federal land has often been attached to discussions of the conservation of special natural places. However, states also protect lands in the United States. To learn more about the history of the establishment of national parks, see https://www.nps.gov/articles/quick-nps-history.htm. Or you can read the Congressional Research Service's report "Federal Land Ownership: Overview and Data."[29]

26 Ibid.
27 Ibid.
28 "Evaluating Federal Land Management in Montana", p. 38; https://www.leg.mt.gov/content/Committees/Interim/2013-2014/EQC/Public-Comment/sj15-publiccommentdraftreport-withoutappendices.pdf
29 https://fas.org/sgp/crs/misc/R42346.pdf

LECTURE REVIEWS

1. Complete Lecture Seven Review Worksheet.

2. Complete Lecture Seven Quiz, including True & False Questions.

GOING DEEPER: SUPPLEMENTAL READING & VIDEO OPTIONS

 Found at www.theamericanview.com/constitution-course-supplemental-assignments which can also be found at the bottom of theamericanview.com under Resources.

CHAPTER EIGHT

OVERVIEW OF THE CONSTITUTION:
ARTICLES II AND III

GENERAL OBJECTIVES

It is our intent and our hope that you will understand the provisions of Articles II and III of the Constitution which establish the Executive and Judicial branches of Federal government and define and distribute their powers.

SPECIFIC OBJECTIVES

☆ *Understand the nature and the limits of the authorities and powers granted to the Executive Branch of the Federal government by the Constitution, i.e. Executive Orders, and usurpations of executive powers.*

☆ *Understand the nature and purpose of the Electoral College.*

☆ *Understand the nature and limits of the judicial authorities and powers granted to the Judicial Branch of the Federal government by the Constitution; usurpations of judicial power, i.e. misconception that Supreme Court decisions are the "law of the land."*

☆ *Explain the jurisdiction of the Federal courts.*

☆ *Develop an appreciation of the checks and balances exercised among various branches of government.*

☆ *Understand the reasons and constitutional methods for impeachment of judges and Federal officers.*

"Thou shalt in any wise set him king over thee, whom the Lord thy God shall choose: one from among thy brethren shalt thou set king over thee."
 –Deuteronomy 17:15

"A feeble Executive implies a feeble execution of the government. A feeble execution is yet but another phrase for a bad execution; and a government ill executed, whatever it may be in theory, must be, in practice a bad government.... The ingredients which constitute energy in the Executive, are, first, unity; secondly, duration; thirdly, an adequate provision for its support; fourthly, competent powers. The ingredients, which constitute safety in the republican sense are, first a due dependence on the people; secondly, a due responsibility."[1]
 –Alexander Hamilton

---

1 "The Executive Department Further Considered." Federalist No. 70. https://www.congress.gov/resources/display/content/The+Federalist+Papers#TheFederalistPapers-70

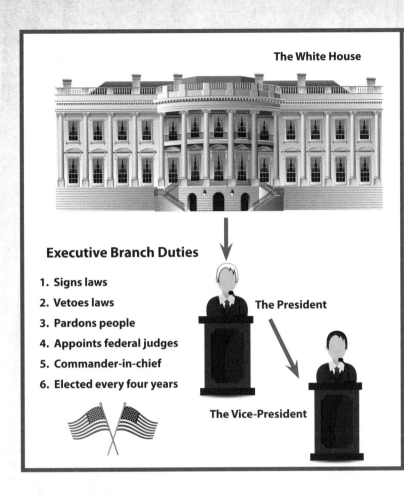

The White House

About the Executive Branch

President

Commander-in-chief of the military
Makes national policies and budgets
Enforces federal laws

Vice-President

Presiding officer of the Senate
Second in line for presidency

Secretary of State

Most senior position in a president's cabinet
Crafts foreign policy

Secretary of Defense

Executes President's defense policies
Advises President about the Army and Navy

Attorney General

Advises President and cabinet on legal matters
Head of the Department of Justice

Executive Branch Duties

1. **Signs laws**
2. **Vetoes laws**
3. **Pardons people**
4. **Appoints federal judges**
5. **Commander-in-chief**
6. **Elected every four years**

The President

The Vice-President

Lecture Eight: Overview of the Constitution: Articles II and III; follow along with the notes in the following section.

ARTICLE II: THE EXECUTIVE BRANCH – PRESIDENCY

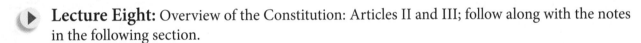

A. **Section 1**. Term, Selection, Qualifications and Succession.

1. President serves four-year term – no limit on terms:

    a. Convention originally voted for two-term limit, but George Washington voted against it.

    b. Convention later eliminated limit.

    c. Washington served two terms and announced that was enough, thus setting tradition of two terms.

    d. Franklin D. Roosevelt was elected to four terms, died in 4th term in 1945. Enactment of 22nd Amendment (1951) limited President to two terms.

2. Electoral College (altered by 12th Amendment, 1804):

    a. Electors chosen by States.

b. Each State's electors equal total number of Senators and Representatives from that State.

c. Electors normally are pledged to support candidate who carried their State, but sometimes violate the pledge.

d. If no candidate receives majority, then race goes to Congress:

- House chooses President, each state casting one vote as majority of that state's Congressmen desire, from top three from electoral college.

- Senate chooses Vice-President, one vote per Senator from top two from electoral college.

e. Electoral college is a state check on Federal power; protects smaller States.

f. With two-party system, one candidate almost always receives majority in electoral college. With multi-party system, elections would more frequently go to Congress.

3. Presidential Qualifications:

a. Natural-born citizen;

b. At least 35 years old; and,

c. Resident of United States for at least 14 years.

4. Succession: (altered by 22nd Amendment, 1951, 25th Amendment, 1967)

a. Vice-President succeeds President and serves as acting President if President is alive but unable to fulfill duties of office.

b. If Vice-Presidency becomes vacant, President nominates Vice-President subject to confirmation by majority of both houses of Congress.

c. If both offices become vacant, Congress by law provides for succession. Congress has provided (Presidential Succession Act 1886, amended 1947, 1948, 1965, 1966, 1970, 1977, 1988) that the order of succession shall then be:

- Speaker of the House.

- President pro tempore of the Senate.

- Cabinet officers according to seniority of their departments.

5. Compensation.

6. Oath to "preserve, protect and defend the Constitution." Washington added "so help me God!,"[2] starting tradition.

B. **Section 2.** Powers and Duties of President:

1. Commander-in-Chief of Army and Navy, and state militias when called into Federal service (only when a war has been officially declared):

a. Power over armed forces is shared among Congress, President and the States:

---

2 There is an interesting article on the topic at: https://wallbuilders.com/george-washington-actually-say-help-god-inauguration/

- Congress makes basic rules for armed forces.

- President gives day-to-day orders and more specific regulations.

- States control militias except when in Federal service.

    b. War Powers Resolution (1973) attempts to define this sharing of power.

2. May require written opinion of cabinet officials. Such officials have two duties:

    a. Administer departments.

    b. Advise President.

3. Pardon offenses:

    a. All Federal offenses (including contempt) except impeachment.

    b. Except impeachment because English king had frustrated Parliament's impeachment power by pardoning impeached officers and restoring them to their positions.

    c. May pardon before, during, or after indictment or conviction.

    d. Means of tempering justice with mercy.

    e. Executive check upon judicial branch.

4. May make treaties with concurrence of 2/3 of Senators:

    a. House concurrence not required because Framers thought this would jeopardize the executive secrecy necessary in negotiating treaties — John Jay[3]

    b. Court created exception: Commercial treaties require only a majority of both Houses (example: NAFTA, GATT).

    c. Court created exception: Executive agreements do not require concurrence of either branch (U.S. v. Belmont, 301 U.S. 324, 1937). This court decision unlawfully removed a critically important check and balance on the office of the Presidency. There exists no international agreement that is not important enough to require Senate approval.

5. Appoint Supreme Court Justice, Ambassadors, and major Federal officers with advice and consent of Senate majority:

    a. Congress may authorize President to appoint lower Federal officers without Senate approval.

    b. President may appoint Justices, Ambassadors, and cabinet officials without Senate approval while Senate is in recess. However, they shall cease to hold office at the end of the Senate's next term, if the Senate does not confirm them.

    c. Congressional check on Executive power.

---

3 The Powers of the Senate. Federalist No. 64. https://www.congress.gov/resources/display/content/The+Federalist+Papers#TheFederalistPapers-64

6. Idea of checks and balances came from John Witherspoon:

   a. John Witherspoon was president of the College of New Jersey (now Princeton University).

   b. Witherspoon taught no less than nine of the delegates to the Constitutional Convention; including James Madison.

   c. Witherspoon's major contribution to the foundation of the Federal government was the idea of checks and balances. Checks and balances provide a way in which the different branches can impede each other, thereby slowing down the actions of government. (For more information, see chapter 6 of *Christianity and the Constitution* by John Eidsmoe.)

C. **Section 3**. Powers and Ceremonial Duties:

   1. Give information to Congress:

      a. State of the Union address, a tradition with no legal force but helps set tone for country.

      b. At such other times as Congress may require.

   2. Recommend legislation, but someone in Congress must introduce it; the President cannot introduce legislation.

   3. Convene emergency session of Congress.

   4. Receive foreign ambassadors.

   5. Faithfully execute all laws of the United States. This is the extent of Executive Orders. They are not laws made by the President, but simply the President seeing to it that the laws made by Congress are faithfully executed.

   6. Commission all Federal officers (with substantially the same oath taken by the President – to support the Constitution).

D. **Section 4**. Impeachment:

   1. Applies to President, Vice-President, and all civil officers.

   2. Only grounds (with original intent definitions of Founders):

      a. **Treason** – to levy war against the United States, adhering to their enemies, giving them aid and comfort.[4]

      b. **Bribery** – giving or taking rewards for corrupt practices, false judgment, testimony or performance of that which is illegal or unjust.[5]

      c. Other high crimes [serious felonies; statutory law] and misdemeanors [misconduct].

---

4 http://webstersdictionary1828.com/Dictionary/treason
5 http://webstersdictionary1828.com/Dictionary/Bribery

"The offences to which the power of impeachment has been and is ordinarily applied as a remedy are… what are aptly termed political offences, growing out of **personal misconduct, or gross neglect, or usurpation, or habitual disregard of the public interest.**"[6] [emphasis added]

3. Procedure for Impeachment:

    a. House votes to impeach (majority required).

    b. Senate then votes to remove from office.

    c. With 2/3 required vote.

    d. With Chief Justice presiding.

4. Used only two times against Presidents:

    a. Andrew Johnson, 1868; Senate fell one vote short of removing him (35 - 19).[7]

    b. William Jefferson Clinton in 1998 was impeached by the House. He was tried by the Senate and acquitted on February 12, 1999; Article I. 45-55, Article II. 50-50.[8]

    c. In 1974, Richard Nixon resigned when the House began preparing articles of impeachment.

5. Used only 11 other times against Federal officials:

    a. These included nine judges, one Senator, one cabinet official.

    b. Senate acquitted all but four; all four were judges.

    c. The Senator was acquitted because Senate-ruled Congress lacked jurisdiction to impeach Senator; proper remedy was expulsion (Article I, Sec 5, Clause 2).

6. Legislative check upon Executive power.

7. Promotes stability by providing orderly means of removing officials without bloodshed.

6 Story, Joseph. *Commentaries on the Constitution of the United States, Vol. II.* (Boston: Hilliard, Gray, and Company, 1833), p. 233-234.
7 https://www.senate.gov/artandhistory/history/common/briefing/Impeachment_Johnson.htm
8 H.Res.611 — 105th Congress (1997-1998) summary. https://www.congress.gov/bill/105th-congress/house-resolution/611

How the Impeachment Process Works

House

1 Any member can introduce a resolution of impeachment if they suspect the President is guilty of **"treason, bribery, or other high crimes or misdemeanors."**

2 The House of Representatives considers the set of charges. If **a simple majority (51%)** support impeachment, the process moves to trial.

Senate

3 **The trial begins.** The Chief Justice of the Supreme Court presides over it, while members of the House form the prosection and Senators act as the jury. The President can appoint defense lawyers.

4 At the end of the trial, a Senate vote delivers the outcome. **If at least two-thirds (67%)** of the Senators find the President guilty, he is removed from office and the Vice -President takes over for the remainder of the term.

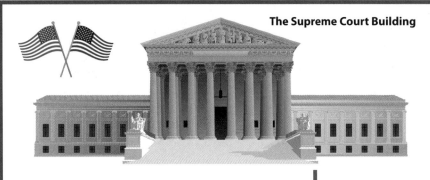

The Supreme Court Building

1. **Dissatisfied parties petition the Court for review**
   Parties may appeal their case to the Supreme Court to review the decision of the lower court.

2. **Justices write opinions**
   The Justices examine the petition and supporting materials.

3. **The Court issues its decision**
   Four Justices must vote in favor for a case to be granted review.

The Supreme Court Justices

★ ★ ★ ★ ★

About the Justices

There are nine Justices

A Chief Justice, the head of the judicial branch

Eight Associate Justices

When a new Justice is needed

The President nominates a candidate, usually a federal judge.

The Senate votes to confirm the nominee.

The Court can continue deciding cases with less than nine Justices, but if there is a tie, the lower court's decision stands.

Justices are not appointed for life, but during good behavior, though they may resign or retire.

They serve an average of 16 years.

ARTICLE III: THE JUDICIAL BRANCH

A. **Section 1**. Establishment of Courts and Judges:

  1. Judicial power vests (permanently resides) in:

     a. Supreme Court.

     b. Lower courts as Congress determines:

        - Congress has established Federal district courts and circuit courts of appeal.

        - Congress could abolish these, or add additional levels of courts.

  2. Judges hold office not for life, but "during good behavior:"

     a. Framers wanted judges to be insulated from political pressure.

     b. Gouverneur Morris: "Those who are charged with the important duties of administering justice, should, if possible, depend only on God."[9]

     c. "[G]ood behavior" means fidelity to the Constitution, or to not practice what Chief Justice Story described as impeachable offenses – "… personal misconduct or gross neglect or usurpation or habitual disregard of the public interest."[10]

  3. Compensation may not be diminished during tenure. This prevents congressional interference with their duties.

---

9 Gouverneur Morris. *To Secure the Blessings of Liberty: Selected Writings of Gouverneur Morris.* Edited and with an Introduction by J. Jackson Barlow (Indianapolis: Liberty Fund, 2012).

10 Story, Joseph. *Commentaries on the Constitution of the United States,* Vol. II. (Boston: Hilliard, Gray, and Company, 1833), p. 234.

B. **Section 2**. Jurisdiction of Courts

1. All cases in law (statute) and equity (general principles of fairness). It should be noted that the judicial branch, including the Supreme Court, presides over and issues opinions on specific cases. Those opinions are binding on the parties of the specific case, and do not become "the law of the land." Only Congress makes law – Article I, Section 1.

    a. Arising under Constitution, Federal laws, or treaties.

     • In Marbury v. Madison, 5 U.S. 1 (1803), Chief Justice John Marshall interpreted this language to authorize judicial review, i.e. the power of the Court to strike down statutes on the ground that they are inconsistent with the Constitution and therefore invalid.[11]

     • Jefferson, who was President at the time, strongly disagreed with this ruling.

    b. Involving foreign officials.

    c. Involving admiralty or maritime law (since these are difficult for states to handle).

    d. Involving controversies between states.

    e. Involving diversity of citizenship (citizens of different States or foreign nations).

    f. Involving suits between a state and a citizen of another state or nation (changed by 11th Amendment, 1795).

2. Types of jurisdiction:

    a. Original – goes directly to the Supreme Court – Narrow range of cases involving foreign officials and states as parties.

    b. Appellate: all other cases, with such exceptions as Congress shall make.

     • Important check on judicial power; Congress can limit the Supreme Court's appellate jurisdiction.

     • Congress has not used this check for over 100 years.

     • Types of cases where Congress could limit Court's appellate jurisdiction (Please refer to Lecture Six Homework, Supplemental material, article by Judge Roy Moore entitled, "The Constitutional Restoration Act.")

3. Right to trial by jury preserved for all Federal crimes except impeachment (and petty misdemeanors). Trial shall be in State where crime was committed. Jury of common citizens was an important check on abuse of government power by judges and prosecutors.

C. **Section 3**. Treason

1. Definition from *Webster's 1828 Dictionary*: "Treason against the United States shall consist only in levying War against them, or in adhering to their enemies, giving them aid and comfort."[12]

---

11 "U.S. Reports: Marbury v. Madison, 5 U.S. (1 Cranch) 137 (1803)." https://www.loc.gov/item/usrep005137/. See also: https://www.loc.gov/rr/program/bib/ourdocs/marbury.html

12 http://webstersdictionary1828.com/Dictionary/treason

a. In England, one could be convicted of having treasonous thoughts. In America, Puritans taught that conscience was beyond government's jurisdiction, so treason had to include acts.

b. Note plural reference to United States as them and their, not it or its. Framers thought of United States as an union in which states were supreme. As Federal power increased, usage gradually changed from plural to singular.

2. Evidence needed for conviction — two witnesses or confession (Compare Deuteronomy 17:6).

3. Congress fixes penalty for treason by statute, but may not include "corruption of blood" — that is, citizenship or inheritance rights of one's family shall not be affected by one's conviction of treason (Compare Deuteronomy 24:16).

PRESIDENTIAL DUTIES AND DETAILS

A Constitutional and Unconstitutional Overview ©Ricki Pepin 2016

According to Article II, Sections 2 and 3 of the U.S. Constitution, the job description of the President of the United States is very simple. It only contains 322 words. More than twice that many words (664, but who's counting?) are used in Article II, Section 1 to define the process of choosing the president. The job description covers only five areas:

One	Two	Three	Four	Five
The president is the commander-in-chief of the military (but only in times of declared war – very important detail!).	The president is responsible for insuring that the laws passed by Congress are executed and enforced as written. (This is the entire scope and authority of Executive Orders. They are not a blank check for the President to write law.)	The president is allowed to grant pardons for crimes other than impeachment.	The president can also make treaties, but only if two-thirds of the Senate agrees to the terms of those treaties. (He cannot act unilaterally.)	The president can nominate ambassadors, Supreme Court justices and other officers (most commonly cabinet secretaries and federal judges – not czars!). But he can only nominate them. The Senate has final approval on any nominations.

What is a czar? The term "czar" is unofficial, something more often used by the media than by the government. This is not a partisan issue. Both Democrats and Republicans have appointed czars for years. In 2009, Senator John McCain asserted that Obama had more czars than the Romanovs. This proved to be true at that time as the Romanovs had 18 and President Obama had 28!

Find the Answer: Research the various czars that served under President Obama – and see if you can discover how much they were paid. Reading these titles and job descriptions reveals the root of the problem: The problem is not the term "czar", but the fact that each of these czars are on the government payroll, appointed by the President, and in almost every instance working in capacities that are outside the federal government's constitutional jurisdiction and authority.

Which President wrote the most Executive Orders? The answer may surprise you.

Find the Answer: This link will take you to a chart listing the number of Executive Orders next to each president. http://www.presidency.ucsb.edu/data/orders.php

The President who wrote the least? William Henry Harrison – 0

The top three Presidents who wrote the most, from lowest to highest?

3. Theodore Roosevelt – 1,081

2. Woodrow Wilson – 1,803

1. Franklin D. Roosevelt – 3,522

Once again, the root of the problem is not the number of Executive Orders. It is the unconstitutional use of them – Presidents writing "law" – not simply insuring laws Congress passes are executed and enforced as written.

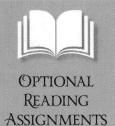

LECTURE EIGHT

OPTIONAL READING ASSIGNMENTS

1. Continue reading *The Law* by Fredric Bastiat. Start at "The Socialists Wish to Play God" and read to "The Idea of Passive Mankind" (pages 263-265).

LECTURE REVIEWS

1. Complete Lecture Eight Review Worksheet.

2. Complete Lecture Eight Quiz, including True & False Questions.

GOING DEEPER: SUPPLEMENTAL READING & VIDEO OPTIONS

 Found at www.theamericanview.com/constitution-course-supplemental-assignments which can also be found at the bottom of theamericanview.com under Resources.

"Where are Executive Orders authorized in the U.S. Constitution?" by Michael Peroutka (https://www.theamericanview.com/q-where-are-executive-orders-authorized-in-the-u-s-constitution-2/)

"A President is not a King and States Must Make Sure of It" by Jake MacAulay (https://www.theamericanview.com/president-not-king-states-must-make-sure-it/)

Law & Liberty (Chapters 1 through 3) by R. J. Rushdoony. This book consists of a series of essays composed of radio addresses in 1966 and 1967. These essays were written as a summary statement of certain concepts of law and liberty and have been proven to be prophetic in the decline of America if Christianity was replaced with Human Secularism.

CHAPTER NINE
THE CASE AGAINST CASE LAW

"Therefore by the deeds of the law there shall no flesh be justified in his sight: for by the law is the knowledge of sin."
                    –Romans 3:20

"The natural liberty of man is to be free from any superior power on Earth, and not to be under the will or legislative authority of man, but only to have the law of nature for his rule."[1]
                    – Samuel Adams

"We must reject the idea that every time a law's broken, society is guilty rather than the lawbreaker. It is time to restore the American precept that each individual is accountable for his actions."[2]
                    – Ronald Reagan

GENERAL OBJECTIVES

Our Founders clearly established a fixed standard of justice for our land; they spoke of an unchanging benchmark. They were not inventing anything new through the War for Independence; they were simply reasserting the ancient rights of Englishmen or more broadly the rights of all men as subjects of the Sovereign Creator of the Universe. So how did we shift off that fixed foundation to the legislative and judicial insanity of our day?

Something has led people who no longer hope to control the legislatures to look to the courts as expounders of the Constitution, and in some courts "new principles" have been discovered outside the Constitution. Now, if the "new principles discovered" are actually "outside" the Constitution, are they not therefore unconstitutional?

SPECIFIC OBJECTIVES

✰ Develop an understanding of what case law is and how it has impacted both the balance of power set forth by the U.S. Constitution and individual rights.

✰ Understand how the actions of a few influential people overturned the prevalent foundation of understanding the law to a more secular and humanistic one.

✰ Discover the link between Charles Darwin and his theory of evolution and the issue of case law.

---

1   https://www.brainyquote.com/quotes/samuel_
    adams_136363?src=t_law
2   https://www.brainyquote.com/quotes/ronald_
    reagan_147706?src=t_law

Introduction:

Most Americans assume that rulings and decisions handed down in cases that come before American courts are based on, and consistent with, the "rule of law." But, regrettably, this is not true.

In American courtrooms today, court rulings are not based on real law. Rather, they are based on an imitation system which is commonly called "case law" or "the case law method." This phony "case law" method of understanding what law is and where law comes from is taught in virtually every law school in America today. Indeed, a careful study reveals that the promotion of the "case law method" is the very reason that the modern law schools were established.

Prior to the 1880s, those who desired to practice law studied under experienced attorneys. Their apprenticeship included both the study of recognized legal scholars such as Blackstone, Montesquieu and Locke, as well as practical experience in writing briefs and memorandums and observing their masters in actual practice before the bar.[3]

Undergirding that system was the universal understanding that law, like truth, is a fixed and certain thing because it is a part of God's creation; and that the principles and precepts of law are found in God's Word and in His Creative Order.

But the "case law" system replaces the wisdom of God's Creative Order with the foolishness of men's evolutionary imaginings.

Law students, who, of course, go on to become lawyers and judges and congressmen, are taught that the source of law is the mind of a judge, which is then changed by the opinion of another judge and then, well… you can tune in tomorrow to see what the law might be then….

▶ **Lecture Nine:** Watch the video lecture The Case Against Case Law; follow along with the notes in the following section.

Back in 1975 two prominent law teachers, Harold Berman of Harvard and John T. Noonan of University of California at Berkley, published an article in which they claimed that the secularization of legal education (the elimination of "the religious dimension") began at Harvard Law School under the leadership of the first dean Christopher Columbus Langdell: "With Langdellian legal education, the older idea that law is ultimately dependent on Divine Providence, that is has a religious dimension, gradually receded, and I think we can say, has ultimately almost vanished."[4]

Just like the rowboat image, many lawyers probably would not have realized that there EVER WAS a religious dimension to the study of law in America. But there was such a dimension — and it is now gone.

WHAT HAPPENED AT HARVARD TO ACCOUNT FOR SUCH A SWEEPING CHANGE?

A. You may not be able to tell it by this rendition but the top two books are face up and the bottom book is face down. This is to symbolize that limits of reason, and the need for God's revelation.

B. Under Increase Mather changed to Christo et Ecclesiae. And the Word "Veritas" was added.

---

3   Ibid.

4   Berman, Harold J. "The Secularization of American Legal Education in the Nineteenth and Twentieth Centuries." Journal of Legal Education, Vol. 27, No. 4 (1976), p. 384.

C. It remained the same for over two hundred years until the presidency of Charles William Eliot 1869 to 1909. During Eliot's time the seal was changed so that only the word "Veritas" remained: any reference to Christ and the church was removed completely. Also the book on the bottom was turned face up.

D. So now the symbolism is completely humanistic. This is in keeping with the tireless efforts of Eliot to free the education at Harvard from "narrow" and "dying" religious views.

1.	Two years after leaving the Harvard presidency, Eliot summarized his position in an article entitled, "The Religious Ideal in Education."
2.	In that article, Eliot contended that the new "ideal" centered upon the "best human thinking and feeling…concerning truth, beauty…and goodness".[5]
3.	Please note that this was a religious view but NOT a Christian one. Rather it was the religion of secular humanism.
4.	But to support this RELIGIOUS GOAL Eliot relied upon the words of Jesus Christ from the Gospel of John: "And ye shall know the truth, and the truth shall make you free." John 8:32.

ELIOT'S MISUSE OF CHRIST'S QUOTE FORGED A NATIONWIDE MOVEMENT THAT SPREAD FROM HARVARD ACROSS AMERICA.

A. These Words of Christ began to appear on college buildings from coast to coast.

B. For example, in 1937 these words were engraved on two stone inlays over the two main entrances to the library building at the University of Oregon.

C. In the later part of the 19th century and the first part of the 20th century, almost all of the private and public institutions in America became linked in a common mission – the pursuit of truth UNAIDED by God and unencumbered by the teachings of the Bible.

D. What had they forgotten? Or cast away?

FAITH IN MAN OR FAITH IN GOD

Then said Jesus to those Jews which believed on him, If ye continue in my word, then are ye my disciples indeed; And ye shall know the truth, and the truth shall make you free.
—John 8:31-32

5 "The Religious Ideal in Education." Eliot, Charles W. The Outlook, Volume 99. Volume XCIXE September-December 1911. (New York: The Outlook Company), p. 411.

A. Christ taught that the truth could not be known apart from God and His revelation. Eliot and his followers believed that man, beginning with himself, could determine all truth by means of the scientific method. (See Psalm 2, same problem described.)

B. Eliot assumed that the key to knowledge was man's observation under the discipline of a scientific mind.

C. NOT God's revelation under the discipline of the Holy Spirit.

D. Therefore Eliot discarded what was left of Harvard's historic commitment to the orthodox Christian FATIH IN GOD and together with other educational leaders of his time, fashioned for American education a new FAITH IN MAN.

E. He outlined this new FAITH IN MAN in an inaugural address celebrating the induction of the first president of Johns Hopkins University in Baltimore.

1. In praising this new secular humanist school and other such "scientifically" oriented institutions, he summarized in that speech the new education's confession of faith:

   a. "They (the new schools) can show how physics with its law of conservation of energy, chemistry with its doctrine of indestructability and eternal flux of atoms, and biology with its principle of evolution through natural selection, have brought about within thirty years a wonderful change in men's conception of the universe.

   b. If the universe, as science teaches, be an organism which has by slow degrees grown to its form of today on its way to its form of tomorrow, with slowly formed habits which we call laws, and a general health which we call the harmony of nature, then, as science also teaches, the life principle or soul of that organism, for which science has no better name than God, pervades and informs it so absolutely that there is no separating God from nature, or religion from science, or things sacred from things secular."[6] —Charles Eliot

F. You can see here that Eliot has used his fallen reason to reduce God to Nature.

G. He has confused the Creator with His creation.

H. He thinks the creature that God has created is, in fact, God himself.

I. Not only did Eliot reduce God to Nature, but he also substituted a new law of evolution for the laws of God.

J. According to him, man and the universe were not governed by fixed and unchangeable laws. They were actually governed by "slowly formed habits." And those slowly formed habits were still evolving.

K. Another way of saying this is that Eliot wanted God to conform to man in order to accommodate his belief that the "scientific spirit, the scientific method" should prevail.

L. If you had questioned Eliot, he would have admitted that man had not scientifically proven the law of evolution.

---

6 "The Darwinization of Law in America." Pastor David Whitney. The American View website. https://www.theamericanview.com/constitution-course-supplemental-assignments/the-darwinization-of-law-in-america/E

M. But, notwithstanding this, he dedicated Harvard, and he encouraged others in Academia to dedicate old and new universities, to promote research and study designed to verify and to validate Charles Darwin's theory of evolution as it had appeared just a few years earlier in his work *Origin of Species*.

N. Until his death in 1926 (after serving 40 years as president of Harvard) Eliot proselytized other colleges, universities, and public secondary schools for the purpose of establishing this new faith in the scientific method and in evolution. He, and others, enjoyed remarkable success.

O. They were so successful that in today's public (and private) school classrooms – with very few exceptions—the scientific method is universally acclaimed as the key to knowledge, and evolution is almost unquestionably accepted as the only reasonable explanation for the origin of the universe and of man.

P. Now, in addition, Eliot promoted science and evolution as the key to truth in all fields of knowledge – history, philosophy, theology, politics and law.

Q. Eliot was not just a man of ideas. He was a man of action.

1. Therefore, he carefully selected men to serve as teachers and leaders at Harvard for the purpose of carrying out his program and ideas.

2. In no other field did he have a more lasting and significant influence than in the field of law.

3. This is because of his selection of the first dean of Harvard Law School of Christopher Columbus Langdell.

   a. Eliot chose Langdell as dean of the law school not because of his qualifications but because he shared Eliot's worldview.

   b. They shared a common commitment to use the scientific method to study and to teach law.

   c. As Langdell himself explained to those attending a Harvard Law School Association on an anniversary occasion:

      i. "Law is a Science…and all the available materials of that science are contained in printed books…Therefore the library is the proper workshop of professors and students alike…It is to us all what the laboratories are to chemists and physicists."[7]

4. Eliot and Langdell introduced a new method of study into the law school.

5. After only 10 months at being a professor, Langdell was elected as the first Harvard Law School Dean. He held this position for 25 years.

6. From this position of leadership, Langdell revolutionized legal education at Harvard AND THROUGHOUT THE UNITED STATES.

---

7 McDowell, Gary L. *The Language of Law and the Foundations of American Constitutionalism*. (Cambridge: Cambridge University Press, 2010), p 22.E.

7. He did this by securing the appointment of other professors who shared his commitment to teaching law as a science, as well as by introducing and championing the CASE LAW METHOD of teaching law.

8. "Simply stated, Langdell's case method required the teacher to collect and classify – or to use another teacher's collection and classification of – opinions written by judges in particular cases. The teacher then presented a 'casebook' to each student to read and study. In the classroom, the reasonings of the judges and the students were questioned, restated, and refined until generalized rules of law could be extracted – either by the teacher or by the student – from the particular cases deliberated."[8]

9. At first the students did not like this new method of studying law. They preferred the old method, in which a teacher gave a lecture setting forth the general legal rules and then illustrated those legal rules by their application in certain cases.

10. The CASE METHOD did not simply revolutionize what happened in the classroom. Rather, the CASE METHOD changed the philosophy of law in America. BECAUSE IT CHANGED THE SOURCE OF LAW.

11. Nowhere has this new philosophy been better stated than in Langdell's own preface to his *1879 Cases on Contracts*, which was the first casebook ever published:

   a. "Law, considered as a science, consists of certain principles or doctrines… Each of these doctrines has arrived at its present state by slow degrees; in other words, it is a growth, extending in many cases though centuries. This growth is to be traced in the main through a series of cases; and much the shortest and best, if not the only way of mastering the doctrine effectually, is studying the case in which it is embodied."[9]

THE ORIGINAL FOUNDATION FOR AMERICAN LAW

From the time of the (first) War for American Independence to the time of the War Between the States, the primary law book in America had been William Blackstone's *Commentaries on the Laws of England*. First published in the 1760s and widely circulated throughout Colonial America, Blackstone's *Commentaries* soon became the basic textbook for teaching law. For generations before Langdell came to Harvard, most American lawyers learned law by reading Blackstone.

A. Blackstone believed that principles and doctrines underlying the common law of England were unchanging. In the introduction to his *Commentaries*, he defined law "in the most general sense" as " a rule of action which is prescribed by some superior, which the inferior is bound to obey."[10]

   1. "When the Supreme Being formed the universe, and created matter out of nothing, He impressed certain principles upon that matter, from which it can never depart, and without which it would cease to be." – Sir William Blackstone[11]

---

8 Titus, Dr. Herb. *God, Man, and Law: The Biblical Principles.*
9 Langdell, C.C. *A Selection of Cases on the Law of Contracts.* (Boston: Little, Borwn, and Company, 1871), p. vi.
10 Blackstone, William. *Commentaries on the Laws of England. Book the First.* Third Edition. (Oxford: Clarendon Press, 1768), p. 38.
11 Ibid.

2. From this example of the laws governing the physical inanimate world, Blackstone drew a parallel to the laws governing man's affairs.

    a. "Man, considered as a creature, must necessarily be subject to the laws of His Creator, for he is entirely a dependent being… As a man depends absolutely upon his Maker for everything, it is necessary that he should, in all points, conform to his Maker's will."[12]

    b. This "Will of the Maker" Blackstone called "the law of nature." This law was fixed when God created man.

    c. "For as God, when He created matter, and endued it with a principle of mobility, established certain rules for the perpetual direction of the motion, so, when He created man, and endued him with the free will to conduct himself in all parts of life, He laid down certain immutable laws of human nature, whereby that free will is in some degree regulated and restrained."[13]

    d. Blackstone therefore concluded that the "law of nature", having been dictated by God, Himself, is "superior" to all others and "binding over all the globe, in all countries, and at all times."[14]

    e. Finally, Blackstone argued that no human laws are of any validity if contrary to God's law, and that no human laws have any authority except as derived from that higher law.

3. Not only did Blackstone believe that God dictated the law governing man, he identified God as the God of the Holy Bible and God's Law as that which is contained within the Bible.

NOW, COULD MAN HAVE DISCOVERED THOSE LAWS BY STUDYING LEGAL CASES AND BY REASONING?

A. Blackstone did not believe so. God, after man's fall, "in compassion to the frailty, the imperfection, and the blindness of human reason," was pleased to enable man "to discover and enforce" His laws "by an immediate and direct revelation."[15]

B. "The Doctrines thus delivered we call the revealed or divine law, and they are to be found only in the Holy Scriptures."[16] —Sir William Blackstone

C. According to Blackstone (and this is reflected in the Declaration of Independence and in the documents of America's founding), human reason is an inadequate mechanism for understanding and implementing Divine law. Therefore we should not expect that knowledge of these truths is attainable by reason.

D. Blackstone did not determine his view of *God and nature, God and man,* and *God and law* through the scientific method.

12 Ibid, p. 39.
13 Ibid.
14 Ibid, p. 41.
15 Ibid.
16 Ibid, p. 42.

E. On the contrary, he did not trust man's power of observation and of reason; nor did he believe that God, nature, man and law were the products of an evolutionary growth process.

F. Instead, he believed in the Genesis account of Creation of the universe and the fall of man.

"This faith in God, creation, and revelation as the foundation for law dominated legal education before Langdell came to Harvard. While law students were encouraged to read court opinions in actual cases, they were advised that the law did not arise out of the cases. Instead they were taught to study the cases in order to understand how general legal principles were applied to particular legal conflicts. Such training was designed to teach the student how to guide a judge to the applicable and governing rules of law and to call the judge's attention to the controlling facts of each case."[17]

—*God , Man and the Law*, Dr. Herb Titus

LET'S CONTRAST THIS VIEW WITH THAT OF LANGDELL:

A. Langdell approached the cases differently. He believed that the cases were the "original sources" of legal doctrines and principles:

B. The case gave birth to the rule of law, which slowly evolved through a series of cases into a full-fledged legal principle.[18] —*God, Man and the Law*, Dr. Herb Titus

C. As John Chapman Gray, one of Langdell's colleagues, stated:

    1. "The law is a living thing, with a continuous history, sloughing off the old, taking on the new."[19]

D. So Langdell wasn't merely introducing a new method for teaching the law. He introduced a new faith concerning law.

E. Under the doctrines of this faith, he believed that man, led by the ablest scholars and judges, could discover and determine the laws governing human affairs.

F. Because he believed that man did not need the aid of God and of the Holy Scripture, Langdell sought to eliminate both from legal education — NOT BY DEFAULT, BUT BY DESIGN.

LANGDELL AND HIS BOSS ELIOT WERE NOT ALONE.

They had embraced the new faith that swept the academic world in the later 1800s – that Darwin's theory of evolution was the key to all of life, including the law.

A. Charles Darwin – let's look at the influence of Darwin on Langdell:

---

17 Titus, Dr. Herb. *God, Man, and Law: The Biblical Principles.*
18 Ibid.
19 McDowell, Gary L. *The Language of Law and the Foundations of American Constitutionalism.* (Cambridge: Cambridge University Press, 2010), p. 25.

1. **FIRST**: Charles Darwin believed that the species of life, the subject of the science of biology, had evolved over centuries by a slow process of growth through variations and natural selection. He rejected any notion that all living species were created specially and separately at some definite point of time.

   a. In the same way, Langdell believed that the science of law contained doctrines and principles that had been developed over centuries by a slow process of growth. These doctrines and principles had NOT been immutably cast at the beginning of the history of man.

2. **SECOND**: Darwin believed that the origin and growth of the species of life could only be discovered by an empirical study of the natural world around him.

   a. Darwin rejected God's revelation of the creation account of life and the governing physical laws of the universe.

   b. Likewise, Langdell believed that the growth of legal principles and doctrines could be traced only by a careful empirical study of the cases already decided by judges and of the law books written by men.

   c. Again, following Darwin's example, Langdell rejected God's revelation of the creation of man and of the governing moral laws of the universe.

B. "Why do the heathen rage, and the people imagine a vain thing? The kings of the earth set themselves, and the rulers take counsel together, against the LORD, and against his anointed, saying, Let us break their bands asunder, and cast away their cords from us." Psalm 2:1-3

C. Both of these beliefs of Darwin have dominated the teaching of law since the early part of the 20th century.

   1. Evolution NOT Creation

   2. Belief in man NOT God

D. Harvard students at first rejected the case law method. (Several critics established a school at Boston University to maintain the traditional methods.)

E. But as Langdell hired colleagues that were sympathetic and as some very influential lawyers became his vocal supporters.

   1. Oliver Wendell Holmes, Jr.

   2. Louis Brandeis

F. By 1914, Langdell's teaching methods prevailed in almost every law school in the country.

HOW DOES THIS APPLY TO US TODAY?

A. So, why do we kill 55 million of our own American babies and declare to ourselves that it is lawful?

B. Why do we have a lawless government that claims it can kill anybody it wants to without any due process required by the Fifth Amendment?

C. Why do we have ridiculous and unjust decisions handed down by judges every day?

D. Why do the nations rage? BECAUSE of one major reason:

1. Virtually all lawyers are trained to find the law in the wrong place. Lawyers (and judges) are trained to believe that LAW can be found in the writings of a judge and then changed by the writings of another judge and then changed again by the opinion of yet another judge and…well… tune in tomorrow to guess what the law might be then.

2. Has it ever seemed odd to you that when there is an important case being decided by the Supreme Court, that cameras line up and crowds form to listen to what the high priests of law will say?

3. We can learn lessons from the classic book and movie — *The Wizard of Oz* — and follow the example of Dorothy's dog, Toto, who had the right idea.

4. Rather than waiting for the Great and Powerful Oz to pronounce the new law we are to follow, we need to be like Toto.

5. Pull back the curtain, see the truth, and act on it accordingly.

topic

CAN JUDGES MAKE LAW?[20] By Jake MacAulay

What would you answer if I asked: "What judge has no lawmaking authority?"

The answer, of course, is any federal judge in these United States of America.

I realize that many Americans have no earthly idea what the delegated powers in Article III of the United States Constitution are and I encourage you to read them.

So few powers are delegated to the Federal Judiciary that it takes less than 400 words to define them – fewer words than the column you are reading right now – while the powers of Congress and President number over 3,300!

So why are Americans allowing these unlawful court opinions to go into effect, which stop lawful presidential orders, and worse, challenging and appealing them in a higher court as if they have authority to do so?

Understand that the Judicial Branch of our constitutional government has no more law-making power than a referee in a football game has the power to make up new rules for the game. Both the court and the referee have a single job to do: discover and apply the rules to the rivalling parties before them.

Judicial Overreach? Consider the following example. President Donald Trump in January of 2017 issued four Executive Orders related to enforcement of existing immigration laws and protection of the border of the United States. Unfortunately, just days later, the head of the Department of Homeland Security, General John F. Kelly, appeared to be taking orders from unelected judges instead of the Commander-in-Chief when he issued a statement promising "compliance"[21] with the court order that challenged the President's executive order. Some have argued that this constituted a "mutiny" against the President. Kelly knows that "the order issued by Trump was both legal and necessary to the security of the United States and that the Commander-in-Chief had the full authority to issue that directive," wrote columnist J.B. Williams.[22]

"It's a mess, a complete mess," is what Trump might say of the rulings against his Executive Order. But as President, he can do something about it. First, he simply issued a series of tweets, one being that "dangerous" foreigners are being allowed into the U.S. because of the judicial rulings. But since when do judges decide the foreign or immigration policies of the United States? Where is that written in law or the Constitution?

On March 6, 2017, President Trump issued a new series of guidelines within an Executive Order Protecting the Nation from Foreign Terrorist Entry into the United States, that rescinded one of the previous Executive Orders from January 2017.[23]

Judicial Overreach? Many legal scholars have clearly explained how the judicial rulings against the order are not based on law or the Constitution. What is lacking is an effort by the administration and Congress to remove or restrict the power of tyrannical judges who present their own personal opinions as expressions of the facts and the law.

20 https://www.theamericanview.com/what-judge-has-no-lawmaking-authority/
21 https://www.dhs.gov/news/2017/01/29/dhs-statement-compliance-court-orders-and-presidents-executive-ord
22 http://www.newswithviews.com/JBWilliams/williams358.htm
23 https://www.whitehouse.gov/presidential-actions/executive-order-protecting-nation-foreign-terrorist-entry-united-states-2/

Congress should impeach federal judges who make outrageous rulings that have no basis in the Constitution. Why? Because just like in this case, it puts all Americans at risk!

In conclusion, Congress should be called upon to begin impeachment proceedings immediately against these judges who have stepped way outside the limits of their authority. This is truly "bad behavior" described in Article III, Section 1, that constitutes an impeachable offense found in Article II, Section 4. Theses judges have directly obstructed (and told others to disobey and disregard) a Congressional Law and Presidential Executive Order to implement it.

Finally, the President and all his administration should begin immediate implementation of Trump's LEGAL Executive Order, while citing its constitutionality.

LECTURE NINE

OPTIONAL READING ASSIGNMENTS

1. Continue reading *The Law* by Frederic Bastiat. Start at "Socialists Ignore Reason and Facts" and read to "A Frightful Idea" (pages 266-267).

LECTURE REVIEWS

1. Complete Lecture Nine Review Worksheet.

2. Complete The Case Against Case Law, Lecture Nine Worksheet 1.

3. Complete Lecture Nine Quiz, including True & False Questions.

GOING DEEPER: SUPPLEMENTAL READING & VIDEO OPTIONS

Found at www.theamericanview.com/constitution-course-supplemental-assignments which can also be found at the bottom of theamericanview.com under Resources.

Note: Use the search term "case law" on the website for more articles and information.

"The Darwinization of Law in America" by Pastor David Whitney.

CHAPTER TEN
OVERVIEW OF THE CONSTITUTION:
ARTICLES IV, V, VI, AND VII

"So I took the chief of your tribes, wise men, and known, and made them heads over you, captains over thousands, and captains over hundreds, and captains over fifties, and captains over tens, and officers among your tribes."

–Deuteronomy 1:15

"...the states should be watchful to note every material usurpation on their rights; denounce them as they occur in the most preemptory terms; to protest against them as wrongs to which our present submission shall be considered, not as acknowledgments or precedents of right, but as a temporary yielding to the lesser evil until their accumulation shall overweigh that of separation."[1]

–Thomas Jefferson

1 *The Jeffersonian Cyclopedia: A Comprehensive Collection of the Views of Thomas Jefferson,* edited by John P. Foley. (New York and London, Funk & Wagnalls Company, 1900), p. 133.

Lecture Ten: Articles IV, V, VI and VII; follow along with the notes in the following section.

ARTICLE IV: RELATIONS AMONG THE STATES

A.   **Section 1**. Full Faith and Credit Between States:

    1. With few exceptions, each state must recognize as valid and give judicial enforcement to the legal enactments of other States.

        a. A Nevada divorce or marriage must be recognized as valid by the State of Alabama.

        b. A will executed in North Dakota, if valid under North Dakota law, must be accepted in Mississippi.

        c. Exception: situations in which legal enactments in one State are manifestly against the public policy of another State. Possible example: "homosexual marriage."

B.   **Section 2**. Privileges and Immunities; Extraditions:

    1. State may not limit rights or privileges to state residents only. Must grant same privilege to non-residents.

        a. Examples include hunting and fishing licenses, or attending State universities.

        b. However, State may charge higher rate for non-residents, as with non-resident tuition, to equalize the fact that the resident has paid taxes to support the universities, hunting lands, etc.

    2. Upon Virginia Governor's request, New York Governor must extradite to Virginia a fugitive from justice found in New York. Exceptions:

        a. If fugitive is also wanted for crime in New York, New York may try him and make him serve sentence before extraditing him to Virginia.

        b. Since Governor is responsible for safety and well-being of all persons within his State, he may refuse to extradite a fugitive if he believes the person will not receive fair and humane treatment in the receiving State.

C.   **Section 3**. Admission of New States:

    1. Restrictions:

        a. No State may be formed entirely within borders of another State, without the consent of the State Legislature.

        b. No State may be formed from territory of another State without that State legislature's consent and the consent of Congress.

    2. Congress may make rules for admission of new states.

        a. Normally passes "enabling act" authorizing territory to hold constitutional convention and specifying certain provisions State constitution must contain.

      b.   Territory then holds convention and adopts constitution, which is sent to Congress for approval.

    3.   Congress has authority to govern territories and other Federal property. Usually establishes territorial government but exercises supervisory control. For example: District of Columbia and military reservations.

D. **Section 4**. Republican Government:
United States guarantees that each State shall have republican government:

    1.   Differences between republic and democracy set forth in Lecture Six.

    2.   Before State is admitted to union, Congress makes sure State has republican constitution: government by elected representatives, separate branches of government, limited government, bills of rights, etc.

    3.   U.S. also protects States against two other threats to republican government:

        a.   Foreign invasion; i.e. Border Patrol.

        b.   Domestic insurrection.

ARTICLE V: AMENDMENT

  A.   George Washington, 1797 Farewell Address:

"If in the opinion of the people the distribution or modification of the Constitutional powers be in any particular wrong, let it be corrected by an amendment in the way which the Constitution designates. But let there be no change by usurpation; for though this, in one instance, may be the instrument of good, it is the customary weapon by which free governments are destroyed."[1]

---

1 "Transcript of President George Washington's Farewell Address (1796)." https://www.ourdocuments.gov/doc.php?flash=false&doc=15&page=transcript

WASHINGTON'S FAREWELL ADDRESS · 1796

B. Recognizing their own fallibility and the possible need for change, the Framers provided two means of amending the Constitution:

   1. Approval of amendment by 2/3 of both Houses of Congress; or,

   2. By application of 2/3 of the State legislatures, Congress "shall call a Convention for proposing Amendments ..."

   3. Whichever means is used, the amendment must also be ratified by 3/4 of the States, either by their legislatures or by State ratifying conventions. Congress shall direct which means shall be used.

C. The Constitution has been amended 27 times by the Congressional route.

D. We have never amended the Constitution by the Convention route, but on several occasions nearly ⅔ of the States have called for a convention.

E. Possible dangers of a new Convention:

   1. Constitution does not specify how delegates would be selected, or what rules of procedure would be followed. Congress would probably determine this.

   2. No guarantee that delegates to new Convention would share the Framers' view of human nature or their concomitant fear of government power.

   3. No assurance that Convention could be limited to a single amendment. Many believe the Convention could consider many amendments, or even whole new constitutions.

   4. James Madison, 1788: *"Having witnessed the difficulties and dangers experienced by the first Convention which assembled under every propitious circumstances, I should tremble for the result of a second..."*[2]

   5. With an amendment carefully limiting what a new Convention could do, the Convention route could be a good check on a Congress unresponsive to the popular will. Without such limits, a new Convention could be dangerous.

F. Certain amendments prohibited:

   1. Ending the slave trade before 1808.

   2. Depriving State of equal representation in the Senate without the State's consent.

ARTICLE VI: GENERAL MATTERS

A. Debts and agreements entered into before Constitution will be recognized as valid.

   1. Unusual, because most new governments disavowed debts of predecessors.

   2. Helped develop foreign confidence in U.S. Government.

---

2 "From James Madison to George Lee Turberville, 2 November 1788." https://founders.archives.gov/documents/Madison/01-11-02-0243

3. Helped restore national unity, since much national debt was owed to former British loyalists.

B. Supremacy clause. Supreme law of the land is:

1. Constitution.

2. Federal laws made under the authority thereof ("thereof" refers to Constitution).

3. Treaties made under authority of United States. Why under authority of the "United States" rather than under the Constitution?

    a. One view: Treaties are superior to the Constitution. But if so, Constitution could be amended by adopting a treaty, which is not what Framers intended (Reid v. Covert, 354 U.S. 1 (1957)).

    b. More logical view: Framers said "under the Authority of the United States" instead of Constitution because they intended to honor treaties made before the Constitution was adopted.

4. Constitution, Federal laws, and treaties take precedence over State Constitutions/laws (but ONLY in those areas specifically listed in Article I, Section 10. In all other matters, State Constitutions rank supreme – See Amendments 9 and 10).

5. State judges are bound by Constitution, Federal laws, and treaties.

C. Oath of Office:

1. All Federal and State judges, legislators and officers must take oath to support Constitution.

2. No religious test for Federal office. But not such prohibition for State office. Why?

a. Many States had established religions and required religious oaths.

b. The established religions and oaths of the various States differed.

c. Framers felt the question of religious tests and oaths was best left to State governments.

ARTICLE VII: RATIFICATION

A. Constitution would be effective when ratified by nine States:

1. Under the Articles of Confederation and Perpetual Union, unanimous consent was required to amend the Articles of Confederation and Perpetual Union.

2. Framers proposed different means of ratification because they were quite certain Rhode Island would not ratify, possibly other States as well.

3. Congress approved this means of ratification and sent Constitution to States for ratification.

4. Constitution became effective when ratified by New Hampshire June 21, 1788.

5. North Carolina did not ratify until November 21, 1789, Rhode Island until May 29, 1790.

B. "Done in Convention by the Unanimous consent of the States present ..."

1. Rhode Island not present.

2. Majority of delegates from each State voted to ratify so all 12 States present ratified.

3. Three individual delegates chose not to sign: Elbridge Gerry of Massachusetts, Edmund Randolph of Virginia, and George Mason of Virginia.

C. "In the Year of our Lord one thousand seven hundred and eighty-seven..."[3] This statement is often left off the newer copies of the Constitution.

1. 1,787 years after the Birth of Christ.

2. "Our Lord" therefore clearly refers to Jesus Christ.

3. Unlike the French Revolutionists, the Framers of our Constitution had no reservations about referring to Jesus Christ as "our Lord" and using His Birth as the central event of history.

---

3 https://www.law.cornell.edu/constitution/signers

topic

DANGERS OF A CONSTITUTIONAL CONVENTION
By Ricki Pepin ©2016

A Constitutional Convention (ConCon) would be an ineffective and risky method for getting the federal government back under control. There are simply too many undefined parameters. Article V gives absolutely no guidelines as to how it will be run, how delegates can be selected and who can do the selecting.

The greatest danger is the level of authority vested in these delegates. Once a ConCon is convened, the chosen delegates have what is known as "Plenipotentiary Power." This gives them the legal power to overrule all existing law-making bodies in a nation, including changing the mechanism for ratification of their new laws. This is precisely what happened in Philadelphia in 1787, bypassing the "iron-clad requirements" to amending the Articles of Confederation simply because they had the authority to do so.

A short online search reveals there are many George Soros' backed anti-constitutional organizations who are also clamoring for an Article V convention, seeking (in their words) – "social justice and restoring true democracy." Conservative Constitutionalists should shudder at the prospect of a convention endowed with power of this magnitude, populated by activist delegates who have a Soros credit card in their pocket with such a commitment and purpose. And even if our best hopes are realized and some well-constructed "liberty amendments" actually pass, we would still be depending on people in power who are ignoring our current Constitution to suddenly adhere to the new one. Not likely.

An Article V Convention is the wrong battlefront. America is not facing a crisis of a lack of laws. There are already too many laws on the books. We are facing a crisis of too few Statesmen with sufficient integrity and moral fortitude to enforce good laws. America is facing a shortfall of character in her lawmakers' hearts and souls, not a shortage of pen and ink to write more laws. Failure for Constitutional Conservatives to prevail at an Article V Convention of States could end America as we know it. In short, it's not worth the risk. The true solution is to defend and enforce constitutional law, and elect more lawmakers who will keep their oaths to do so.

LECTURE TEN

OPTIONAL
READING
ASSIGNMENTS

1. *The Law* by Frederic Bastiat. Start at "The Leader of the Democrats" and read to "A Temporary Dictatorship" (pages 268-270).

LECTURE REVIEWS

1. Complete Lecture Ten Review Worksheet.

2. Complete Lecture Ten Quiz, including True & False Questions.

GOING DEEPER: SUPPLEMENTAL READING & VIDEO OPTIONS

 Found at www.theamericanview.com/constitution-course-supplemental-assignments which can also be found at the bottom of theamericanview.com under Resources.

Law & Liberty (Chapters 5 through 8) by R. J. Rushdoony. This book consists of a series of essays composed of radio addresses in 1966 and 1967. These essays were written as a summary statement of certain concepts of law and liberty and have been proven to be prophetic in the decline of America if Christianity was replaced with Human Secularism.

CHAPTER ELEVEN
THE BILL OF RIGHTS AND THE FIRST AMENDMENT

GENERAL OBJECTIVES

It is our intent and our hope that you will understand the historical background of the Bill of Rights including the arguments favoring and opposing the adoption of the first ten Amendments to the Constitution. Also, we desire that you will be able to understand the purpose and function of the First Amendment and the restrictions it places on the Federal government.

SPECIFIC OBJECTIVES

✰ *Articulate the reasons why some of the Framers, including James Madison of Virginia, argued that a Bill of Rights was unnecessary. And why other Framers thought it might prove dangerous to the people's liberty.*

✰ *Understand the process by which the Constitution can be legitimately amended and the Founders' concern the methodology not be evaded nor abused.*

✰ *Understand, appreciate and be prepared to dispel myths and falsehoods by the government schools and the media regarding "Separation of Church and State."*

✰ *Develop a proper framework for understanding the opinions of the Supreme Court in what are considered to be leading First Amendment cases and the tests that the courts used to decide.*

"Where the spirit of the Lord is, there is liberty."
                    –2 Corinthians 3:17

"... in 1768, Patrick Henry rode for miles on horseback to a trial in Spottsylvania County. He entered the rear of a courtroom where three Baptist ministers were being tried for having preached without the sanction of the Episcopalian Church. In the midst of the proceedings, he interrupted; 'May it please your lordship, what did I hear? Did I hear an expression that these men, whom your worships are about to try for misdemeanor, are charged with preaching the gospel of the Son of God?'"[1]
                    –William J. Federer

1 William J. Federer, *American's God and Country Encyclopedia of Quotations* (Coppell, TX: Fame, 1994), p. 287.

112

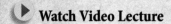 **Watch Video Lecture**

Lecture Eleven: The Bill of Rights and the First Amendment; follow along with the notes in the following section.

THE DEVELOPMENT OF THE BILL OF RIGHTS

A. Historically, Englishmen occasionally thought it necessary to reassert their ancient rights:

1. Magna Carta, 1215.

2. Englishmen's Bill of Rights 1689: Reasserted "true, ancient, and indubitable rights and liberties of the people."

B. Why no Bill of Rights in the original Constitution?

1. James Madison argued: Bill of Rights was unnecessary since Federal government had only limited delegated powers. No need to prohibit government from doing what government has no authority to do anyway.

2. Alexander Hamilton concluded: A Bill of Rights could be dangerous, because it could not possibly list all rights, and a future government might conclude that rights not listed were forfeited to the government. Rights are better protected by relying upon established English and American common law.

C. But many wanted a Bill of Rights:

1. Lack of Bill of Rights was a principal objection of Anti-Federalists (opponents of Constitution) like Patrick Henry and George Mason.

2. Writing from France, Thomas Jefferson generally liked the Constitution but regretted the lack of Bill of Rights.

3. During ratification debates, Federalists (supporters of Constitution) promised to support a Bill of Rights if the Constitution were ratified.

4. State ratifying conventions proposed about 350 amendments, many of which duplicated each other.

5. James Madison worked these into 12 amendments and introduced them in Congress in 1789.

6. Congressional committees reworked these amendments and passed them.

7. The necessary 3/4 of the States ratified the first ten amendments in 1791. They became known as the Bill of Rights.

8. James Madison's 11th Amendment dealt with congressional reapportionment and was never ratified.

9.	James Madison's 12th Amendment dealt with congressional pay raises and likewise did not receive much initial support. In recent years, interest in this amendment was renewed, and it finally was ratified by 3/4 of the states in 1992. It is now the 27th Amendment.
10.	Each of these first ten amendments limits Federal power. Most of the remaining amendments expand Federal power.
11.	Initially, the Bill of Rights limited only the Federal government, not State or local governments. Recently, courts have ruled on what is referred to as the Incorporation Doctrine, namely that the Bill of Rights are incorporated into the 14th Amendment and thereby applied to the States (See Lecture 13).

THE FIRST AMENDMENT: RELIGIOUS FREEDOM AND OTHER FREEDOMS

Congress shall make no law respecting an establishment of religion, or prohibiting the free exercise thereof; or abridging the freedom of speech, or of the press; or the right of the people peaceably to assemble, and to petition the government for a redress of grievances.

A. "Congress shall make no law respecting an establishment of religion..." This statement sets up a jurisdictional separation of government/State (Congress) and church (religion).

1. This separation is a biblical concept:

a. Old Testament – Kings (civil government) always came from tribe of Judah, priests (church) always came from tribe of Levi.

b. New Testament – "Render therefore unto Caesar (civil government) the things that are Caesar's; and unto God (church/religion) the things that are God's." (Matthew 22:21)

c. Civil government is ordained by and derives its authority from God.

- Daniel 2:21: "And he changeth the times and the seasons: he removeth kings, and setteth up kings: he giveth wisdom unto the wise, and knowledge to them that know understanding."

- Daniel 4:25b: "...till thou know that the most High ruleth in the kingdom of men, and giveth it to whomsoever he will."

- Romans 13:1-2, 4: "Let every soul be subject unto the higher powers. For there is no power but of God: the powers that be are ordained of God. Whosoever therefore resisteth the power, resisteth the ordinance of God: and they that resist shall receive to themselves damnation. For he is the minister of God to thee for good. But if thou do that which is evil, be afraid; for he beareth not the sword in vain: for he is the minister of God, a revenger to [execute] wrath upon him that doeth evil."

d. All law is based upon moral values which have their roots in religion.

"The statement, 'You can't legislate morality,' is a dangerous half-truth and even a lie, because all legislation is concerned with morality... Laws against manslaughter and murder... echo the commandment, 'Thou shalt not kill.' Laws against theft are commandments against stealing. Slander and libel laws, perjury laws, enact the moral requirement, 'Thou shalt not bear false witness.' Traffic laws are moral laws also: their purpose is to protect life and property... We may disagree with the morality of a law, but we cannot deny the moral concern of law. Law is concerned with right and wrong; it punishes and restrains evil and protects the good, and this is exactly what morality is about. It is impossible to have law without having morality behind that law, because all law is simply enacted morality." –Rousas John Rushdoony.[2]

2. Colonial charters acknowledged God as Source of governmental authority; many had State churches:

   a. New England colonies (Massachusetts, Connecticut, New Hampshire) established Congregational (Puritan) church.

   b. Southern colonies (Virginia, North Carolina, South Carolina, and Georgia) established Church of England (Episcopal).

   c. Middle colonies (Rhode Island, Delaware, New Jersey, Maryland, Pennsylvania, New York) often had greater degree of religious freedom but still publicly recognized God and often required citizens to affirm Trinitarian faith to vote and hold office.

3. Between 1620 and 1789 the American climate moved toward religious liberty for several reasons:

   a. Puritan thinkers like John Bunyan (who wrote *Pilgrim's Progress*) and John Milton (who authored *Paradise Lost*).

   b. The First Great Awakening (Christian revival of 1740s with preachers like Jonathon Edwards and George Whitefield) led many to leave the established Church of England and join dissenting churches (Presbyterian, Methodist, Baptist). They then objected to supporting Church of England.

   c. James Madison, Patrick Henry and others defended Baptists accused of preaching without Episcopal ordination; this led them to press for religious liberty in Virginia.

   d. Concerns over England's attempt to install an Archbishop over the colonies.

   e. Perhaps most important: Which church would be the established church of the United States? The many different churches and establishments in the various colonies led to agreement that establishment of religion should be a State matter, not a Federal matter.

4. Meaning of establishment clause:

   a. Separationist view: "Wall of separation between Church and State." – Debunking the Jefferson myth

      • Thomas Jefferson penned these words in 1803, 14 years after First Amendment adopted.

---

2   Rushdoony, R.J. "Can We Legislate Morality?" *Law & Liberty*. (Vallecito, CA: Chalcedon Foundation, 2009).

- Thomas Jefferson was in France while First Amendment adopted, had no direct hand in it.

- Thomas Jefferson saw the "wall of separation" as protecting the church from the state – the very opposite as it is portrayed today.

- Thomas Jefferson's words, virtually forgotten for nearly 150 years, are now quoted out of context as though they represent the true spirit of the First Amendment.

b. Non-preferential treatment by the national government of one denomination over others.

- James Madison's explanation on floor of Congress, Floyd's Summary, 1789. *"Mr. Madison said, he apprehended the meaning of the words to be, that Congress should not establish a religion and enforce the legal observation of it by law, nor compel men to worship God in any manner contrary to their conscience."*[3]

- Justice Joseph Story, *Commentaries on the Constitution*, 1833: *"Probably at the time of the adoption of the Constitution, and of the amendment to it now under consideration, the general, if not the universal sentiment was, that Christianity ought to receive encouragement from the state, so far as was not incompatible with the private right of conscience and the freedom of religious worship. An attempt to level all religions, and to make it a matter of state policy to hold all in utter indifference, would have created universal disapprobation, if not universal indignation ... The real object of the First Amendment was not to countenance, much less to advance, Mohammedanism, or Judaism, or infidelity, by prostrating Christianity; but to exclude all rivalry among Christian sects, and to prevent any national ecclesiastical establishment which should give to a hierarchy the exclusive patronage of the national government."*[4]

c. Supreme Court's invention of the "*Lemon test*," Lemon vs. Kurtzman, 403 U.S. 602 (1971) – turning original intent on its head by re-defining church as any religious activity vs. denominational preference.[5]

- Statute must have a secular purpose.

- Its primary effect must not be to advance or inhibit religion.

- It must not constitute excessive entanglement of government with religion.

d. *Lemon Test* is framework for analysis, not ironclad rule.

e. Justice Scalia said on the *Lemon Test*: "When we wish to strike down a practice it forbids, we invoke it. When we wish to uphold a practice it forbids, we ignore it entirely."

3 "Amendments to the Constitution, [15 August] 1789." https://founders.archives.gov/documents/Madison/01-12-02-0224
4 Story, Joseph. *Commentaries on the Constitution*. (Boston: Hilliard, Gray, and Company, 1833), p 700.
5 "U.S. Reports: Lemon v. Kurtzman, 403 U.S. 602 (1970)." https://www.loc.gov/item/usrep403602/

Free Speech

    f. Through the decision of the *Lemon Test* the Supreme Court ignored the simple language – "Congress shall make no law establishing a [religious DENOMINATION]" and basically re-wrote the law into virtually muzzling religious ACTIVITY according to their ever-changing whims.

B.   "Or Prohibiting the Free Exercise thereof ..."

    1. "Exercise" implies not just conscience, but words and actions; i.e. school plays, student essays, erecting monuments in parks, etc.

    2. Supreme Court *"Yoder Test,"* Wisconsin v. Yoder, 406 U.S. 205 (1972):[6]

        a. Does individual have sincere religious belief (This "test" is clearly outside civil government's authority. An individual's thoughts are not subject to government regulation.)

        b. Does government action impose substantial burden upon exercise of that religious belief?

        c. Does government have compelling interest that cannot be achieved by less restrictive means?

C.   "Or abridging the freedom of speech... ."

    1. General principle is that speech is protected, but States which ratified First Amendment had similar provisions in their State constitutions yet prohibited blasphemy, obscenity, etc.

    2. Certain forms of expression are outside protection of First Amendment:

        a. Speech presenting clear and present danger to national security or public safety;

---

6 "U.S. Reports: Wisconsin v. Yoder, 406 U.S. 205 (1972)." https://www.loc.gov/item/usrep406205/

     b. Speech soliciting crime or violence;

     c. Fighting words;

     d. Obscenity; and,

     e. Defamation.

3. Without freedom of thought, there can be no such thing as wisdom – and no such thing as public liberty without freedom of speech. —Benjamin Franklin[7]

D. "Or the press … ."

1. Supreme Court Justice Potter Stewart View: This clause gives the press special protection or preferred status as check on government power.

2. Supreme Court Justice Warren Burger (Majority) View: This clause gives the press no special status or protection; it simply extends the protections of the free speech clause to the print and broadcast media.

E. "Or the right of the people peaceably to assemble…" King George's insensitivity to colonists' grievances was one factor leading to the Declaration of Independence. Public presentation of grievances can be a safety valve against violence.

1. There are many modern day examples of peaceable assembly, such as the 2009 Tea Party gathering at Washington, D.C.

2. Protests that involve rioting and/or property damage are NOT a "peaceable" assembly, and therefore, are not constitutionally protected (i.e. 2015 Ferguson, Missouri riots). Participants in such protests are breaking the law and should be arrested accordingly.

F. "… and to petition the Government for a redress of grievances."

1. There are also examples of the people petitioning for redress of grievances such as "We the People…" petition advanced by Robert Schultz and also by Dr. Mike Hargadon of Maryland.

---

7 as Silence Dogood, No.8; https://founders.archives.gov/documents/Franklin/01-01-02-0015

topic

CHRISTIANS, PATRIOTS, AND POLITICS

When was the last time you heard a sermon on any of these topics?

The Law of Nature and Nature's God – 1669 – Rev. John Davenport

Government is Limited by Law – 1692 – Rev. Gershom Bulkley

Duties of Civil Rulers – 1754 – Rev. Jonathan Mayhew

Right to Resist Tyranny – 1742 – Rev. Nathaniel Appleton

Civil Disobedience – 1738 – Rev. Jared Eliot

A Just War in Self-Defense – 1768 – Rev. Jonas Clarke

Natural, Equal Rights of Life, Liberty and Property – 1759 – Rev. Samuel Langdon

These are historic, PATRIOTIC sermons that were the source of the colonist's education and passion to defend their God-given rights. These teachings gave them the integrity and courage to fight against the strongest military power in the world (and win)!

These sermons are examples of pastors who were fulfilling the second half of the Great Commission: The Cultural Mandate – taking their Country for Christ! (Matthew 28:18-20)

Patriotism. Love of one's country; the passion which aims to serve one's country, either in defending it from invasion, or **protecting its rights and maintaining its laws and institutions** in vigor and purity. Patriotism is the characteristic of a good citizen, the noblest passion that animates a man [emphasis added]. (*Webster's 1828 Dictionary*)

How can we protect or maintain our rights and laws – the Constitution and Bill of Rights – if we don't know what they say?

Should Christians be involved in politics?

To answer that, we need to define exactly what politics is:

Politics. The science of government; that part of ethics [doctrines of morality!] which consists in the regulation and government of a nation or state for the preservation of its safety, peace and prosperity…also for the protection of its citizens in their rights, with the preservation and improvement of their morals. (*Webster's 1828 Dictionary*)

Who is called and equipped to "preserve and improve morals"?

Answer – The church/Christians in the Great Commission (Matthew 28:18-20)

Here are some organizations to help you, your pastor and church to do so:

Institute on the Constitution – www.theamericanview.com – Offering many educational resources, including a One-Day Seminar for Pastors, church and other leaders called "Our American Christian Heritage – The Truth of America's Biblical Founding." Using primary source documents including the Bible, excerpts from Columbus' diary, *Webster's 1828 Dictionary*, the Mayflower Compact, the Declaration of Independence and the U.S. Constitution, learn the huge role God and the Bible played in the founding of America. Call 866-730-9796 to schedule a seminar or if you have questions.

Providence Foundation – www.providencefoundation.com – Restoring America as the land of liberty – 434-978-4535 – Order additional copies of Watchmen on the Walls. Providence Foundation is a Christian educational organization whose mission is to train and network leaders to transform their culture for Christ and to teach all citizens how to disciple the nations. Please share a copy of *Watchmen on the Walls* with your pastor!

Wallbuilders – www.wallbuilders.com – Wallbuilders is dedicated to presenting forgotten history and heroes, with an emphasis on the moral, religious and constitutional foundation in which America was built. Their goal is to exert a direct and positive influence in government through both education and developing public policies which reflect biblical values, and encouraging Christians to be involved in the civic arena.

The National Black Robe Regiment – Educating & Equipping Pastors for Spiritual & Cultural Transformation. They are building a nationwide network of member churches who are encouraged to participate in their biblical and historical role to stand boldly for righteousness and transform society through spiritual and cultural engagement. Watch a video about this organization at: http://www.youtube.com/watch?v=0UYpH5ey-jY

American Renewal Project – Pastor David Lane – www.theamericanrenewalproject.com

Family Research Council

Culture Impact Ministry Team (FRC) – www.CultureImpact.org

Watchmen on the Wall (FRC) – www.watchmenPastors.org

Vision America (FRC) – www.visionAmerica.org

20:28 Pastors Outreach (FRC) – www.2028Pastors.com

Liberty Counsel – www.lc.org – Liberty Counsel is an international nonprofit litigation, education and policy organization dedicated to advancing religious freedom, the sanctity of life and the family since 1989 by providing free assistance and representation on these and related topics. Their purpose is to preserve religious liberty and help create and maintain a society in which everyone will have the opportunity to discover the truth that will give true freedom.

LECTURE ELEVEN

OPTIONAL READING ASSIGNMENTS

1. Continue reading excerpts of *The Law* by Frederic Bastiat. Start at "Socialists Want Equality of Wealth" and read to "The Socialists Want Dictatorship" (pages 270-272).

LECTURE REVIEWS

1. Complete Lecture Eleven Review Worksheet.

2. Complete Lecture Eleven Quiz, including True & False Questions.

GOING DEEPER: SUPPLEMENTAL READING & VIDEO OPTIONS

 Found at www.theamericanview.com/constitution-course-supplemental-assignments which can also be found at the bottom of theamericanview.com under Resources.

- *Letters to/from Thomas Jefferson.* To learn where the phrase "a wall of separation between church and state" came from and what it originally meant.

- *Law & Liberty* (Chapters 13 through 14) by R. J. Rushdoony. This book consists of a series of essays composed of radio addresses in 1966 and 1967. These essays were written as a summary statement of certain concepts of law and liberty and have been proven to be prophetic in the decline of America if Christianity was replaced with Human Secularism.

- *The First Amendment: Its Original Text and Meaning which have not changed* (DVD) by Herb Titus. This video will provide a deeper understanding of the text of the First Amendment.

- *Why No Church Should Be a 501c3 Organization* (DVD) by Pastor David Whitney. This video will help to understand the reason behind the silence of most churches in our day and what can be done to remedy that problem.

CHAPTER TWELVE
AMENDMENTS II - X

It is our intent and our hope that you will understand the historical background of the Bill of Rights specifically including the Second through the Tenth Amendments and their original purpose in restricting the authority and power of the central (Federal) government.

SPECIFIC OBJECTIVES

☆ *Understand the historical purpose behind each early Amendment and the critical importance of the need to restrict and limit government power and the extent of government's intrusion into the lives of the people.*

☆ *Appreciate the intent of the Framers of the early Amendments (before the War Between the States) to limit government authority.*

☆ *Develop a proper framework for understanding the opinions of the Supreme Court in what are considered to be leading Constitutional Law cases and the tests that the courts use to decide these cases.*

"The God who gave us life gave us liberty at the same time... Can the liberties of a nation be thought secure when we have removed the only firm basis, a conviction in the minds of the people that these liberties are ... the gift of God? That they are not to be violated but with His wrath?"[1]

–Thomas Jefferson

From the Preamble to the Bill of Rights: "The Conventions of a number of the States, having at the time of their adopting the Constitution, expressed a desire, in order to prevent misconstruction or abuse of its powers, that further declaratory and restrictive clauses should be added: And as extending the ground of public confidence in the Government, will best ensure the beneficent ends of its institution."

---

1 "Quotations on the Jefferson Memorial." https://www.monticello. org/site/research-and-collections/quotations-jefferson-memorial

Watch Video Lecture

 Lecture Twelve: Amendments II-X; follow along with the notes in the following section.

THE BILL OF RIGHTS

Football Field Analogy

A. Using the analogy that the Constitution with its Seven Articles is like a football field, we can make the following comparisons.

B. The side lines and end zone define the field of play. When the ball is out of bounds the play stops.

1.	The limits on the powers and the exercise of those powers are clearly defined in the Seven Articles of the Constitution.
2.	The problem is that those boundaries on the football field consist only of some white chalk on the grass.
3.	Likewise many during the ratification debates feared that the Seven Articles of the Constitution were very weak limits on Federal power.

C. Then the Bill of Rights erected a thick brick wall on the side lines and end zone to go beyond merely defining the field of play, but moreover to prohibit the ball from ever going out of bounds.

| 1. | Those desiring to tyrannize our land have had to punch holes in and create doorways through that thick brick wall to achieve their purpose of unlimited Federal government. |
| 2. | Many of the subsequent Amendments to the Bill of Rights accomplished that destructive purpose. |

THE SECOND AMENDMENT

The Right to Keep and Bear Arms

"A well-regulated militia, being necessary to the security of a free state, the right of the people to keep and bear arms, shall not be infringed."

A. Two Views:

| 1. | **The Collectivist View:** Second Amendment protects only the right of the people collectively to bear arms by the state maintaining a national guard or police force. |
| 2. | **The Individualist View:** Second Amendment protects the individual's rights to bear arms; it mentions the militia only as a reason for this right. |

B. The meaning of "militia":

| 1. | Not just a national guard or state police force. |

2.	*Webster's 1828 Dictionary*: "The militia of a country are the able-bodied men organized into companies, regiments and brigades, with officers of all grades, and required by law to attend military exercises on certain days only, but at other times left to pursue their usual occupations."[2]
3.	English law, at least from the reign of Alfred the Great (871 - 899 A.D.), required all able-bodied men to purchase weapons and be available for military duty.

C. If the Second Amendment protects only a collective right of the State to maintain a police force, it is out of place in a Bill of Rights which protects individuals.

D. The Framers saw individual ownership of firearms as a protection of freedom against both foreign invasion and domestic tyranny.

1.	Samuel Adams: "The Constitution shall never be construed ... to prevent the people of the United States who are peaceable citizens from keeping their own arms."[3]
2.	Thomas Jefferson: "No free men shall ever be debarred the use of arms."[4]
3.	Noah Webster: "Before a standing army or a tyrannical government can rule, the people must be disarmed; as they are in almost every kingdom in Europe. The supreme power in America cannot enforce unjust laws by the sword; because the whole body of the people are armed, and constitute a force superior to any band of regular (or professional) troops that can be, on any pretense, raised in the United States." (1787)[5]

E. A 20-year history of "Right to Carry Laws" across America.

F. Principle/Agency nature of power to bear arms by Sheriff and police.

THE THIRD AMENDMENT

Quartering Troops

"No soldier shall, in time of peace be quartered in any house, without the consent of the owner, nor in time of war, but in a manner to be prescribed by law."

A. Prohibits British practice of forcing private citizens to house soldiers.

B. Exceptions to it include the following:

1.	Owner's consent.
2.	Wartime, but even then in manner prescribed by law.
3.	The experiences of the War for Independence shaped this Amendment:

---

2 http://webstersdictionary1828.com/Dictionary/militia
3 "Samuel Adams, Quotes on the Second Amendment." The James Madison Research Library and Information Center. http://www.madisonbrigade.com/s_adams.htm
4 "I. First Draft by Jefferson, [before June 1776]" https://founders.archives.gov/documents/Jefferson/01-01-02-0161-0002
5 "Noah Webster, Quotes on the Second Amendment." The James Madison Research Library and Information Center. http://www.madisonbrigade.com/n_webster.htm

> *"Robert Combs, a tavern keeper in Pennington, can inform you, of a Rape committed on the Wife and Daughter of one John Christopher, by the Enemy while they lay there; One Philip Parmer's daughter of that Neighbourhood, was also ravished by 6 Soldiers; Thomas Keynes's daughter was treated in the same Manner."[6]*

THE FOURTH AMENDMENT

Unreasonable Search and Seizure

"The right of the people to be secure in their persons, houses, papers, and effects, against unreasonable searches and seizures, shall not be violated, and no warrants shall issue, but upon probable cause, supported by oath or affirmation, and particularly describing the place to be searched, and the persons or things to be seized."

A. Background – the Laws of Nature and Nature's God – the Bible:

1. "A man's house is his castle, and God's law, as well as man's, sets a guard upon it; he that assaults it does so at his peril." – Matthew Henry's Commentary on Exodus 22.

2. In Book 4, Chapter 16 of Sir William Blackstone's *Commentaries on the Laws of England*: "And the law of England has so particular and tender a regard to the immunity of a man's house, that it stiles [considers] it his castle, and will never suffer it to be violated with immunity… For this reason no doors can in general be broken open to execute any civil process; though, in criminal causes, the public safety supersedes the private… [A]lso… that a man may assemble people together lawfully … in order to protect and defend his house [against rioters or other lawbreakers]; which he is not permitted to do in any other case."[7]

B. Protects against invasions of privacy.

C. Key word: "unreasonable." Does not protect against all searches and seizures, only against those that are unreasonable.

D. To be reasonable, a search normally must:

1. Be accompanied by a warrant.

2. Be supported by probable cause.

3. Have probable cause set forth in affidavit.

4. Be authorized by a neutral and detached magistrate.

E. In urgent circumstances, the requirement of a warrant does not apply. Examples include:

1. Search incident to lawful arrest.

---

6 Excerpt from a letter from George Washington to Governor of New Jersey, William Livingston, March 3, 1777. https://founders.archives.gov/documents/Washington/03-08-02-0524

7 Blackstone, William. *Commentaries on the Laws of England. Book the Fourth*. Fourth Edition. (Oxford: Clarendon Press, 1770), p. 223-224.

2.   Hot pursuit of a fleeing felon.

3.   A bona fide emergency.

F.   Lesser invasions of privacy, like "stop and frisk," can be justified with less than probable cause.

G.   Applies wherever there is a reasonable expectation of privacy, not to items in plain view.

H.   Exclusionary rule: Evidence seized in violation of the Fourth Amendment cannot be used in court, unless good faith error:

1.   Exclusionary rule not specifically stated in Fourth Amendment.

2.   Courts adopted exclusionary rule because they thought it necessary to make sure police respect Fourth Amendment.

I.   The Fourth Amendment limits government's authority to invade individual citizen's person and property without good cause.

J.   What about the "Patriot Act" and its reauthorization?

1.   Opponents of the law have criticized its authorization of indefinite detentions of immigrants; searches through which law enforcement officers search a home or business without the owner's or the occupant's permission or knowledge; the expanded use of National Security Letters, which allows the FBI to search telephone, email, and financial records without a court order; and the expanded access of law enforcement agencies to business records, including library and financial records.

2.   Since its passage, several legal challenges have been brought against the act, and Federal courts have ruled that a number of provisions are unconstitutional.

3.   In 2013, Edward Snowden, a Federal contractor, released documents asserting that the National Security Agency (NSA) was "spying" on American citizens communications without any evidence of a crime or a warrant.

THE FIFTH AMENDMENT

Personal and Property Rights

"No person shall be held to answer for a capital, or otherwise infamous crime, unless on a presentment or indictment of a grand jury, except in cases arising in the land or naval forces, or in the militia, when in actual service in time of war or public danger; nor shall any person be subject for the same offense to be twice put in jeopardy of life or limb; nor shall be compelled in any criminal case to be a witness against himself, nor be deprived of life, liberty, or property, without due process of law; nor shall private property be taken for public use, without just compensation."

A.   Grand jury indictment for capital or other infamous crimes:

1.   Grand jury is a buffer between the citizen and the State.

2. Means no one should go through the expense, trauma and jeopardy of a trial unless a grand jury of common citizens determines there is probable cause.

3. As a fact-finding body, the grand jury also acts as check on government.

4. Military cases excepted.

5. Fifth Amendment expressly recognizes capital punishment.

B. Double jeopardy:

1. Cannot be tried twice by the same jurisdiction for the same offense.

2. Designed to prevent government harassment.

C. No compulsory self-incrimination:

1. Coerced confessions can be false – might confess just to stop torture.

2. Coerced confessions violate human dignity by forcing a person to cooperate in his own self-destruction.

3. Courts have recently ruled that custodial interrogation is inherently coercive, therefore police must read Miranda rights to suspect to ensure any waiver of his Fifth Amendment rights is truly voluntary and intelligent.

D. Cannot be deprived of life, liberty or property without due process of law. "Due process" means procedures essential to fundamental fairness.

E. Cannot take private property for public use without just compensation.

1. What is a "taking"?

2. If government doesn't take title to your property, but limits your use, is that a "taking"? (For example, when unelected, unconstitutional entities like Regional Planning Commissions prohibit you from building or conducting business on your own property, or when they use eminent domain to take part of your private property for public purposes.)

THE SIXTH AMENDMENT

Rights of Criminal Defendants

"In all criminal prosecutions, the accused shall enjoy the right to a speedy and public trial, by an impartial jury of the state and district wherein the crime shall have been committed, which district shall have been previously ascertained by law, and to be informed of the nature and cause of the accusation; to be confronted with the witnesses against him; to have compulsory process for obtaining witnesses in his favor, and to have the assistance of counsel for his defense."

A. Speedy trial – but what is "speedy" depends on all circumstances.

B. Public trial – less likely to be arbitrary and unfair if press and public are present.

C. Jury of State and district (See Lecture Eight).

D. Habeas Corpus – Be informed of charges (with sufficient particularity and sufficiently in advance to prepare a defense).

E. Confront and cross-examine accusers.

F. Subpoena (force) witnesses to testify for defense.

G. Assistance of counsel, right to qualified attorney, at State expense if defendant cannot afford one.

THE SEVENTH AMENDMENT

Rights of Civil Cases

"In suits at common law, where the value in controversy shall exceed twenty dollars, the right of trial by jury shall be preserved, and no fact tried by a jury, shall be otherwise reexamined in any court of the United States, than according to the rules of the common law."

A. Right to jury trial in cases involving common law and more than $20.

B. Judge cannot substitute his opinion for that of the jury, unless he determines that the case was erroneously submitted to the jury or that no reasonable jurors could have reached that verdict.

THE EIGHTH AMENDMENT

Criminal Punishment

"Excessive bail shall not be required, nor excessive fines imposed, nor cruel and unusual punishments inflicted."

A. No excessive bail:

   1. Defendant is presumed innocent; therefore his right to be free until conviction unless he poses a danger to public safety or is likely to flee.

   2. Purpose of bail is to make sure defendant doesn't flee pending trial.

   3. Bail should be no more than necessary to ensure defendant's appearance. That amount depends on all circumstances; nature of offense, defendant's record; defendant's ties to the community, etc.

B. No excessive fines:

   1. Excessive is that which is unreasonable considering nature of offense.

   2. Magna Carta describes excessive fines as forfeitures that deprive defendant of his ability to earn a living.

C. No cruel and unusual punishment:

    1. Used by the Framers to prohibit unreasonable torture; disemboweling, mutilation, etc.

    2. Framers would not have considered capital punishment cruel and unusual (See Fifth Amendment).

        a. However, Justices Brennan and Marshall have argued that the Eighth Amendment must be interpreted according to an "evolving standard of decency" and that society has evolved to the point that capital punishment is cruel and unusual today. Furman v. Georgia, 408 U.S. 238 (1972) (concurring opinion).[8]

        b. This "evolving standard" is dangerous! It disregards absolute truth, and society could evolve downward as well as upward.

THE NINTH AMENDMENT

Un-enumerated Rights

"The enumeration in the Constitution, of certain rights, shall not be construed to deny or disparage others retained by the people."

A. Alexander Hamilton had objected that a Bill of Rights could be dangerous because all rights could not be listed, and in the future the government might assume that all rights not listed were forfeited.

B. To satisfy Alexander Hamilton's objections, James Madison offered the Ninth Amendment.

C. Key word: "Retained." Ninth Amendment does not give courts the authority to create "new" rights. Rather, Ninth Amendment protects only those rights which were already recognized and protected under then-existing English and American common law.

THE TENTH AMENDMENT

Undelegated Powers are Reserved

"The powers not delegated to the United States by the Constitution, nor prohibited by it to the states, are reserved to the states respectively, or to the people."

A. Cornerstone of freedom.

B. Sets in concrete the Framers' view of the covenantal nature of government by which the Federal government has only such power as "We the People" delegate to it through the Constitution.

C. States rights are a powerful check and balance on Federal power, but it is up to the States to use it to protect their citizens.

---

8 "U.S. Reports: Furman v. Georgia, 408 U.S. 238 (1972)." https://www.loc.gov/item/usrep408238/

A "New Bill of Rights"

If the Bill of Rights so clearly limits Federal power, how did we come to the fine mess we are in today?

A.   Franklin Delano Roosevelt (FDR) in his annual address to Congress – January 1944:

"The one supreme objective for the future…can be summed up in one word: Security.…This Republic had its beginning, and grew to its present strength, under the protection of certain inalienable rights – among them the right of free speech, free press, free worship, trial by jury, freedom from unreasonable searches and seizures. They were our rights to life and liberty. As our nation has grown in size and stature, however – as our industrial economy expanded – these political rights proved inadequate to assure us equality in the pursuit of happiness.… so to speak, a second Bill of Rights under which a new basis of security and prosperity can be established for all…Among these are:

We have accepted, the right to a useful and remunerative job…

The right to earn enough to provide adequate food and clothing and recreation.…

The right of every family to a decent home;

The right to adequate medical care…

The right to adequate protection from the economic fears of old age, sickness, accident, and unemployment;

The right to a good education. All these rights spell security."[9]

B.   "Those who would give up essential liberties to purchase a little temporary safety deserve neither liberty nor safety." –Benjamin Franklin[10]

C.   FDR's unconstitutional New Bill of Rights has been increasingly implemented — devastating our economy and work ethic — so that today the federal government is creating dependency by <u>providing for individuals' personal needs</u> in ever-growing social welfare programs. This is the antithesis of the Bill of Rights' original intent of <u>protecting individuals' rights and property</u>.

Review of the Bill of Rights

A.   Five Foundational Freedoms; Religion, Speech, Press, Assembly, Petition – First Amendment.

B.   Keep and Bear Arms – Second Amendment.

C.   My home is my castle – Third Amendment.

D.   No warrant, no search – Fourth Amendment.

E.   Personal and Property Rights – Fifth Amendment.

F.   Criminal Defendants – Sixth Amendment.

G.   In Civil Cases – Seventh Amendment.

9   "State of the Union Message to Congress; January 11, 1944." Franklin D. Roosevelt Presidential Library and Museum. http://www.fdrlibrary.marist.edu/archives/address_text.html
10   https://www.brainyquote.com/quotes/benjamin_franklin_136955

H. When punished – Eighth Amendment.

I. Un-enumerated Rights – Ninth Amendment.

J. Undelegated Powers – Tenth Amendment.

SUPREME COURT DECISIONS – THE LAW OF THE LAND?...NO!
By Ricki Pepin ©2016

On June 26, 2015, the U.S. Supreme Court issued an opinion (Obergefell v. Hodges) that the fundamental right to marry is guaranteed to same-sex couples. Nine months later, Chief Justice Roy Moore and the Alabama's Supreme Court issued their own ruling, rejecting the U.S. Supreme Court decision.

Mat Staver, Founder and Chairman of Liberty Counsel, said of this ruling: *"The recent opinion by the Alabama Supreme Court calling the U.S. Supreme Court's marriage opinion 'illegitimate' will be remembered in history as the pro-marriage 'shot heard around the world.'"*[11]

This ruling from Alabama is a step in re-establishing religious liberty and the Constitution-based Rule of Law. It defies federal overreach and exerts its rightful claim to State Sovereignty as stated in the Tenth Amendment. The State court, by design of our Founders, is a higher authority than a U.S. Supreme Court (or any other agent of the federal government) that attempts to exercise authority that is not attributed to it by the U.S. Constitution.

This action on the part of the Alabama Supreme Court is known as: *Nullification – the act of making something void; the action of a state in abrogating a federal law on the basis of state sovereignty* (*Black's Law Dictionary*). This court is setting an example for Sheriffs and Governors to follow, realizing they are shirking their duties when they allow a federal government to demand anything for which it has no authority.

Plainly stated, the U.S. Supreme Court Obergefell v. Hodges ruling is without legal authority.

Here is an excerpt from Alabama Chief Justice Moore's opinion in rejecting it:

"I agree with the Chief Justice of the United States Supreme Court, John Roberts, and with Associate Justices Scalia, Thomas and Alito, that the majority opinion in Obergefell has no basis in the law, history or tradition of this country. Obergefell is an unconstitutional exercise of judicial authority that usurps the legislative prerogative of the States to regulate their own domestic policy. Additionally, Obergefell seriously jeopardizes the religious liberty guaranteed by the First Amendment to the U.S. Constitution."[12]

Here are a few other constitutional points regarding the Supreme Court's overreach:

The Supreme Court does not make law. **Article I, Section 1** clearly states that *all legislative authority* rests with Congress.

Congress, who does have the authority to make law, has *no authority* over marriage. It is not within their 18 enumerated powers in **Article I, Section 8.**

11 "Alabama Supreme Court Rejects U. S. Supreme Court's Marriage Opinion." March 4, 2016. https://www.lc.org/newsroom/details/alabama-supreme-court-rejects-u-s-supreme-courts-marriage-opinion
12 Ibid.

Any marriage regulations/laws (e.g. bigamy, polygamy, incest, etc.) are the State government's jurisdiction. See **Amendments 9 and 10.**

Many states have passed Defense of Marriage Acts – DOMA – their citizens voting to define marriage as being a union between one man and one woman. The federal government has *no authority* to overrule State governments and their citizens in this regard. Once again, see **Amendments 9 and 10**.

Lastly, but actually primarily, no one — repcat, NO ONE — has the authority to overrule the *Laws of Nature and of Nature's God* – the foundation for all law in America as stated in the **Declaration of Independence**.

Judges take an oath to uphold and defend the U.S. Constitution. Their opinions must comply with the principles stated within this document. When they write opinions that have no legal foundation, then their opinions lack legal legitimacy. That is exactly what happened when these five lawyers issued their opinion, ignoring the Constitution and a millennia of human history. Marriage predates religion and civil government. No civil authority, including the Supreme Court, has the authority to redefine marriage.

Resources:

Foundation for Moral Law – http://morallaw.org – Legal foundation dedicated to the defense of the U.S. Constitution. Founded by Justice Roy Moore.

Tenth Amendment Center – www.tenthamendmentcenter.com – State's Rights group established to restrain the federal government to its constitutionally-enumerated powers.

Rutherford Institute – www.rutherford.org – Dedicated to the defense of civil liberties and human rights. Founded by John Whitehead.

Campaign for Liberty – www.campaignforliberty.org – Promoting and defending the American principles of individual liberty, constitutional government and free markets by means of educational and political activity. Founded by Ron Paul.

Liberty Counsel – www.lc.org – Non-profit litigation, education and policy organization dedicated to advancing religious freedom, sanctity of human life and the family.

Alliance Defending Freedom – www.adflegal.org – Defending Faith. Defending Justice. Founder and CEO – Alan Sears.

1851 Center for Constitutional Law – www.ohioconstitution.org

LECTURE TWELVE

OPTIONAL READING ASSIGNMENTS

1. Continue reading excerpts of *The Law* by Frederic Bastiat. Start at "Dictatorial Arrogance" and read to "The Doctrine of the Democrats" (pages 272-274).

LECTURE REVIEWS

1. Complete Lecture Twelve Review Worksheet.

2. Complete Lecture Twelve Quiz, including True & False Questions.

GOING DEEPER: SUPPLEMENTAL READING & VIDEO OPTIONS

 Found at www.theamericanview.com/constitution-course-supplemental-assignments which can also be found at the bottom of theamericanview.com under Resources.

Law & Liberty (Chapters 19 through 22) by R. J. Rushdoony. This book consists of a series of essays composed of radio addresses in 1966 and 1967. These essays were written as a summary statement of certain concepts of law and liberty and have been proven to be prophetic in the decline of America if Christianity was replaced with Human Secularism.

Interposition (DVD) by Michael A. Peroutka. This video explains the vital role the lesser magistrates are under oath to play in protecting the citizens from a higher magistrate who is violating the law.

CHAPTER THIRTEEN
AMENDMENTS XI - XXVII

GENERAL OBJECTIVES

It is our intent and our hope that you will understand the historical background of the Amendments that followed the War Between the States; specifically including the 11th through the 27th Amendments, and their generally intended purpose of expanding the authority, influence and power of the central (Federal) government.

SPECIFIC OBJECTIVES

☆ *Understand the historical purpose behind each post-war Amendment and the progressive manner in which the central government's power has been grossly and inappropriately enlarged through their adoptions and interpretations.*

☆ *Grasp the continuing and critical need to restrict and limit government power and the extent of government's intrusion into the lives of the people.*

☆ *Appreciate the intent of the Framers of the early Amendments (before the War Between the States) to limit government authority.*

☆ *Develop a proper framework for understanding the opinions of the Supreme Court in what are considered to be leading constitutional law cases and the tests that the courts use to decide these cases.*

"Anyone who has 'studied law,' who has not studied the Bible, has not studied law."
    —Michael Anthony Peroutka

"Where the Spirit of the Lord is, there is Liberty."
    —2 Corinthians 3:17

Watch Video Lecture

 Lecture Thirteen: Amendments XI - XXVII; follow along with the notes in the following section.

THE ELEVENTH AMENDMENT (1798)

Lawsuits Against States

The Judicial power of the United States shall not be construed to extend to any suit in law or equity, commenced or prosecuted against one of the United States by Citizens of another State, or by Citizens or Subjects of any Foreign State.

A. States may not be sued in Federal court by citizens of another jurisdiction, without State's consent.

B. Amends Article III, Section 2, Clause 1 which allowed such suits.

C. Resulted from reaction against lawsuit against state, Chisholm v. Georgia, 2 U.S. 419 (1793).

1. In 1792 in South Carolina, Alexander Chisholm, the executor of the estate of Robert Farquhar, attempted to sue the state of Georgia in the Supreme Court over payments due to him for goods that Farquhar had supplied Georgia during the American Revolutionary War. United States Attorney General Edmund Randolph argued the case for the plaintiff before the Court. The defendant, Georgia, refused to appear, claiming that as a "sovereign" a state did not have to appear in court to hear a suit against it to which it did not consent.

2. Mostly because of Chisholm v. Georgia, the 11th Amendment was ratified in 1795, which removed Federal jurisdiction in cases where citizens of one State attempt to sue another State.

THE TWELFTH AMENDMENT (1804)

Electoral College

"The Electors shall meet in their respective states, and vote by ballot for President and Vice-President, one of whom, at least, shall not be an inhabitant of the same state with themselves; they shall name in their ballots the person voted for as President, and in distinct ballots the person voted for as Vice-President, and they shall make distinct lists of all persons voted for as President, and all persons voted for as Vice-President and of the number of votes for each, which lists they shall sign and certify, and transmit sealed to the seat of the government of the United States, directed to the President of the Senate.

The President of the Senate shall, in the presence of the Senate and House of Representatives, open all the certificates and the votes shall then be counted.

The person having the greatest Number of votes for President, shall be the President, if such number be a majority of the whole number of Electors appointed; and if no person have such majority, then from the persons having the highest numbers not exceeding three on the list of those voted for as President, the House of Representatives shall choose immediately, by ballot, the President. But in choosing the President, the votes shall be taken by states, the representation from each state having one vote; a quorum for this purpose shall consist of a member or members from two-thirds of the states, and a majority of all the states shall be necessary to a choice. And if the House of Representatives shall not choose a President whenever the right of choice shall devolve upon them, before the fourth day of March next following, then the Vice-President shall act as President, as in the case of the death or other constitutional disability of the President.

The person having the greatest number of votes as Vice-President, shall be the Vice-President, if such number be a majority of the whole number of Electors appointed, and if no person have a majority, then from the two highest numbers on the list, the Senate shall choose the Vice-President; a quorum for the purpose shall consist of two-thirds of the whole number of Senators, and a majority of the whole number shall be necessary to a choice. But no person constitutionally ineligible to the office of President shall be eligible to that of Vice-President of the United States."

A. Amends Article II, Section 1, to provide that Electors should vote separately for President and Vice-President. (See Lecture Eight.)

B. In the original language, members of the Electoral College could only vote for President; each elector could vote for two candidates, and the Vice-President was the person who received the second largest number of votes during the election.

THE THIRTEENTH AMENDMENT (1865)

Slavery Abolished

Section 1. Neither slavery nor involuntary servitude, except as a punishment for crime whereof the party shall have been duly convicted, shall exist within the United States, or any place subject to their jurisdiction.

Section 2. Congress shall have power to enforce this article by appropriate legislation.

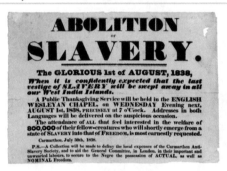

A. The Emancipation Proclamation didn't free slaves; it was only a political document.

B. Early courts ruled that 13th Amendment simply abolished the institution of slavery, not other forms of segregation or discrimination. *The Civil Rights Cases*, 103 U.S. 3 (1883).

C. But Justice Harlan, dissenting, in *The Civil Rights Cases* argued that the 13th Amendment did more than abolish slavery as an institution; it also abolished the "badges and incidents" of slavery that are reminiscent of the slavery era; Segregation, denial of civil rights, etc.

D. Justice Harlan's dissenting view in 1883 eventually became the majority view. Jones v. Mayer, 392 U.S. 409 (1968).[1]

E. "Congress shall have power to enforce this article by appropriate legislation." This provision, which also appears in Amendments 14, 15, 18, 19, 23, 24, and 26, has been used to greatly expand Federal power at the expense of State and individual rights.

F. The Income Tax (1913) (conscription of labor) and the Draft (1917) (conscription of persons) present two bodies of argument indicating that slavery rather than being abolished has been expanded to all individuals.

---

1 "U.S. Reports: Jones et ux. v. Alfred H. Mayer Co. et al., 392 U.S. 409 (1968)." https://www.loc.gov/item/usrep392409/

THE FOURTEENTH AMENDMENT (1868)

Due Process, Equal Protection

Section 1. *All persons born or naturalized in the United States, and subject to the jurisdiction thereof, are citizens of the United States and of the State wherein they reside. No State shall make or enforce any law which shall abridge the privileges or immunities of citizens of the United States; nor shall any State deprive any person of life, liberty, or property, without due process of law; nor deny to any person within its jurisdiction the equal protection of the laws.*

Section 2. *Representatives shall be apportioned among the several States according to their respective numbers, counting the whole number of persons in each State, excluding Indians not taxed. But when the right to vote at any election for the choice of electors for President and Vice-President of the United States, Representatives in Congress, the Executive and Judicial officers of a State, or the members of the Legislature thereof, is denied to any of the male inhabitants of such State, being twenty-one years of age, and citizens of the United States, or in any way abridged, except for participation in rebellion, or other crime, the basis of representation therein shall be reduced in the proportion which the number of such male citizens shall bear to the whole number of male citizens twenty-one years of age in such State.*

Section 3. *No person shall be a Senator or Representative in Congress, or elector of President and Vice-President, or hold any office, civil or military, under the United States, or under any State, who, having previously taken an oath, as a member of Congress, or as an officer of the United States, or as a member of any State legislature, or as an executive or Judicial officer of any State, to support the Constitution of the United States, shall have engaged in insurrection or rebellion against the same, or given aid or comfort to the enemies thereof. But Congress may by a vote of two-thirds of each House, remove such disability.*

Section 4. *The validity of the public debt of the United States, authorized by law, including debts incurred for payment of pensions and bounties for services in suppressing insurrection or rebellion, shall not be questioned. But neither the United States nor any State shall assume or pay any debt or obligation incurred in aid of insurrection or rebellion against the United States, or any claim for the loss or emancipation of any slave; but all such debts, obligations and claims shall be held illegal and void.*

Section 5. *The Congress shall have power to enforce, by appropriate legislation, the provisions of this article.*

A. This Amendment is very destructive, particularly because it erodes the protections in the Bill of Rights. It was destructive of the limits established on the Federal government and the powers reserved to the State governments.

B. States must respect rights of all U.S. citizens.

C. Problems in the Ratification of the 14th Amendment:

1. Proposed by an unconstitutional Congress – The United States Constitution, Article V provides: *"No State, without its consent, shall be deprived of its equal suffrage in the Senate."* The fact that 23 Senators had been unlawfully excluded from the U.S. Senate, in order to secure a two-thirds vote for adoption of the Joint Resolution proposing the 14th Amendment is shown by Resolutions of protest adopted by eight State legislatures: New Jersey, Alabama, Texas, Arkansas, Georgia, Florida, South Carolina, North Carolina.

2.	Never presented to President Andrew Johnson – see his speech June 22, 1866.
3.	Never ratified by 3/4 of States – 15 of 37 States rejected it – Texas, Georgia, Florida, Alabama, North Carolina, Arkansas, South Carolina, Kentucky, Virginia, Louisiana, Delaware, Maryland, Michigan, Ohio, New Jersey.
4.	Congress illegally removed 10 Southern State Legislatures by military force and installed puppet governments which "ratified" the 14th Amendment.
5.	Supreme Court has never dealt with the constitutional problems. Some of which were presented in the Coleman v. Miller (1939) case.[2]
6.	"The legislatures of Georgia, North Carolina and South Carolina had rejected the amendment in November and December 1866. New governments were erected in those States (and in others) under the direction of Congress. The new legislatures ratified the amendment that had been rejected on the following dates: North Carolina on July 4, 1868, South Carolina on July 9, 1868, and Georgia on July 21, 1868."[3]

D. The States may not deprive anyone of life, liberty or property without due process of law:

1.	The Fifth Amendment contains similar provision for Federal government. This applies to States.
2.	Courts have subsequently ruled that "liberty" and "due process" include most of the rights guaranteed in the Bill of Rights, and that the Bill of Rights applies to government action at all levels.
3.	Since municipalities, counties, and school districts are subdivisions of State government, judicially active courts have held that the "Incorporation Doctrine" means the Bill of Rights applies to government action at all levels. This has been the justification for such actions as removing prayer and the Bible from local public schools.
4.	Debate rages as to whether the "Incorporation Doctrine" accurately reflects the intent of the authors of the 14th Amendment.

E. Original intent can be seen by examining primary source writings.

1.	Congressman John Bingham, a sponsor of the 14th Amendment, was asked if he feared it might open the door for the federal government to usurp rights away from the States. He replied, *"I repel the suggestion… that the [14th] Amendment will… take away from any State any right that belongs to it."*[4]
2.	In 1875, seven years after the 14th Amendment was "ratified," Republican Congressman James Blaine proposed a constitutional amendment (which was never ratified). This Blaine Amendment would have forbidden public funding of private, denominational schools by the States [Note the similarity to the First Amendment]:

2 "U.S. Reports: Coleman v. Miller, 307 U.S. 433 (1939)." https://www.loc.gov/item/usrep307433/
3 Source sweetliberty.org/fourteenth.amend.htm
4 "American Minute - Whatever Happened to the Bill of Rights?" Bill Federer, 12/15/15

a. Blaine Amendment proposed text – *"No State shall make any law respecting an establishment of religion, or prohibiting the free exercise thereof; and no money raised by taxation in any State for the support of public schools, or derived from any public fund therefor, nor any public lands devoted thereto, shall ever be under the control of any religious sect; nor shall any money so raised or lands so devoted be divided between religious sects or denominations."*[5]

b. The First Amendment declares the following: *"Congress shall make no law respecting an establishment of religion, or prohibiting the free exercise thereof; or abridging the freedom of speech, or of the press; or the right of the people peaceably to assemble, and to petition the Government for a redress of grievances."*

3. The Blaine Amendment became pivotal in State debates on the role of religion in public education, religious establishment and religious expression. If the original intent of the 14th Amendment was to actually incorporate the First Amendment (as well as the others of the Bill of Rights) into State governments, then this Blaine Amendment attempt would have been completely unnecessary.

F. States may not deny anyone equal protection of the law.

G. Those who aided the Confederacy may not vote or hold office unless pardoned by Congress.

H. Debts owed to Union soldiers are valid; debts owed to Confederate soldiers are invalid; this was another way of stripping away the wealth of those that were part of the Confederacy.

THE FIFTEENTH AMENDMENT (1870)

Voting Rights for Former Slaves

Section 1. The right of citizens of the United States to vote shall not be denied or abridged by the United States or by any State on account of race, color, or previous condition of servitude.

Section 2. The Congress shall have power to enforce this article by appropriate legislation.

U.S. citizens may not be deprived of right to vote because of race, color, or previous servitude.

THE SIXTEENTH AMENDMENT (1913)

Income Tax

The Congress shall have power to lay and collect taxes on incomes, from whatever source derived, without apportionment among the several States, and without regard to any census or enumeration.

A. Congress passed income tax in 1893; Supreme Court ruled it unconstitutional in 1895 (Article I, Section 9) (no capitation taxes).

5 "Blaine Amendment," https://en.wikipedia.org/wiki/Blaine_Amendment. Also see: https://ij.org/issues/school-choice/blaine-amendments/answers-frequently-asked-questions-blaine-amendments/

B. Congress then passed the 16th Amendment in 1909; "ratified" 1913.

C. Ratification problems with the 16th Amendment – Bill Benson's research was included in a 1985 book co-written with Martin Beckman entitled: *The Law That Never Was: The Fraud of the 16th Amendment and Personal Income Tax.* Bill Benson is a former investigator for the Illinois Department of Revenue who began his research when assisting his attorney with a tax case.

D. In his research, Bill Benson discovered the following problems:

1.	Seven State legislatures did not ratify the amendment and reported it as such. (Connecticut, Florida, Oregon, Pennsylvania, Rhode Island, Utah, Virginia)
2.	Two State legislatures did not ratify the amendment, but reported it as ratified to the Secretary of State. (Kentucky, Tennessee)
3.	Six other States failed to have the Governor sign the amendment as required by the State Constitution after it was approved. (Idaho, Iowa, Kentucky, Minnesota, Missouri, Washington)
4.	Only 13 States were required for the amendment to fail, and there are 14 with substantive ratification issues.
5.	There are still other States with violations of their State Constitutions in the ratification process, including eight States reported by Secretary of State Knox as having ratified the amendment. These States actually have missing or incomplete records of the ratification procedures or votes, and there is no conclusive record that they ratified the amendment or reported any ratification to the Secretary of State. (Delaware, Michigan, Nevada, New Hampshire, South Dakota, Tennessee, Vermont, Wyoming)
6.	In 25 States, the legislature violated a provision of their State Constitutions during the ratification process. (Arizona, Arkansas, California, Colorado, Georgia, Idaho, Illinois, Kansas, Kentucky, Louisiana, Maryland, Massachusetts, Michigan, Mississippi, Missouri, Montana, New Jersey, New Mexico, North Dakota, Tennessee, Texas, Vermont, Washington, West Virginia, Wyoming)
7.	Twenty-nine States violated their State Constitutions, laws or procedural rules during the ratification process thereby seemingly voiding the legislation. (Arizona, Arkansas, California, Colorado, Georgia, Idaho, Indiana, Iowa, Kentucky, Louisiana, Maryland, Massachusetts, Minnesota, Mississippi, Missouri, Montana, Nebraska, New Jersey, New Mexico, New York, Ohio, Oklahoma, South Carolina, South Dakota, Tennessee, Texas, Vermont, West Virginia, Wyoming)
8.	Other issues include syntax and punctuation issues which violate the Article V process:

    a. Twenty-two States approved the Amendment with changes in syntax, accepting this inexact version as the original for ratification.

    b. One State approved the Amendment with variations in spelling accepting this inexact version as the original for ratification.

    c. At least 26 approved the Amendment with changes in punctuation accepting this inexact version as the original for ratification.

9. When counting States with issues in the ratification process, 45 of the 48 States had some type of issue. There are 31 with significant violations and seven others not approving the Amendment for a total of 38 States which did not constitutionally ratify the 16th Amendment.

Constitution Article I, Section 9, contains a list of actions that are forbidden to Congress. In that list, Clause 4 provides: "No capitation, or other direct, tax shall be laid, unless in proportion to the census or enumeration herein-before directed to be taken."[6]

This constitutional prohibition means that no Federal tax on the people or their earnings is allowed! This provision clearly forbids any Federal direct tax unless it is levied upon, and apportioned among, the State governments in proportion to the population of each State as required in Article I, Section 2, Clause 3. "Representatives and direct Taxes shall be apportioned among the several states which may be included within this Union, according to their respective Numbers…"

10. Tariffs were the principle means by which the Federal government funded its work except in times of war. The Federal government apportioned the tax bill to each State according the proportions determined by the census. Each State would raise the revenue in its State by the means its legislature determined and forward the proceeds to Washington, D.C. The States had a powerful check on Federal spending, as Senators were appointed by the State Legislatures and subject to recall whenever they acted contrary to the wishes of the State Legislature. The States could stop any and every act of Federal spending they were unwilling to raise from the sweat and tears of their citizens. By taxing them to pay the Federal Tax bill, the States were obligating themselves to pay through the votes of their Senators.

E. The "Original Purpose" of the 16th Amendment is revealed when reviewing the Trust Busters:

1. Sherman Anti-Trust Act enacted in 1890.

2. Congress enacted an income tax law that imposed a tax on the income of corporations in 1894.

3. 1895 in the case of Pollock v. Farmers Loan and Trust CO., 157 U.S. 420, the Supreme Court declared that tax unconstitutional because it imposed a tax on income derived from property. Understanding the Pollock decision:[7]

   a. To tax income when the source of the income was property, imposes a Federal tax burden on the property itself. This is forbidden by limitations on direct taxation in the Constitution.

   b. Article I, Section 2, Clause 3 provides: "Representatives and direct Taxes shall be apportioned among the several states which may be included within this Union, according to their respective Numbers…"

---

6 *Black's Law Dictionary*, 5th Edition, defines "capitation tax" as "a tax or imposition on the person."
7 "U.S. Reports: Pollock v. Farmers' Loan and Trust Co., 158 U.S. 601 (1895)." https://www.loc.gov/item/usrep158601/

4.	President William Howard Taft gave a message to a joint session of Congress on June 16, 1909 which was published in the Congressional Record (Senate) on pages 3344 and 3345. President Taft explained that the purpose and function of his proposed 16th Amendment was to assure the constitutionality of his proposed Corporation Income Act which was passed in the same 1909 sessions of Congress. The Amendment did not authorize any income tax on U.S. Citizens. In President Taft's June 16, 1909, message to a joint session of Congress, he called for a bill to impose a tax of only 2% income of corporations. He described his proposed corporation income tax bill as being: *"...in form and substance almost exactly the same character as that..."* income tax law involved in the Pollock decision of the U.S. Supreme Court, wherein the law was ruled to be unconstitutional. President Taft considered it unlikely that the Court would be willing to reverse the Pollock ruling.[8]
5.	Therefore, in order to assure the constitutionality of an income tax on corporations, he proposed a constitutional amendment that would override the crux of the Pollock decision and thereby assure the constitutionality of his newly proposed 1909 Corporation Income Tax Act.

F.   Court opinion on the 16th Amendment: Brushaber v. Union Pacific, 240 U.S. 1 (1916): The cornerstone decision relied upon by the Internal Reveune Service (IRS)[9] that established the constitutionality of the income tax (but only as an excise tax) under the 16th Amendment. This case involved withholding from monies accruing to non-resident aliens, but not to citizens! The Brushaber court explained that the 16th Amendment states that the tax authorized by the Amendment must be laid "without apportionment," and because the Constitution still requires that all direct taxes must be apportioned among the States, the income tax cannot stand constitutionally as a direct tax (a tax on citizens). The Court stated that the income tax is constitutional only as an indirect tax in the nature of an excise.

G.   In 1916 the U.S. Supreme Court held, in Stanton v. Baltic Mining, 240 U.S. 103 (1916), that the "16th Amendment created no new power of taxation."[10]

H.   Other Supreme Court cases:

1.	Have ruled that the income tax is an excise tax imposed on activities involving the exercise of a government granted privilege, such as the activities of corporations or activities of non-resident aliens working or doing business in this nation and that income is the measurement for determining the amount of the tax for such corporations or non-resident aliens.
2.	1918 U.S. Supreme Court decision of Peck & CO. v. Lowe, 247 U.S. 165 (1918), states that *"The 16th Amendment does not extend the power of taxation to new or excepted subjects…Neither can the tax be sustained as a tax on the person, measured by income. Such a tax would be by nature a capitation rather than an excise."*[11]

I.   Capitation taxes are still forbidden by Article I, Section 9, Clause 4 of the Constitution! Nothing in the 16th Amendment repealed or nullified the constitutional limitations on the imposition of direct taxes which still prohibit the imposition of any Federal taxes on individual citizens of this country or on their property.

8   https://www.govinfo.gov/content/pkg/GPO-CRECB-1909-pt3-v44/pdf/GPO-CRECB-1909-pt3-v44-21-1.pdf
9   "U.S. Reports: Brushaber v. Union Pac. R. R., 240 U.S. 1 (1916)." https://www.loc.gov/item/usrep240001/
10   "U.S. Reports: Stanton v. Baltic Mining Co., 240 U.S. 103 (1916)." https://www.loc.gov/item/usrep240103/
11   "U.S. Reports: Peck & Co. v. Lowe, 247 U.S. 165 (1918)." https://www.loc.gov/item/usrep247165/

J. Compare the language of the 21st Amendment. It specifically states that the 18th Amendment is nullified. In order for the language of Article I, Section 9 to be nullified, the 16th Amendment would have had to specifically and clearly state that the prohibitions in Article I were rescinded, just as the 21st Amendment does.

K. This was understood to be a very limited tax. In 1913 the standard exemption was $4,000 (about $60,000 in 1994 dollars). Those making less paid no tax. After deductions were subtracted, the first $20,000 of income was taxed (about $300,000 in 1994 dollars) which was 1%. In addition, those who were very wealthy paid a graduated "super tax." For those making $500,000 or more (about $7,500,000 in 1994 dollars) this "super tax" was just 6%.

L. The Federal income tax has served as a vehicle of tyranny by confiscating the people's money through seizure by the central government and returning it to the States in a manner that coerces the States to be the agent of Federal tyranny.

THE SEVENTEENTH AMENDMENT (1913)

Senators Popularly Elected

Clause 1. The Senate of the United States shall be composed of two Senators from each State, elected by the people thereof, for six years; and each Senator shall have one vote. The electors in each State shall have the qualifications requisite for electors of the most numerous branch of the State legislatures.

Clause 2. When vacancies happen in the representation of any State in the Senate, the executive authority of each State shall issue writs of election to fill such vacancies: Provided That the legislature of any State may empower the executive thereof to make temporary appointments until the people fill the vacancies by election as the legislature may direct.

Clause 3. This amendment shall not be so construed as to affect the election or term of any Senator chosen before it becomes valid as part of the Constitution.

A. Formerly they were chosen by State legislatures, thus giving State legislatures powerful influence over Congress.

B. The 17th Amendment eliminated an important State check on Federal power.

C. When Bill Benson was researching the ratification of the 16th Amendment, he discovered that were even more problems with the process that "certified" the 17th Amendment. He prepared an article entitled "Proof the 17th Amendment was not Ratified" documenting his findings from the National and various State archives which has now been deleted from the web.

D. However, others have taken up the cause of having the 17th Amendment repealed and began to conduct research into the 17th Amendment.

E. Certified documents can be found online;[12] summaries of the documents include the following:

    1. Eleven States did not ratify the 17th Amendment in violation of Article V:

        a. Utah explicitly rejected the amendment.

---

12 http://www.devvy.com/new_site/17th_amendment_docs_march_2010.html

b. Alabama, Florida and Georgia refused to vote on the amendment.

c. Kentucky, Maryland, Mississippi, Rhode Island, South Carolina and Virginia did not vote on the amendment.

d. Since several States were out of session at the time of the vote, have they been deprived of equal Suffrage in the U.S. Senate because they did not participate in the ratification of this amendment?

2. Four other States had substantial issues as well. No action was taken in Delaware and no records exists for Oregon, Vermont or Washington.

3. Minnesota was determined to fully meet the ratification requirement by the Secretary of State in the official Federal records although official notice from the State seems to have not been sent.

4. Thirty-six other States have a list of errors in the various Resolutions of State Legislatures. (Arizona, Arkansas, California, Colorado, Connecticut, Idaho, Illinois, Indiana, Iowa, Kansas, Maine, Massachusetts, Michigan, Minnesota, Missouri, Montana, Nebraska, Nevada, New Hampshire, New Jersey, New Mexico, New York, North Carolina, North Dakota, Ohio, Oklahoma, Oregon, Pennsylvania, South Dakota, Tennessee, Texas, Vermont, Washington, West Virginia, Wisconsin, Wyoming)

The Executive Branch, under the Secretary of State, ruled that these errors were immaterial to the adoption of the amendment. It is clear that the proper procedure in proclaiming the adoption of the proposed amendment was not followed. Nevertheless, the Secretary of State was allowed to disregard the errors in violation of the ratification process. Does this not violate the very document it seeks to amend – our Constitution?

F. Since several States were out of session at the time of the vote, have they been deprived of equal Suffrage in the U.S. Senate because they did not participate in the ratification of this amendment? Is fraud (non-ratification) enough to allow a state to declare it null and void in their State?

G. Secretary of State William Jennings Bryan declared the 17th Amendment ratified at 11:00 am, May 31, 1913, by proclamation.

THE EIGHTEENTH AMENDMENT (1919)

Prohibition of Alcohol

Section 1. After one year from the ratification of this article the manufacture, sale, or transportation of intoxicating liquors within, the importation thereof into, or the exportation thereof from the United States and all territory subject to the jurisdiction thereof for beverage purposes is hereby prohibited.

Police raid confiscating illegal alcohol.

Section 2. The Congress and the several States shall have concurrent power to enforce this article by appropriate legislation.

Section 3. This article shall be inoperative unless it shall have been ratified as an amendment to the Constitution by the legislatures of the several States, as provided in the Constitution, within seven years from the date of the submission hereof to the States by the Congress.

A. This amendment gave the Federal government authority over a matter of law enforcement that was better left to the States or to Family Government.

B. "The powers delegated by the proposed Constitution to the federal government are few and defined. Those which are to remain in the State governments are numerous and indefinite."[13] –James Madison

THE NINETEENTH AMENDMENT (1920)

Women's Suffrage

The right of citizens of the United States to vote shall not be denied or abridged by the United States or by any State on account of sex.

Congress shall have power to enforce this article by appropriate legislation.

Right to vote cannot be denied on the basis of sex. This was already true in some States.

Woman Suffrage Headquarters, Cleveland, 1913

THE TWENTIETH AMENDMENT (1933)

Presidential Succession

Section 1. The terms of the President and Vice-President shall end at noon on the 20th day of January, and the terms of Senators and Representatives at noon on the 3d day of January, of the years in which such terms would have ended if this article had not been ratified; and the terms of their successors shall then begin.

Section 2. The Congress shall assemble at least once in every year, and such meeting shall begin at noon on the 3d day of January, unless they shall by law appoint a different day.

Section 3. If, at the time fixed for the beginning of the term of the President, the President elect shall have died, the Vice-President elect shall become President. If a President shall not have been chosen before the time fixed for the beginning of his term, or if the President elect shall have failed to qualify, then the Vice-President elect shall act as President until a President shall have qualified; and the Congress may by law provide for the case wherein neither a President elect nor a Vice-President shall have qualified, declaring who shall then act as President, or the manner in which one who is to act shall be selected, and such person shall act accordingly until a President or Vice-President shall have qualified.

Section 4. The Congress may by law provide for the case of the death of any of the persons from whom the House of Representatives may choose a President whenever the right of choice shall have devolved upon them, and for the case of the death of any of the persons from whom the Senate may choose a Vice-President whenever the right of choice shall have devolved upon them.

Section 5. Sections 1 and 2 shall take effect on the 15th day of October following the ratification of this article.

Section 6. This article shall be inoperative unless it shall have been ratified as an amendment to the Constitution by the legislatures of three-fourths of the several States within seven years from the date of its submission.

---

13 The Federalist Papers, No. 45.

A. President and Vice-President take office on January 20th instead of March 4th. Improved transportation made the earlier date feasible, and also reduced opportunities for "lame duck" Presidents and Congressmen to exert last-minute influence.

B. Presidential succession altered again! (See Lecture Eight.)

THE TWENTY-FIRST AMENDMENT (1933)

Prohibition Repealed

Section 1. The eighteenth article of amendment to the Constitution of the United States is hereby repealed.

Section 2. The transportation or importation into any State, Territory, or possession of the United States for delivery or use therein of intoxicating liquors, in violation of the laws thereof, is hereby prohibited.

VOTE FOR PROPOSAL NUMBER ONE TO REPEAL EIGHTEENTH AMENDMENT

1. For the delegates favoring the pending amendment to the Constitution of the United States.
2. For the delegates opposing the pending amendment to the Constitution of the United States.

MISSOURI ASSOCIATION AGAINST PROHIBITION
ORGANIZED IN 1921

Board of Directors
Chilton Atkinson   Malcolm McMenamy
James W. Byrnes   John S. Lehmann
D. L. Grey   Fletcher R. Harris
                     A. L. Shapleigh

HERE COMES MISSOURI!

Section 3. This article shall be inoperative unless it shall have been ratified as an amendment to the Constitution by conventions in the several States, as provided in the Constitution, within seven years from the date of the submission hereof to the States by the Congress.

A. The 18th Amendment was repealed. It was not popular and Juries were nullifying government prosecutions.

B. However, enforcement authority over violations of State law seems to be retained by Section 2.

C. Despite repeal, the IRS and Bureau of Alcohol, Tobacco, Firearms and Explosives (BATFE) remain. BATFE was formerly the ATF (Alcohol, Tobacco, and Firearms).

THE TWENTY-SECOND AMENDMENT (1951)

Two-Term Limit for President

Section 1. No person shall be elected to the office of the President more than twice, and no person who has held the office of President, or acted as President, for more than two years of a term to which some other person was elected President shall be elected to the office of the President more than once. But this article shall not apply to any person holding the office of President when this article was proposed by the Congress, and shall not prevent any person who may be holding the office of President, or acting as President, during the term within which this article becomes operative from holding the office of President or acting as President during the remainder of such term.

Section 2. This article shall be inoperative unless it shall have been ratified as an amendment to the Constitution by the legislatures of three-fourths of the several States within seven years from the date of its submission to the States by the Congress.

Two-term tradition was broken by Franklin Delano Roosevelt during crisis of Depression and World War II. But when FDR died a few weeks into his fourth term, Americans decided to make the two-term tradition a solid rule.

THE TWENTY-THIRD AMENDMENT (1961)

District of Columbia Electors

Section 1. The District constituting the seat of Government of the United States shall appoint in such manner as the Congress may direct:

A number of electors of President and Vice-President equal to the whole number of Senators and Representatives in Congress to which the District would be entitled if it were a State, but in no event more than the least populous State; they shall be in addition to those appointed by the States, but they shall be considered, for the purposes of the election of President and Vice-President, to be electors appointed by a State; and they shall meet in the District and perform such duties as provided by the twelfth article of amendment.

Section 2. The Congress shall have power to enforce this article using appropriate legislation.

> District of Columbia now has electors equal to the number of electors from the least populous state (three electors). District of Columbia residents may now vote for the President. But District of Columbia still has no voting representatives in Congress, and is still not a State.

THE TWENTY-FOURTH AMENDMENT (1964)

Poll Tax Amendment

Section 1. The right of citizens of the United States to vote in any primary or other election for President or Vice-President, for electors for President or Vice-President, or for Senator or Representative in Congress, shall not be denied or abridged by the United States or any State by reason of failure to pay any poll tax or other tax.

Section 2. The Congress shall have power to enforce this article by appropriate legislation.

> Poll taxes ($1 or $2 in order to vote) were used to cover the costs of elections. But because they were sometimes used to deny people the right to vote, they were eliminated by this amendment.

President Lyndon B. Johnson signing the Constitutional Amendment on the Poll Tax.

THE TWENTY-FIFTH AMENDMENT (1967)

Presidential Succession

Section 1. In case of the removal of the President from office or of his death or resignation, the Vice-President shall become President.

Section 2. Whenever there is a vacancy in the office of the Vice-President, the President shall nominate a Vice-President who shall take office upon confirmation by a majority vote of both Houses of Congress.

Section 3. Whenever the President transmits to the President pro tempore of the Senate and the Speaker of the House of Representatives his written declaration that he is unable to discharge the powers and duties of his office, and until he transmits to them a written declaration to the contrary, such powers and duties shall be discharged by the Vice-President as Acting President.

Section 4. Whenever the Vice-President and a majority of either the principal officers of the executive departments or of such other body as Congress may by law provide, transmit to the President pro tempore of the Senate and the Speaker of the House of Representatives their written declaration that the President is unable to discharge the powers and duties of his office, the Vice-President shall immediately assume the powers and duties of the office as Acting President.

Thereafter, when the President transmits to the President pro tempore of the Senate and the Speaker of the House of Representatives his written declaration that no inability exists, he shall resume the powers and duties of his office unless the Vice-President and a majority of either the principal officers of the executive department or of such other body as Congress may by law provide, transmit within four days to the President pro tempore of the Senate and the Speaker of the House of Representatives their written declaration that the President is unable to discharge the powers and duties of his office. Thereupon Congress shall decide the issue, assembling within forty-eight hours for that purpose if not in session. If the Congress, within twenty-one days after receipt of the latter written declaration, or, if Congress is not in session, within twenty-one days after Congress is required to assemble, determines by two-thirds vote of both Houses that the President is unable to discharge the powers and duties of his office, the Vice-President shall continue to discharge the same as Acting President; otherwise, the President shall resume the powers and duties of his office.

Presidential succession revised again! (See Lecture Eight.)

THE TWENTY-SIXTH AMENDMENT (1971)

18-Year-Old Vote

Section 1. The right of citizens of the United States, who are eighteen years of age or older, to vote shall not be denied or abridged by the United States or by any State on account of age.

Section 2. The Congress shall have the power to enforce this article by appropriate legislation.

A. The right to vote may not be denied on the basis of age, for anyone who is over 18.

B. This does not prevent States from setting a voting age lower than 18, but they may not set a voting age higher than 18.

C. Voting is now increasingly seen as a universal right, rather than as a means of protecting rights and a privilege to be exercised by those who can vote responsibly, by stakeholders in the administration of justice.

D. The dilution of the franchise leads to the increase of legal plunder. (Read Frederic Bastiat's book *The Law*.)

THE TWENTY-SEVENTH AMENDMENT (1992)

Congressional Pay Increase

No law, varying the compensation for the services of the Senators and Representatives, shall take effect, until an election of Representatives shall have intervened.

A. No congressional pay increases will take effect until after the next election.

B. This is a check of the people upon their lawmakers; it gives the people an opportunity to express their disapproval of the pay increase by voting the lawmakers out of office.

C. This was originally the 11th Amendment of the Bill of Rights, but it was not ratified by 3/4 of the States.

D. In the 1980s and 1990s, as people became upset with congressional pay increases, interest in this Amendment was renewed, and it was ratified by the 38th State in 1992.

E. The 27th Amendment was certified by the Director of the U.S. Archives.

CHRISTIANITY IN THE CLASSROOM? SOMETHING TO THINK ABOUT By Ricki Pepin ©2014

We're told by progressives and many public educators that God, specifically the Judeo-Christian God of the Bible, has no place in the classroom. Not only, they say, is this a bad idea, but it's actually breaking the law — a violation of students' religious liberties. Really?

I was recently invited to teach a 12-week Constitution course using a room at a local public high school in Springboro, Ohio. The class was open to the public – parents, grandparents, students. A few community agitators seized this opportunity to flex their politically correct muscles by calling in the ACLU and threatening a lawsuit if we did not cancel the class.

The ACLU informed us that if we proceeded with this class we would be violating the students' First Amendment rights. I was stunned. Teaching the Constitution was to be deemed unconstitutional by the ACLU? Their objections stemmed from what they referred to as the "religious content" within the course. This objection proved to be a classic illustration of either a desire to indoctrinate students, historical ignorance, or both.

In order to best understand the Constitution, our course teaches American history alongside. For accuracy purposes, we use many primary source documents – what the founders themselves wrote — not a modern historian's rewrite of events. Here's where the rubber meets the road (or for revisionists, where the fingernails meet the chalkboard): In seeking the original intent of our founders and using their writings, you cannot leave out the Bible and Christianity. Their writings are overflowing with both.

To our utter amazement, the objections and lawsuit threats of the ACLU to our teaching this course stemmed from the "religious content" contained within the founders' own writings! For example:

- The Mayflower Compact – The Pilgrims wrote that the reason for their voyage and their purpose in founding a new nation was *"for the glory of God and to advance the Christian faith."* This direct quotation of the Pilgrims presents a profound and powerful truth from history: America was actually birthed for the purpose of advancing Christianity. Were you taught this in school? The ACLU is doing all they can to be sure no one is.

- The Declaration of Independence – Within this document the Founders wrote that all men are *"created equal and endowed by their Creator with certain unalienable rights…"* This statement pre-supposes a Creator God. They further wrote the basis of law would be *"The Laws of Nature and Nature's God"* – the 10 Commandments and your God-given conscience. They were continuing the purpose of this new nation as stated by the Pilgrims – *advancing the Christian faith.* Were you taught this in school?

- The Constitution, which many refer to as a godless document, is signed *"in the year of our Lord 1787"* – thus referring to Jesus Christ as the standard of dating all of history. Were you taught this in school? They did not say the Lord, but rather *our Lord*, once again expressing their religious views and standards, something the ACLU apparently finds threatening, frightening and illegal.

Christianity in the classroom is a historical fact. Noah Webster was the Founder known as "the Schoolmaster of the Nation." Author of many textbooks, his most famous "blue-backed speller" set a publishing record of a million copies a year for 100 years and contained a "moral Catechism" with rules from Scripture. He declared, *Education is useless without the Bible*" and "*The Bible was America's basic text book in all fields.*"

Indeed, prior to 1964 when the Bible was removed from the classroom, the main disciplinary problems in schools were chewing gum and throwing spit wads. Today we have metal detectors at high schools in an attempt to stop such unthinkable, horrific events as students shooting other students (i.e. Paducah, Kentucky; Columbine, Colorado; Virginia Tech in Blacksburg, Virginia; Nickel Mines, Pennsylvania; Parkland, Florida; Newtown, Connecticut; etc.).

Christianity in the classroom is not about bringing in doctrine from different denominations. It's about teaching Christian values such as integrity, kindness, loyalty, courage, and purity. How would schools be different and student's behavior improved if we returned to teaching the moral values found in Scripture? Spit wads or bullets? Which would you choose for your children to face on a daily basis? Maybe it's time to bring Christianity back to the classroom.

Something to think about.

LECTURE THIRTEEN

OPTIONAL
READING
ASSIGNMENTS

1. *The Law* by Frederic Bastiat. Start at "The Socialist Concept of Liberty" and read to "The Cause of French Revolutions" (pages 275-276).

LECTURE REVIEWS

1. Complete Lecture Thirteen Review Worksheet.

2. Complete Lecture Thirteen Quiz, including True & False Questions.

GOING DEEPER: SUPPLEMENTAL READING & VIDEO OPTIONS

 Found at www.theamericanview.com/constitution-course-supplemental-assignments which can also be found at the bottom of theamericanview.com under *Resources*.

Surprising Facts About The Sixteenth Amendment by John Sasser. To gain a constitutional understanding of what the 16th was supposed to accomplish according to the legislators, President and Supreme Court when it was proposed.

Defects in the Ratification of the 16th Amendment by Bill Benson. To examine the amazing evidence against the 16th's legal ratification by the required number of States.

CHAPTER FOURTEEN
THE CRISIS OF THE CONSTITUTION:
FROM BIBLICAL ABSOLUTES TO EVOLUTIONARY HUMANISTIC RELATIVISM

GENERAL OBJECTIVES

You should appreciate the broad sweep of historical events and influences that have altered the way in which Americans think about truth and law and government.

SPECIFIC OBJECTIVES

☆ *Appreciate and articulate the influences of Rousseau, Hegel, Comte, Darwin, and Spencer on American thinking.*

☆ *Grasp the significance of the application of these changing views of truth on the American legal system, including the training of lawyers since the 1870s.*

☆ *Understand and be able to demonstrate legal positivism in the decisions of American courts.*

☆ *Develop a learned understanding of the dangerous ramifications of the "Living Constitution" approach to jurisprudence in American courts and American education and culture.*

"If the foundations be destroyed, what can the righteous do?"
– Psalm 11:3

"In law, the moment of temptation is the moment of choice, when a judge realizes that in the case before him his strongly held view of justice, his political and moral imperative, is not embodied in a statute or in any provision of the Constitution. He must then choose between his version of justice and abiding by the American form of government. Yet the desire to do justice, who's nature seems to him obvious, is compelling, while the concept of constitutional process is abstract, rather arid, and the abstinence it counsels unsatisfying. To give in to temptation, this one time, solves an urgent human problem, and a faint crack appears in the American foundation. A judge has begun to rule where a legislator should."[1]
–Robert H. Bork

1 Robert H. Bork, *The Tempting of America.*

▶ **Lecture Fourteen:** The Crisis of the Constitution: From Biblical Absolutes to Evolutionary Humanistic Relativism; follow along with the notes in the following section.

THE FRAMERS' VIEW OF THE CONSTITUTION

A. Law, like truth, is unchanging, absolute, and God-ordained.

   1. Derived this view partly from the biblical view of truth.

   2. Old Testament: Truth (emeth) is fixed, unchanging, meets the test of time.

   3. New Testament: Truth (aletheia) is identified with Jesus Christ (John 14:6), who is "the same yesterday, and today, and forever" (Hebrews 13:8).

B. Derived this view partly from Sir Isaac Newton (1642 - 1727) who taught that the universe is governed by fixed, absolute, God-ordained laws – scientific laws like the laws of motion, gravity, mathematics, chemistry, physics, etc; moral laws for the governance of man. Newton was a devout Christian who wrote extensively on Bible prophecy, and his views were eagerly embraced by Christians and Deists alike as "the Laws of Nature and of Nature's God."

C. Derived this view in part from legal and political thinkers like Sir William Blackstone, Baron Charles Montesquieu, and John Locke, who taught that man's laws must conform to the Revealed Law of Scripture and the Law of Nature, both of which were dictated by God Himself.

D. The Framers therefore believed the Constitution was to be interpreted according to a fixed standard, its plain meaning interpreted by the intent of those who drafted and ratified it. This is called "the Jurisprudence of Original Intent."

   1. James Madison: *"(If) the sense in which the Constitution was accepted and ratified by the Nation ... be not the guide in expounding it, there can be no security for a faithful exercise of its powers."*[2]

   2. Thomas Jefferson: *"The Constitution on which our Union rests, shall be administered by me according to the safe and honest meaning contemplated by the plain understanding of the people of the United States, at the time of its adoption."*[3]

   3. George Washington: *"If, in the opinion of the people, the distribution or modification of the Constitutional powers be at any particular wrong, let it be corrected by an Amendment in the way the Constitution designates. But let there be no change by usurpation; though this may in one instance be the instrument of good, it is the customary weapon by which free governments are destroyed."*[4]

A CHANGING VIEW OF TRUTH

A. Jean-Jacques Rousseau (1712 - 1778):

---

2 "From James Madison to Henry Lee, 25 June 1824." https://founders.archives.gov/documents/Madison/04-03-02-0333
3 "From Thomas Jefferson to Providence Citizens, 27 March 1801."https://founders.archives.gov/documents/Jefferson/01-33-02-0410
4 From Washington's *Farewell Address to the People of the United States.*

1. Rejected concept of sin.

2. Stressed goodness of man.

3. Blamed human institutions for existence of evil.

B. George Wilhelm Friedrich Hegel (1770 - 1831):

1. Rejected concept of absolute, unchanging truth.

2. Believed truth evolves from age to age.

3. Means by which truth changes is the "dialectic" (thesis/antithesis/synthesis). The November 2009 debate about Healthcare (House Bill 3200) is an example of the Hegelian Dialectic in play in modern America. When faced with a Democrat/Liberal "antithesis," the Republican/Conservative response is not an argument in favor of the "thesis" but a capitulation to a "synthesis." The synthesis shares the same philosophical basis as the antithesis.

C. Auguste Comte (1789 - 1857):

1. Father of Positivism.

2. Positivism: The only meaningful truth is that which can be empirically verified.

3. Renders concepts such as God, divine law, natural law, natural right, equality, human dignity meaningless.

D. Charles Darwin (1809 - 1883):

1. Popularized evolutionary model of origins through *On the Origin of Species by Means of Natural Selection, or the Preservation of Favoured Races in the Struggle for Life* (1859).

2. Overproduction.

3. Struggle for survival.

4. Survival of the fittest.

5. Reproduction of like kinds.

6. Did not develop this model into a philosophical worldview; others did.

E. Herbert Spencer (1820 - 1903):

1. Made Darwin's model a philosophy and worldview.

2. Wrote extensively showing how evolution is the unifying principle affecting and underlying every academic discipline:

a. Economics: Laissez-faire Social Darwinism (tooth-and-claw, cut-throat competition), Crony Capitalism (political favors for political support); both unlike biblical capitalism which stresses compassion and moral responsibility (e.g. the Proverbs 31 woman).

b. Freudian and Jungian psychology.

c. Sociology.

d. Anthropology.

e. Even liberal biblical criticism, viewing Bible as evolving document developing as man evolved, rather than revelation given by God to man.

THE RISE OF LEGAL POSITIVISM

A. 1870s: Dean Christopher Columbus Langdell of Harvard Law School pioneered a new theory of law known as legal positivism, replacing natural law theory. Two of his notable disciples were Roscoe Pound and Oliver Wendell Holmes Jr.

B. Principles of legal positivism:

1. There are no divine absolutes in law, or if there are, they are irrelevant to the modern legal system.

2. Law is simply man-made – whatever the state says, is law.

3. Law evolves as man evolves.

4. Judges guide the evolution of law by writing decisions.

5. To study law the "scientific" way, get to the original sources: Study the decisions of judges (case law method of legal study).

C. Result: "Living Constitution" view that judges are not bound by the intent of the Framers but rather are free to give new meanings to the Constitution. Some legal scholars have even called the Court a "continuing constitutional convention."

1. Judges who hold this view feel free to create new "rights" not found in the Constitution, like abortion and homosexual conduct.

2. Radical offshoots of Legal Positivism:

a. Legal Realism: Argues that since no divine absolutes or natural law principles exist, legal system should stop pretending to be neutral and objective and instead openly work to advance the causes and clients it favors.

b. Critical Legal Studies Movement (often Marxist): Argues that the legal system be openly partial to the poor and "oppressed" and should openly work against the rich, the religious establishment, etc.

c. But God's Law states in Leviticus 19:15: *"Ye shall do no unrighteousness in judgment: thou shalt not respect the person of the poor, nor honour the person of the mighty: [but] in righteousness shalt thou judge thy neighbour."*

Example: Furman v. Georgia, 408 U.S. 238 (1972): Justices Brennan and Marshall argued (concurring opinion) that capital punishment is "cruel and unusual punishment" barred by the 8th Amendment. Although the Framers clearly didn't intend that, Brennan and Marshall said, *"The Amendment must draw its meaning from the evolving standards of decency that mark the progress of a maturing society."*[5]

DANGERS OF THE "LIVING CONSTITUTION APPROACH"

A. Human rights are not secure. The same court that can read into the Constitution rights that aren't there (like abortion and homosexual conduct), can read out of the Constitution rights that are there (like property rights, contract rights, firearms, and free exercise of religion).

1. There is no guarantee that history will always move upward toward greater recognition of human rights, human dignity, and human equality.

2. History could just as easily move downward toward a new age of barbarism (as much of the 20th and 21st centuries would indicate).

3. Nor is there any guarantee that judges will always be more "enlightened" and forward looking than the general population on matters of human equality and human rights. In fact, during much of history, judges have been behind the general public in that regard. See for example the Nuremberg Trials of the Nazi Judges.

4. The fixed standard of the Constitution is a far better guarantee of human rights than any evolving judge-made standard.

B. A "Living Approach" leads to "Big Government."

1. Through strained interpretations of the General Welfare Clause, Interstate Commerce Clause, Necessary and Proper Clause, Contract Clause, Due Process Clause, and others, courts have opened the door to vast expansions of the size and scope of government at all levels.

2. In 1789 the Federal Government under President Washington had 350 Federal civilian employees; today they number in the millions.

3. In 1832 the total Federal budget was $11 million, roughly $1.30 per person. In 2015 the total Federal Budget including debt was about $17 trillion, *multiplying more than 1,000,000 times and increasing the per person debt to $53,125!*

4. Since 1900 the total number of government laws and regulations the average citizen is required to obey has increased 3,000%.

5. The increase of government control and government services leads to a corresponding decrease of individual liberty and individual responsibility.

C. If the state is the highest authority and there is no higher law, there is no such thing as an unjust law.

---

5. "U.S. Reports: Furman v. Georgia, 408 U.S. 238 (1972)." https://www.loc.gov/item/usrep408238/

D. It leads to judicial tyranny.

1.	Alexander Hamilton argued that the Judiciary is the "least dangerous" branch of government because its powers are limited to interpreting the Constitution and Laws (*The Federalist Papers, Numbers 78, 81*).
2.	Justice Felix Frankfurter: "*What governs is the Constitution, and not what we have written about it.*"[6]
3.	Justice (formerly Chief Justice) William Rehnquist: "*No amount of repetition of historical errors in judicial opinions can make the errors true.*"[7]
4.	But if judges are not bound by the fixed standard of the plain meaning of the Constitution and the intent of the Framers, they are free, in the words of Chancellor James Kent, to "*roam at large in the trackless fields of their own imaginations.*"[8]
5.	Lino Graglia, Professor of Constitutional Law, University of Texas, School of Law: "*... judicial usurpation of legislative power has become so common and so complete that the Supreme Court has become our most powerful and important instrument of government in terms of determining the nature of quality of American life. Questions literally of life and death (abortion and capital punishment), of public morality (control of pornography, prayer in the schools, and government aid to religious schools), of public safety (criminal procedure and street demonstrations), are all, now, in the hands of judges under the guise of questions of Constitutional Law. The fact that the Constitution says nothing of, say, abortion, and indeed, explicitly and repeatedly recognizes the capital punishment of the court has come close to prohibiting, has made no difference. The result is that the central truth of Constitutional Law today is that it has nothing to do with the Constitution except that the words 'due process' or 'equal protection' are almost always used by the judges in stating their conclusions. Not to put too fine a point on it, **Constitutional Law has become a fraud, a cover for a system of government by the majority vote of a nine-person committee of lawyers, unelected and holding office for life.*"* [emphasis added][9]
6.	Chief Justice Charles Evans Hughes: "*We are under a Constitution, but the Constitution is what the judges say it is.*"[10]
7.	Lewis Carroll, *Through the Looking Glass*: "*When I use a word,*" Humpty Dumpty said in rather a scornful tone, "*it means just what I choose it to mean — neither more nor less.*" "*The question is,*" said Alice, "*whether you can make words mean different things.*" "*The question is,*" said Humpty Dumpty, "*who is to be master — that is all.*"

THE SOLUTION: BACK TO BASICS

A. Back to the Constitution as interpreted by the Framers.

B. Back to the biblical principles the Framers held.

---

6 The Federalist Papers. https://www.congress.gov/resources/display/content/The+Federalist+Papers
7 In Wallace v. Jaffree, 472 U.S. 38 (1985). https://supreme.justia.com/cases/federal/us/472/38/
8 "Safeguarding the Constitution from the Court." New York Times letter to the editor. October 10, 1984. https://www.nytimes.com/1984/10/10/opinion/l-safeguarding-the-constitution-from-the-court-258484.html
9 Lino A. Graglia, "Judicial Review on the Basis of 'Regime Principles': A Prescription for Government by Judges," *South Texas Law Journal, Vol. 26, No. 3* (Fall 1985). Page 441.
10 https://www.brainyquote.com/quotes/charles_evans_hughes_402462

topic

CONSTITUTIONAL LITERACY – DOES IT MATTER? SOMETHING TO THINK ABOUT By Ricki Pepin ©2014

Pop quiz: What holiday do Americans celebrate on September 17? If you said, "Constitution Day," congratulations! You are among a very small minority of Americans who know something of their history. But, is that really important? Why celebrate the Constitution? Who even knows what it says?

A couple years ago the Ohio General Assembly passed legislation (SB-165) that mandated teaching directly from a few of the founding documents, one of which was the U.S. Constitution. While this made some patriots happy, I had to ask, "Why does the State have to pass legislation to mandate this? Shouldn't this already be part of every student's history or government class? Does this mean that they haven't been reading (much less studying) our founding documents? If so, how long has this been going on?"

To answer these questions, I'd like to share a story of a conversation I had recently on an airplane with a fellow passenger. During the usual genial conversation about what we do and why we were traveling, I shared with this gentleman the fact that I was on my way to teach a group how to lead a 12-week Constitution class. He stiffened a bit, pulled back ever so slightly in his seat and asked me, "Are you a lawyer?" I smiled and answered, "No, I'm not." His demeanor turned sharply condescending when he declared, "Well, I am."

While I knew from his body language and tone that this was intended as a declaration of superiority and even a challenge as to how I thought I was qualified to teach such things, I just smiled even bigger and replied, "That's great! It's interesting you should say that because I have had several attorneys take my class, and do you know they tell me that all through law school they never even read, let alone studied the Constitution?"

My words hit the bullseye. His face looked as though I had just punched him in the stomach. He sank down in his seat. The wind was out of his sails. I could see his mind racing back to law school classes, thinking, remembering, and then the startling confession that obviously stunned him more so than me: "No…we never did…"

His mind had opened, so I took the opportunity to stir it up some more: "Isn't that incredible?" I asked. "When I go to a doctor, I naturally assume that they have studied anatomy. If not, I'm in trouble! When I hire a CPA to do my taxes, I naturally assume they have taken accounting courses. If not, I'm in trouble. So, how is it that an attorney can graduate from law school and never study the law of America, the Constitution of the United States? Maybe this is part of the reason our nation is in so much trouble today?"

His eyes got even bigger, but he remained speechless, and then turned away to read a book.

While I didn't exactly make a new best friend, I do believe I gave him a lot to think about.

What about the rest of us? What's the take-home point here? While this issue certainly needs to be addressed in schools, I'd like to direct your thoughts to some applications to adults, specifically to you and your legislators.

When Congress is considering any bill, their criteria should not be the latest Gallup poll, your opinion, or their opinion about whether or not this potential legislation is a good or bad idea. Their sole concern should be keeping their oath of office when they pledged to Almighty God that they would *protect and defend the Constitution of the United States*. All legislation (to be lawful) must fall within the 18 parameters listed in Article I, Section 8. The criteria is conforming to the Constitution, not opinion – yours or theirs.

But the bigger question is, are you constitutionally literate enough to hold your elected representatives accountable to this standard? If not, today is the day to do something about it. Take the *Institute on the Constitution* course that focuses on history and original intent. Help students start *American Clubs*. Restoration of America begins with constitutional literacy of all generations. Imagine…knowledge of and adherence to the Constitution! Now that would be something to celebrate!

Something to think about.

LECTURE FOURTEEN

OPTIONAL
READING
ASSIGNMENTS

1. *The Law* by Frederic Bastiat. Start at "The Enormous Power of Government" and read to "The Basis for Stable Government" (pages 277-279).

LECTURE REVIEWS

1. Complete Lecture Fourteen Review Worksheet.

2. Complete Lecture Fourteen Quiz, including True & False Questions.

GOING DEEPER: SUPPLEMENTAL READING & VIDEO OPTIONS

 Found at www.theamericanview.com/constitution-course-supplemental-assignments which can also be found at the bottom of theamericanview.com under Resources.

Write a short essay completing this statement: "The most important thing I can do as a result of this course is…"[11]

The Darwinization of Law in America by Pastor David Whitney. This essay examines the machine by which our legal system was subverted and transformed into that which our Framers never intended.

---

11 If you are interested in having your essay possibly published online, you can submit them to TheAmericanView.com website; they will not be published without receiving the permission of the student and parents.

CHAPTER FIFTEEN
STATE'S POWERS IN OUR CONSTITUTIONAL REPUBLIC

SPECIFIC OBJECTIVES

Many assume that the Constitution is all about the powers and structure of the Federal government. While that is part of it, there are also some very important rights spelled out within the document about the rights and powers of the states. We will look at:

★ Language in the text of the Constitution that supports the rights of states

★ Opinions among the Founding Fathers about the balance of Federal and State power

★ The importance of "interposition" in terms of keeping in check Federal over-reach

You should be able to answer the following questions:

★ Why did the Founders believe the Articles of Confederation were not sufficient and a new Constitution was necessary?

★ What is the balance of power between the States and the Federal government, and why was it needed?

★ How does the Electoral College support the rights of States and the balance of power among them?

"The heart of the prudent getteth knowledge; and the ear of the wise seeketh knowledge."
    –Proverbs 18:15

"While imperfect, the electoral college has generally served the republic well. It forces candidates to campaign in a variety of closely contested races, where political debate is typically robust."[1]
    –William M. Daley

"The Electoral College is a process, not a place. The founding fathers established it in the Constitution as a compromise between election of the President by a vote in Congress and election of the President by a popular vote of qualified citizens."
    –National Archives

---

1 www.brainyquote.com/authors/william_m_daley

Our founders had a distinctive understanding of human nature, which formed the basis for the decisions they made in framing our civil government. Their understanding was based upon a plain reading of the Bible and they knew (and believed) what the Apostle Paul wrote in Romans 3:10-18, 23:

> As it is written, There is none righteous, no, not one: there is none that understandeth, there is none that seeketh after God. They are all gone out of the way, they are together become unprofitable; there is none that doeth good, no, not one. Their throat is an open sepulchre; with their tongues they have used deceit; the poison of asps is under their lips: whose mouth is full of cursing and bitterness: their feet are swift to shed blood: destruction and misery are in their ways: and the way of peace have they not known: there is no fear of God before their eyes.
> . . . for all have sinned, and come short of the glory of God.

These statements have sobering implications and the founders took them seriously as they crafted a new form of civil government for these United States. Since all men are sinners, no man (or group of men) could ever be entrusted with unchecked powers. Moreover, history and their own experience convinced them that safety and prudence would only be served by the establishment of multiple checks from multiple sources on the exercise of any power or prerogative entrusted into the hands of any man.

Although most citizens are aware that the Constitution provides for *horizontal* checks and balances between and among the three branches — Legislative, Executive and Judicial — on the federal level, most do not realize that, in the opinion of the founders, the more important check was a *vertical* one. That is to say, between the higher and lower *levels* of government, federal, state, and local. Inasmuch as they feared the accumulation and consolidation of power, they wanted to ensure that if the federal government would attempt to act beyond the powers granted to it in the Constitution, the state governments would stand in the gap against that overreach. In this chapter we will explore three categories of checks and balances:

- The greater powers of the state governments
- Interposition
- The state legislature's powers via the electoral college

THE GREATER POWERS OF THE STATE GOVERNMENTS

We must remember that it was the states which created the federal government. When independence was declared on July 4, 1776, the former colonial governments of all 13 colonies were officially abolished. Each state proceeded to form a new government based upon a State Constitution ratified by the citizens of those states. Those states sent delegates to craft a form of government that would govern the relationships between the newly formed states. That first agreement, The Articles of Confederation, was not ratified by all 13 states until March 1, 1781, after four years of bickering among the states over its terms. (This was barely six months before the surrender of Lord Cornwallis at Yorktown and the virtual end of the War for Independence.)

Despite its claim to establish a "perpetual union," the agreement itself was not long lived. Voices calling for a convention to consider amendments to the Articles reached enough force to bring delegates together from 12 states in May 1787. That convention through the long, hot Philadelphia summer produced our Constitution. James Madison, rightly called the Father of our Constitution, was one of three authors writing the Federalist Papers, which argued for the ratification of this new form of central government to replace the Articles of Confederation. In Federalist Paper #45, Madison explains the relationship between the Sovereign States and the proposed new government which would be inaugurated by the Constitution.

The powers delegated by the proposed Constitution to the federal government are few and defined. Those which are to remain in the State governments are numerous and indefinite. The former will be exercised principally on external objects, as war, peace, negotiation, and foreign commerce; with which last the power of taxation will, for the most part, be connected.

The powers reserved to the several States will extend to all the objects which, in the ordinary course of affairs, concern the lives, liberties, and properties of the people, and the internal order, improvement, and prosperity of the State. The operations of the federal government will be most extensive and important in times of war and danger; those of the State governments, in times of peace and security. As the former periods will probably bear a small proportion to the latter, the State governments will here enjoy another advantage over the federal government.[2]

Clearly, Madison and the other delegates to the Philadelphia convention envisioned a balance of powers between the existing states and the newly proposed federal government under the Constitution, where the states retained their "numerous and indefinite" powers. The federal government would only possess "few and defined" powers that are clearly set out in the text of the Constitution. There are 22 powers that relate to taxing and spending and three others that relate to elections, immigration, and importation, as well as implementing certain amendments to the Constitution. The federal government's powers were small in number and very restricted in scope in contrast to those held by the state governments: "The powers reserved to the several States will extend to all the objects which, in the ordinary course of affairs, concern the lives, liberties, and properties of the people, and the internal order, improvement, and prosperity of the State." To seal the restrictions on the federal government, the Bill of Rights was ratified as the first ten amendments to the Constitution.

The Tenth Amendment forcefully states,

> The powers not delegated to the United States by the Constitution, nor prohibited by it to the States, are reserved to the States respectively, or to the people.

The Tenth Amendment frames and is firmly fixed on the principle that the federal government possesses no powers except those specifically enumerated in the Constitution, and that the states retained all powers which they possessed before the Constitution was ratified and did not surrender by means of the Constitution's specific terms.

In light of these purposes and intentions, the question then presents itself: what did the founders expect would happen when the federal government, given the fallen nature of man, began to encroach upon the powers of the state governments and the God-given rights of the people? The answer is "interposition."

INTERPOSITION

The doctrine of interposition is known by a few names. Author and Pastor Matt Trewhella refers to "The Doctrine of the Lesser Magistrates" in his book by that title.[3] Dr. Paul Jehle, Founder and Director of the Plymouth Rock Foundation, speaks of the "Applied Doctrine of Interposition."[4] And while the term is not widely known or used in modern discussions among politicians or pundits, it is a well-established and well-documented remedy against unlawful actions by those men or groups of men who are charged with upholding and defending the law.

Webster's 1828 Dictionary defines interposition (in part):

> A being, placing or coming between; intervention; as the interposition of the Baltic sea between Germany and Sweden. The interposition of the moon between the earth and the sun occasions a solar eclipse.[5]

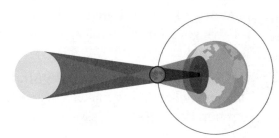

2   https://www.congress.gov/resources/display/content/The+Federalist+Papers#TheFederalistPapers-45
3   Trewhella, Matthew J. *The Doctrine of the Lesser Magistrates: A Proper Resistance to Tyranny and a Repudiation of Unlimited Obedience to Civil Government.* North Charleston: CreateSpace Independent Publishing Platform, 2013.
4   https://plymrock.org/; https://www.pilgriminstitute.org/index.php/home/our-mission/bios/speakers-bios/paul-jehle
5   http://webstersdictionary1828.com/Dictionary/interposition

And as recently as 1966, *Random House Dictionary* included this historically important idea in its definition of "interposition":

> *U.S.* Doctrine that an individual State may oppose any federal action it believes encroaches on its sovereignty.[6]

Furthermore, *Black's Law Dictionary* defines interposition as "The action of a State while exercising its sovereignty in rejecting a federal mandate that it believes is unconstitutional or overreaching."[7]

Whatever the formal name, it is vital that we citizens be able to understand and to describe the concept of interposition and the "Doctrine of the Lesser Magistrates" to be able to articulate the duty of the lesser magistrate to stand against and to protect the citizen from a tyrannical government, and to be fully equipped to judge the ability of those seeking office to assume the responsibilities of the lesser magistrate.

Why is interposition so important? Because it is the lawful remedy for unlawful civil government.

Let me describe it with an illustration from your front yard — what I call "Interposition and the Family Dog."

You're a good parent. So, let's suppose you think it wise to buy a watchdog so that when your little girl plays in the front yard the dog can protect and defend her from any intruders who may wish to do her harm.

After a little time goes by, the puppy you bought becomes a full-grown animal. His muscles become fully developed, his teeth are big and sharp, and now he towers over your little girl. You are worried that he is becoming too aggressive and one day you look out the door and witness your worst fear — you see the dog attacking your child.

As you burst out the front door, your daughter has gotten free and is cowering in the corner of the fence by the tree. The dog is charging across the yard and in a few seconds will be on her again. You just have time to do what your instincts tell you to do. You get your body — you insert yourself — between the dog and the child — between the danger and the daughter.

You don't stop to think what will happen to you. Your desire and your duty come together in an instant. You thrust yourself between the aggressor and the victim.

What you just did was an act of interposition.

You interposed between the agency that was originally a protector, but had become a threat, and the person or persons you have the duty to protect.

Interposition is as American as apple pie, baseball, and jazz. When we hire civil government to protect and defend our God-given rights, if at any level it ever turns into the aggressor, we need a separate level of civil government to interpose on our behalf, protecting us from the dangerous invasion of our God-given rights.

In *The Doctrine of the Lesser Magistrates*, Pastor Matt Trewhella explains that when the superior or higher civil authority makes a decree (or undertakes some action under the color of law) which is either immoral or unjust, the lesser or lower-ranking civil authority has both the right and the duty to refuse

---

6 *The Random House Dictionary of the English Language: The Unabridged Edition* was edited by Jess Stein and released in October of 1966. This definition of interposition is still included from The Random House Unabridged Dictionary at https://www.dictionary.com/browse/interposition.

7 Black, Henry Campbell. *Black's Law Dictionary*. Fourth Edition. (St. Paul: West Publishing Company, 1968), p. 953. You read about interposition earlier in Chapter 7 of this book and it was paired with the idea of nullification, defined as "the action of making something void; the action of a state in abrogating a federal law on the basis of state sovereignty." Black, Henry Campbell. *Black's Law Dictionary*. Fifth Edition. (St. Paul: West Publishing Company, 1979), p. 963.

obedience to that superior authority. Moreover, in some cases, the lower authority may actively resist the superior authority.[8]

According to Dr. Archie Jones: "The doctrine of interposition is based on the biblical truth that the powers that be, the rulers of civil government, are ordained by God and are His ministers."[9]

Romans 13:3-5 clearly establishes this fact.

> For rulers are not a terror to good works, but to the evil. Wilt thou then not be afraid of the power? do that which is good, and thou shalt have praise of the same: For he is the minister of God to thee for good. But if thou do that which is evil, be afraid; for he beareth not the sword in vain: for he is the minister of God, a revenger to execute wrath upon him that doeth evil. Wherefore ye must needs be subject, not only for wrath, but also for conscience sake (Romans 13:3–5).

Dr. Jones continues, "As God's ministers they are to serve Him — not anyone else. They are to serve Him by protecting and giving praise to those who do good, and by punishing, and therefore restraining, those who do evil. As God's ministers they must follow, obey, and apply His definitions and standards of what is good and what is evil: not their own, nor anyone else's definitions or standards of good and evil."[10]

Interposition by the lower magistrate has been practiced since before the time of Christ. However, it was Christians establishing Western civilization who formalized and embedded the Doctrine of the Lesser Magistrates into their political institutions. Furthermore, interposition by the lesser magistrate is the appropriate biblical and constitutional method to resist tyranny. Properly understood and implemented, it can provide a pathway for citizens to rein in lawless acts by civil government so that justice can be restored, justice being defined as "giving to everyone what is his due" according to *Webster's 1828 Dictionary*.[11]

MAGNA CHARTA PRESENTED TO KING JOHN.

There are many historic examples of interposition and the doctrine of the lesser magistrates.

Consider the Magna Carta of 1215, where the Christian Noblemen who confronted King John at Runnymeade forced the king (who had acted as a tyrant) to sign a treaty acknowledging certain rights for men. The Magna Carta made it clear that all authority comes from God, that all men are subject to the law, and that civil government's role was a limited one.

During the Reformation, both John Calvin in his *Institutes of the Christian Religion* and John Knox in his *Appellation* wrote about the necessity for interposition. Knox cited over 70 passages from Scripture supporting the doctrine. In his famous work *Lex Rex*, published in 1644, Samuel Rutherford also contributed to the importance and necessity of interposition.

Also consider the founding of these United States. According to Dr. Paul Jehle (Plymouth Rock Foundation), the Declaration of Independence is a premier example of a document of interposition because it clearly addresses the five components of Applied Interposition Doctrine. Dr. Jehle argues that lawful interposition must address these five questions:

8 Book description, https://lessermagistrate.com/lesser-magistrates-book/
9 Jones, Dr. Archie. *Gateway to Liberty: The Constitutional Power of the 10th Amendment*. American Vision: 2010
10 Ibid.
11 http://webstersdictionary1828.com/Dictionary/justice

1. What are the sources of the rights violated?
2. Under what authority are you interposing? (Who is the Lesser Magistrate?)
3. How have you demonstrated submissive appeals for a reasonable period?
4. To what specific abuses do you attribute your resistance and how are these abuses unlawful?
5. To what higher authority are you appealing?

One area in which interposition is vitally needed today is for the protection and defense of property rights. There is an agenda crafted by the UN Commission on Sustainable Development, and the UN General Assembly's "Earth Summit+5" Special Session generally known as Agenda 21 (although recently touted as 2030). Sustainable Development is the tool to implement this agenda and was apparently developed as a means of restructuring the world population to lessen environmental impact and achieve an improved supposed quality of life. In one major aspect it either takes direct control of private property or defeats the purpose for owning property at all. This agenda is in nearly every county in our land most commonly (but not limited to) the name of "Regional Planning Commissions," where unelected bureaucrats usurp elected county representatives' authority and openly attack citizen's property rights through random regulations.

Many other examples could be given to illustrate areas where interposition is called for in response to Federal overreach. Why isn't it happening? For one, many elected officials have no understanding that interposition is their power and their duty. Constitutional education can correct this problem. Thomas Jefferson taught us with his clear-eyed exhortation,

> "…the States should be watchful to note every material usurpation on their rights; denounce them as they occur in the most peremptory terms; to protest against them as wrongs to which our present submission, shall be considered, not as yet acknowledgments or precedents of right, but as a temporary yielding to the lesser evil until their accumulation shall overweigh that of separation."[12]

Also, James Madison in Federalist Paper #51 stated,

> "Ambition must be made to counteract ambition…In the compound republic of America, the power surrendered by the people is first divided between two distinct governments, and then the portion allotted to each subdivided among distinct and separate departments. Hence a double security arises to the rights of the people. The different governments will control each other, at the same time that each will be controlled by itself." [13]

Now the second and more difficult issue is the perennial one – taxes. Our Founders structured the taxing powers of the federal government in a fashion which prohibited direct taxation upon the citizens themselves. Thus in Art. I Sec. 9 our Constitution forbids "Capitation or other direct taxes." A Capitation Tax is "an imposition levied upon the person simply."[14] Tax revenue at the Federal level was primarily through Tariffs. If any taxation of citizens was to take place, it could not be against the citizens directly but only as a tax levied upon the States "laid … in proportion to the Census or Enumeration herein before directed to be taken" (Art. I Sec. 9). So the States would be sent a tax bill from the Federal government proportional to their population as determined by the Census. Each State Legislature would then determine the method by which they would raise the fund necessary to pay the Federal tax owed by the State.

This all relates to the failure of interposition today because when Washington, D.C, takes money

---

12 Young, Andrew. *The American Statesman: a Political History, Exhibiting the Origin, Nature and Practical Operation of Constitutional Government in the United States.* (New York: J.C. Derby & N.C. Miller, 1866), p. 432.
13 https://www.congress.gov/resources/display/content/The+Federalist+Papers#TheFederalistPapers-51
14 *Black's Law Dictionary,* 3rd ed.

directly from the citizens, it turns around and offers to give some of that money through grants to the State and Local governments. But that grant money always comes with strings attached. Those State and Local governments are then unwilling to interpose Federal overreach knowing they might lose that revenue stream. One example of this was the National Maximum Speed Law enacted in January 1974. States had to agree to the limit the speed on their highways to the National Standard (55 mph at the time) if they wanted to continue receiving federal funding for highway repair.

One State that tested this was Nevada. On June 1, 1986, Nevada posted a 70mph limit on 3 miles of Interstate 80. They quickly discovered the consequences as the Federal Highway Administration immediately withheld highway funding for Nevada, and Nevada quickly backed down submitting to the National Standard. We see then that States and Local governments are virtually bribed by the Federal government to turn a blind eye to any Federal overreach. The solution to this problem is to elect legislators at State and Local levels that refuse the bait offered by the Federal government and to work with State governments to join in the cause of restoring the taxing powers to the State governments by eliminating Capitation Taxes.

STATE LEGISLATURE'S POWERS AND THE ELECTORAL COLLEGE

In addition to the duty of interposition there are two specific checks assigned by our Constitution to the State Legislature — one against the Federal Legislature and a second against the Federal Executive. The first check was that the senators were appointed by the state legislators, not elected by the people directly as is done today. In this power, the state legislator could instruct their senators regarding their wishes, such that in essence the only federal legislation adopted would be that which a majority of state legislatures approved. This unwisely was taken away by the 17th Amendment, weakening a very important check the states had against federal overreach.

The other powerful check the state legislatures were to have on the federal government was a check against the executive branch. That check is the electoral college. It was our founders' method for electing a president.

When we hear the word "college," an image of ivy-covered walls arises. But the meaning to our founders was not limited to an educational institution. In *Webster's 1828 Dictionary*, college is defined as:

> In a general sense, a collection, assemblage, or society of men, invested with certain powers and rights, performing certain duties, or engaged in some common employment, or pursuit.[15]

The electors in this assemblage, or society of men, were designed to be a check on the federal government executive branch by the state legislatures. Their powers were limited to only electing a president. When that work was done, they were disbanded.

As a body, the electors were chosen by the method determined by each state legislature and tasked to

15 http://webstersdictionary1828.com/Dictionary/college

ELECTORAL POLL

elect the president and vice-president of the United States. As laid out originally in the Constitution, the election process was meant to be a contest of individuals, not of political parties. Before 1804, when an elector cast his ballot he listed his top two choices for president. The choices weren't ranked as "first choice" or "second choice" and no mention of vice-president was made on the ballot. One list was then drawn up that included both names from every elector's ballot. Each elector voted for two persons. The person with the majority of votes cast by the total number of electors was named president. The person with the next highest number of votes was named vice-president. There were no "running mates" in this original system.

Article II Section 1 of our Constitution provided that state legislatures should decide the manner in which their electors were chosen. Even those that did use the method of the popular vote, as most states do today, had widely varying restrictions based upon property ownership.

In the first presidential election of 1788–89 the different states chose differing methods to choose their electors.

- Five states chose electors by direct appointment of the state legislature — Connecticut, Georgia, New Jersey, New York, and South Carolina.

- In two states, the legislature divided the state into electoral districts, with one elector chosen per district by the voters of that district — Virginia and Delaware.

- In two states, the legislature decided the electors would be chosen at large by voters — Maryland and Pennsylvania.

- One state chose two electors appointed by state legislature and each remaining elector was chosen by state legislature from top two candidates in each U.S. House district — Massachusetts.

- In one state each elector was chosen by voters statewide; however, if no candidate won a majority, the state legislature appointed electors from the top two candidates — New Hampshire.

- North Carolina and Rhode Island had not yet ratified the Constitution, remaining their own country under the Articles of Confederation.

In the votes cast by the electoral college:

- George Washington received 69 votes, one from each elector
- John Adams received 34 votes
- John Jay received 9 votes
- Robert H. Harrison received 6 votes
- John Rutledge received 6 votes
- John Hancock received 4 votes

- George Clinton received 3 votes
- Samuel Huntington received 2 votes
- John Milton received 2 votes
- James Armstrong received 1 vote
- Benjamin Lincoln received 1 vote
- Edward Telfair received 1 vote

In the second presidential election in 1792, there were 132 electors as North Carolina, Rhode Island, Vermont, and Kentucky had joined the Union.

- Nine states chose electors by appointment by the state legislature — Connecticut, Georgia, New Jersey, New York, Delaware, North Carolina, Rhode Island, Vermont, and South Carolina.
- In two states, the legislature divided the state into electoral districts, with one elector chosen per district by the voters of that district — Virginia and Kentucky.
- In two states, the legislature decided the electors would be chosen at large by voters — Maryland and Pennsylvania.
- In one state, each elector was chosen by voters statewide; however, if an insufficient number of electors were chosen by majority vote, a runoff was held between the top $2n$ vote-getters, where n is the number of vacancies remaining — New Hampshire.
- In one state, two congressional districts chose five electors each; the remaining two districts chose three electors. Each elector was chosen by majority vote of voters in a congressional district. If an insufficient number of electors were chosen by majority vote, remaining electors would be appointed by the state legislature — Massachusetts.

In this election:

- George Washington received 132 electoral votes, one from each elector
- John Adams received 77 votes
- George Clinton received 50 votes
- Thomas Jefferson received 4 votes
- Aaron Burr received 1 electoral vote

In the third presidential election of 1796:

- Eight states chose electors by appointment by the state legislature — one state with voter input.
- In four electoral districts, voters choose electors.
- In three states, electors were chosen by voters statewide. Remember, the voters are not directly voting for the president and vice-president but for electors in the electoral college who are indicating they will vote in the electoral college for those they deem most suited to be president and vice-president.
- In one it was done by popular vote, but the county voters chose delegates and the delegates then chose electors.

So, you can see in these first three presidential elections the wide variation between the states. The point is that the state legislatures were in the driver's seat; they could determine the method by which to select their electors to the electoral college. Such a system produced a wide ranging outcome from the electoral college in 1796:

- John Adams received 71 votes
- Thomas Jefferson received 68 votes
- Thomas Pinckney received 59 votes
- Aaron Burr received 30 votes
- Samuel Adams received 15 votes
- Oliver Ellsworth received 11 votes
- George Clinton received 7 votes

- John Jay received 5 votes
- James Iredell received 3 votes
- Samuel Johnson received 2 votes
- John Henry received 2 votes
- George Washington received 2 votes
- Charles Cotesworth Pinckney received 1 vote

One odd note here is that George Washington received 2 votes when he had declared that he was not running. But two out of the 138 electors believed that he would be the best president. That was their job as electors. It was not a popularity contest to choose a homecoming king, but to evaluate the character, ability, and track record of leading men in the country to determine who would be the best president for our country.

The fourth presidential election, in 1800, saw the rise of the political parties and the jockeying for electoral college votes to produce the party's desired nominee for president. The Democratic-Republican Party had chosen Thomas Jefferson as the party's candidate for president and Aaron Burr was to be his vice-president. But evidently some electors did not obey what their party bosses determined. The result in the electoral college was a tie between Thomas Jefferson and Aaron Burr. This resulted in the election being decided by the House of Representatives as Article II Section 1 Clause 3 calls for. It took 36 ballots before the tie could be broken in the House of Representatives and Thomas Jefferson chosen as president.

This election of 1800 caused a great stir, which ultimately changed the electoral college. The 12th Amendment was proposed in 1803 and ratified in 1804. It sought a solution to the problem created by the rise of political parties in that the Constitution did not require electors to vote for president and vice-president separately. The 12th Amendment changed the system so that the electors would indicate their choice separately for president and vice-president. Thus, the party system was, in effect, constitutionally recognized by the Amendment.

Fast forward to our day, and all but two state legislatures have chosen a state-wide selection process with the winner take all (that is, all the state's electors are given to the electors committed to the slate for president and vice-president that received the majority in the November election for electoral college candidates).

State legislators can change this structure at any time. Two states have done so in recent memory. Maine changed its method of selecting electors in advance of the 1972 presidential election, while Nebraska enacted a change starting with the 1992 election. In both States, the winner does not take all the electors, instead they are using the "congressional district method." These states allocate two electoral votes to the state popular vote winner, and then one electoral vote to the popular vote winner in each congressional district (2 in Maine, 3 in Nebraska). This creates multiple popular vote contests in these two states. Consider the difference this made in 2008: Obama won Nebraska's 2nd Congressional District (Omaha and its suburbs), gaining a Democratic electoral vote in that state for the first time since 1964. Also, in 2016, Donald Trump won Maine's 2nd Congressional District, which covers most of the state away from Portland, Augusta, and nearby coastal areas. Statewide, Maine last voted Republican in 1988.

Moving States to this congressional district method for selecting electors for the electoral college would give those outside the heavily populated urban areas true representation in the electoral college. It would make the presidential campaigns nationwide, and not laser focused on the swing states and those urban areas with the greatest population. This chart gives a proportional understanding of the weighting of each state in the electoral college. (Note: Red = Republican, Blue = Democrat, Yellow = swing State; also note Maine and Nebraska with their congressional district plan for selecting electors.)

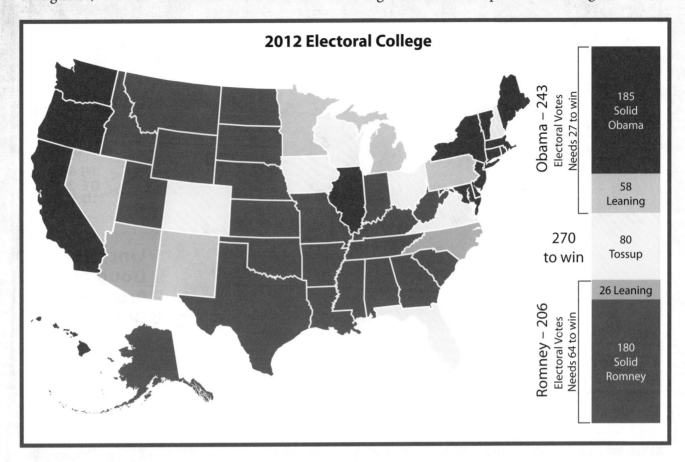

But a growing movement today is calling for the abolition of the electoral college. They want it crushed and the national popular vote to be established as the way we elect a president.

Recognizing the difficulty of amending the Constitution, the advocates are pursuing an unconstitutional initiative, hoping to persuade enough states to pass laws assigning all of their electoral votes to the winner of the national popular vote. The strategy would kick in when states with enough electoral college votes to put a candidate in the White House join the movement. Ten Democrat-leaning states and the District of Columbia have joined so far, representing 165 electoral votes. States representing another 105 electoral votes would be needed to secure the 270 electoral votes required to win the presidency. But this is an illegitimate route, as they would be circumventing the Constitution rather than amending it.

The results of a national popular vote would mean that the system of representation by each state in the selection of a president would be destroyed. A popular vote system nationwide would guarantee the president would be chosen by the major population centers and the great majority of the states would have no say in that election.

The last time in our history a candidate became president without receiving one vote from one elector in the electoral college from nearly half the country resulted in the bloodiest war that our land ever experienced. The states of AL, AR, FL, GA, LA, MS, NC, SC, TN, and TX did not cast one vote for Abraham Lincoln. The geographical divide, where more than half the country did not cast a single vote for the man who became president, demonstrated the reality of secession, even before those states voted to secede.

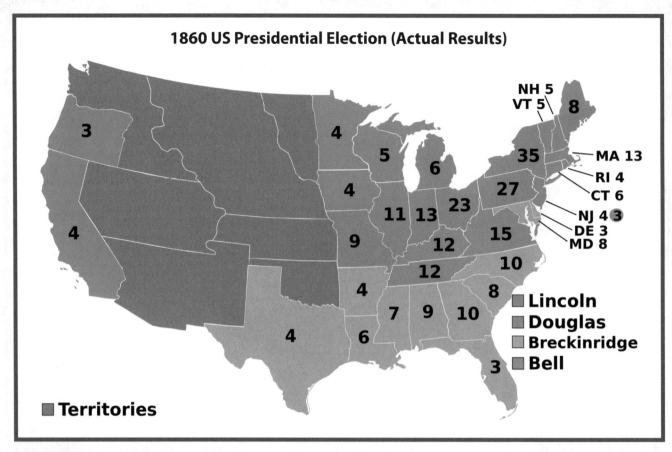

1860 US Presidential Election (Actual Results)

NH 5
VT 5
8
MA 13
35
RI 4
27
CT 6
NJ 4 3
DE 3
MD 8

3
4
5
6
4
11 13 23
15
4
9
12
12
10
4
8
7 9 10
4 6
3

■ Lincoln
■ Douglas
■ Breckinridge
■ Bell

■ **Territories**

The national popular vote would bring a similar geographic divide in our country. Consider what that divide looks like between counties with more than one million in population, versus counties with less. Half of the population in the United States lives in the counties in blue. A national popular vote would enable a tiny minority of counties to determine our Presidential election outcome, virtually nullifying the votes of the vast majority of the other counties.

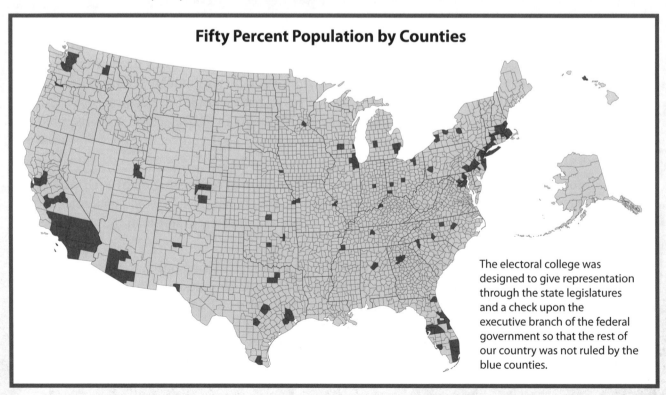

Fifty Percent Population by Counties

The electoral college was designed to give representation through the state legislatures and a check upon the executive branch of the federal government so that the rest of our country was not ruled by the blue counties.

172

For a closer comparison between the electoral college and the popular vote, consider the balance in national representation applied to the 2016 presidential election between Donald Trump and Hillary Clinton, in which Donald Trump won the election with 290 electoral votes while Hillary Clinton won the popular vote by just over 1 million. This chart shows the actual results of which candidates carried which states. Trump clearly won far more states than Clinton, even though Clinton won the national popular vote.

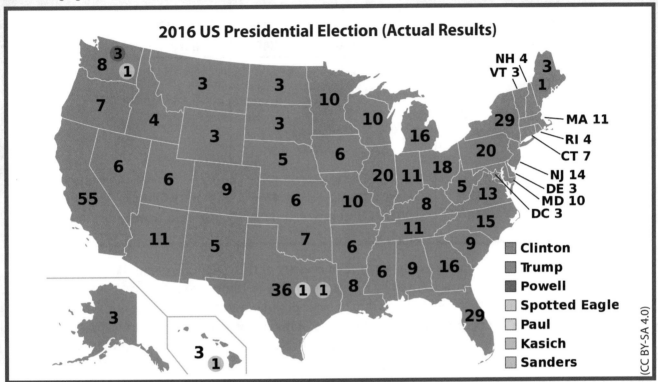

The electoral college was originally created by our Founding Fathers to ensure equal representation of all states, rather than all individuals (the difference between a republic and a democracy). Why is that necessary? It assures that all states have a reasonable representation, that larger states cannot silence the voice of the smaller. Originally, this was based on state size, now census-based population data has become the key factor. The number of electoral votes per state is equal to their representation in Congress: 2 votes per state plus the number of representatives they have in the House.

Realistically, this allows each state to popularly vote for the candidate of their choice and receive a constitutional share of the electoral votes.

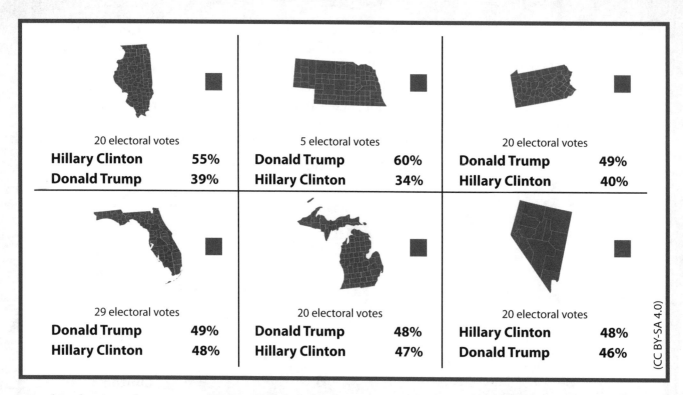

20 electoral votes	**5 electoral votes**	**20 electoral votes**
Hillary Clinton — 55%	Donald Trump — 60%	Donald Trump — 49%
Donald Trump — 39%	Hillary Clinton — 34%	Hillary Clinton — 40%
29 electoral votes	**20 electoral votes**	**20 electoral votes**
Donald Trump — 49%	Donald Trump — 48%	Hillary Clinton — 48%
Hillary Clinton — 48%	Hillary Clinton — 47%	Donald Trump — 46%

In this election, there are multiple examples of the necessity of the electoral system. Looking at the following state maps, Trump was favored by the vast majority of Illinois counties, yet Clinton won the state by a huge margin: 55% to 39%. This is due to large population centers — huge numbers of people in small areas that do not necessarily reflect the needs of the majority of the state. In Nebraska, Clinton won 34% of the vote while winning only two counties. In Nevada, she won the entire state with only two counties! In Pennsylvania, Florida, and Michigan, Trump won the vast majority of the state, but still took less than 50% of the popular vote.

Imagine if this were to happen country-wide instead of state-wide. The majority of the states would not be accurately represented. A popular vote would guarantee a president chosen by population centers, while completely ignoring the majority of the country.

In this election, the country (and most of the states) came out vastly "red," yet Trump lost the popular vote by a minuscule margin (less than 1%), thus proving that the popular vote does NOT accurately represent either the individual states' or the country's demographics.

So, what are the "real" statistics of this election?

Trump won 29 states; Clinton won 21. This is a 16% majority.

Trump won 290 electoral votes; Clinton won 232. This is an 11% majority.

Trump received 61.0 million popular votes to Clinton's 62.1 million popular votes. This was a difference of .9% (9/10ths of 1%).[16]

---

16 https://elections16.usatoday.com/results/president.

Hillary Clinton campaigns in Raleigh, North Carolina

Donald Trump's campaign rally in Phoenix, Arizona

The outcome of the electoral college vote in 2016:

Presidential Electoral Votes:

- Donald Trump – 304 (306)
- Hillary Clinton – 227 (232)
- Colin Powell – 3
- Bernie Sanders – 1 [2 failed votes]
- John Kasich – 1 [1 failed vote]
- Ron Paul – 1
- Faith Spotted Eagle – 1

Vice-President Electoral Votes:

- Mike Pence – 305 (306)
- Tim Kaine – 227 (232)
- Elizabeth Warren – 2
- Susan Collins – 1
- Carly Fiorina – 1
- Winona LaDuke – 1
- Maria Cantwell – 1

So, as you can see, some electors understand they have the power to vote contrary to the popular vote which was cast in their state. We must be reminded of the great danger our founders warned against — the danger of mobocracy. Gouverneur Morris, penman of the final draft of our Constitution, famously stated, "I see with fear and trembling, that [we may be] under the worst of all possible dominions . . . the domination of a riotous mob."[17]

And James Madison sagely wrote in *Federalist Papers* No. 55:

> As there is a degree of depravity in mankind which requires a certain degree of circumspection and distrust, so there are other qualities in human nature which justify a certain portion of esteem and confidence. Republican government presupposes the existence of these qualities in a higher degree than any other form. . . .[18]

Madison also warned in *The Federalist Papers*, No. 10:

> . . . democracies have ever been spectacles of turbulence and contention; have ever been found incompatible with personal security, or the rights of property; and have in general been as short in their lives as they are violent in their deaths.[19]

Our constitutional structure was designed to prevent the cities from ruling the rest of our country. The electoral college's purpose as a state check on the executive branch at the federal level was to assure that our God-given rights are not quashed by demagogues who may gain ascendency in the urban areas of our land.

---

17   Sparks, Jared. *The Life of Gouverner Morris with selections from his correspondence and miscellaneous papers, Vol. 1* (Boston: Gray & Bowen, 1832), p. 25.
18   https://www.congress.gov/resources/display/content/The+Federalist+Papers#TheFederalistPapers-55
19   https://www.congress.gov/resources/display/content/The+Federalist+Papers#TheFederalistPapers-10

CONCLUSION

As we have seen, our founders held a biblical worldview, especially regarding the nature of mankind. They knew men to be fallen, sinful, and far too ready to abuse any power entrusted to their hands.

They wisely crafted a system of multiple checks and balances from multiple sources on anyone holding any office of profit or trust in this constitutional republic. They clearly structured the state governments to have powerful checks on the federal government. They limited the federal government to only those delegated, enumerated powers specified in the Constitution. States held the trump card in the balance of powers between federal and state governments.

Our founders believed, taught, and practiced the doctrine of interposition. States officials were duty-bound by their oath of office to interpose on behalf of their citizens whenever the federal government stepped outside the boundaries clearly established by the Constitution.

Our founders also structured two very powerful tools by which state legislatures held a check upon the powers of the federal government. As we have seen, it was their design that the state legislators appoint their state's senators in the United States Congress to do the bidding of

Engraving on the Federal Building that shows a praying George Washington.

that legislature. That check was destroyed by the 17th Amendment. The second check was the electoral college by which each state legislature could determine the method by which they would be represented in the selection the president and vice-president of the United States. It should surprise no one then that this check is now under attack by the same forces that desire all power centralized in Washington, D.C. without any checks on that power by the state legislatures.

Today as never before it is critical that every freedom-loving American learn these foundation principles of freedom, teach them to others, and work to maintain the powers We the People delegated to our state governments to protect our God-given rights from an over-reaching mobocracy centralized in Washington, D.C. It is We the People that must enforce the Tenth Amendment:

> The powers not delegated to the United States by the Constitution, nor prohibited by it to the States, are reserved to the States respectively, or to the people.

LECTURE FIFTEEN

OPTIONAL
READING
ASSIGNMENTS

1. Continue reading *The Law* by Fredric Bastiat. Start at "Justice Means Equal Rights" and read to "Let Us Now Try Liberty" (pages 279-281).

LECTURE REVIEWS

1. Complete Lecture Fifteen Review Worksheet.

2. Complete Lecture Fifteen Quiz, including True & False Questions.

GOING DEEPER: SUPPLEMENTAL READING & VIDEO OPTIONS

 Found at www.theamericanview.com/constitution-course-supplemental-assignments which can also be found at the bottom of theamericanview.com under Resources.

Multiplying the Message (DVD) by Ricki Pepin. Watch this video to see how you can participate in this great work of restoring our constitutional republic.

PROPER EDUCATION: THE PATH TO AMERICA'S GREATNESS

GENERAL OBJECTIVES

☆ Understand the definition and purpose of education.

☆ Learn the consequences of both good and bad educational philosophy.

SPECIFIC OBJECTIVES

☆ Become familiar with the history and heritage of education in America.

☆ Discover when and how "reformers" stepped in to usurp parental authority and replace it with government indoctrination.

☆ Define and contrast Socialism and Republican forms of government and their relation to education .

☆ See examples of revisionist history and subsequent loss of heritage.

☆ Consider solutions to returning to educational excellence.

"See to it that no one takes you captive through philosophy and empty deception, according to the tradition of men, according to the elementary principles of the world, rather according to Christ."
          –Colossians 2:8; NASB

"The education of youth [is] an employment of more consequence than making laws and preaching the gospel, because it lays the foundation on which both law and gospel rest for success."[1]
          –Noah Webster

---

1 Noah Webster, *American Magazine*, March 1788.

178

WHAT IS EDUCATION AND WHOSE RESPONSIBILITY IS IT?

If a nation expects to be ignorant and free . . . it expects what never was and never will be.

—Thomas Jefferson[2]

Education can lead people to freedom or enslavement, depending on who is doing the educating and what they are teaching. Every civil government is based upon some religion or philosophy of life. Education provides the foundation for an individual's presuppositions, those underlying beliefs upon which they base all their thinking, opinions, and decisions. It is for this reason that understanding this subject is absolutely critical in understanding what it means to be an American and how to maintain freedom.

In an effort to understand education in general, and specifically in America, we need to study not only its origins, but its precise definition and purpose. We've used *Webster's 1828 Dictionary* throughout this course because it is a primary source, authored by Founding Father Noah Webster who was the master of 27 languages. Compare his definition to a more modern version.

The *Tormont Webster's Illustrated Encyclopedic Dictionary* (1990 edition) defines education as "the act or process of imparting knowledge or skill; systematic instruction."[3]

This seems to indicate that the main purpose of education is memorizing some data, and job training. Not a bad goal, but is this really the upshot of good education? Why do we want to impart knowledge? Why do we want to learn a skill? Is there anything else we need to master to succeed in life?

Webster's 1828 Dictionary provides a much more thorough and enlightening definition: "The bringing up, as of a child; instruction; formation of manners. Education comprehends all that series of instruction and discipline which is intended to enlighten the understanding, correct the temper, and form the manners and habits of youth, and fit them for usefulness in their future stations. To give children a good education in manners, arts and science is important; to give them a religious education is indispensable; and an immense responsibility rests on parents and guardians who neglect these duties."[4]

This definition answers the most important questions about education: What is the purpose of education? It's not just about memorizing facts and job training; it's about developing character while training for *life* — manners, discipline, controlling your temper, forming good habits — in addition to arts and science. Both of these types of education — academic and character formation — are to fit children for their usefulness in their future stations, *whatever* they may choose. And undergirding it all is a religious education. America's founders understood the purpose of education was first and foremost to know God. "The fear of the LORD is the beginning of wisdom" (Proverbs 9:10).

This Webster definition also specifies whose job this is — "*an immense responsibility rests on* parents and guardians. . . .*" The definition makes it clear that education is NOT the job of government, federal or state, but rather parents. This jurisdictional responsibility is backed up by the Bible in Deuteronomy 6:7, 9, which says in part: "Teach [these commands] to your children and talk about them when you sit

2 https://www.brainyquote.com/quotes/thomas_jefferson_136269
3 *The Tormont Webster's Illustrated Encyclopedic Dictionary* (Montreal, Canada: Tormont Publications, 1990), p. 538.
4 http://webstersdictionary1828.com/Dictionary/education

at home and walk along the road, when you lie down and when you get up. Write them down..." (NCV). Ephesians 6:4, "Fathers, do not provoke your children to anger but bring them up in the discipline and instruction of the Lord" (ESV). In summary, true education is to be based on biblical principles and taught by parents. Did America's founders comply with this?

HISTORY OF EDUCATION IN AMERICA

Colonial America did not practice a one-size-fits-all education plan as we see in modern-day America. Individuality was embraced and personal responsibility demonstrated as parents instructed their own children, particularly in the Bible. The first community schools were started in 1647 in Massachusetts by the passing of legislation entitled, "The Old Deluder Act." This act established a school once a community reached a population of 50 households. Parents who chose to use these schools paid for them. The main aim was to educate in the Bible so young people would not be "deluded by satan."[5]

During the years of 1776–1835 in America, various educational choices were established that brought about a 70–100% literacy rate in the colonies, much higher than existed in Europe which had many universities, and higher than our modern-day American students. During the founding era, churches (NOT the government) became involved and established charity schools for the poor in communities that could not afford to pay teachers. These were known as Free Schools. Other options included:

Dame Schools for ages 5–7 where students were taken to the teacher's home

Elementary Schools for ages 7–10 where instructors often boarded with the families of their pupils, and moved from one family to another throughout the community

Grammar Schools for ages 10–14 with the specific aim of preparation for university

The Northwest Ordinance — written prior to our U.S. Constitution — clearly sets out the importance our founders placed on education *and* its content: "Article 3 — Religion, morality, and knowledge, being necessary to good government and the happiness of mankind, schools and all means of education shall forever be encouraged."[6] Take note that religion (meaning Christianity) and morality were the top two criteria in relation to government and education. Knowledge took third place. These things were to be "encouraged" by the government, but not supplied by them.

John Adams expressed this sentiment when he said, "Our Constitution was only made for a religious and moral people. It is wholly inadequate for the governance of any other."[7] Liberty cannot be maintained in an immoral society.

Benjamin Rush (left), a Founding Father who was prominent in establishing America's educational institutions, said, ". . . the only foundation for a useful education in a *republic* is to be laid in religion. Without this there can be no virtue, and without virtue there can be no liberty, and liberty is the object and life of all republican governments. . . . But the religion I mean to recommend in this place is that of the New Testament" (emphasis added).[8] Both of these quotations make it clear that America's founders wrote our Constitution according to the principles of a *republican* form of government. What did they understand that to be?

5 Mark A. Beliles & Stephen K. McDowell, *America's Providential History* (Charlottesville, Virginia: Providence Foundation, 1992 (third printing)), p. 104.
6 https://www.ourdocuments.gov/doc.php?flash=false&doc=8&page=transcript
7 From John Adams to Massachusetts Militia, 11 October 1798." https://founders.archives.gov/documents/Adams/99-02-02-3102
8 Ibid, p. 543.

Republic — A state in which the exercise of the sovereign power is lodged in representatives elected by the people . . . it differs from a democracy . . . in which the people exercise the powers of sovereignty in person.[9]

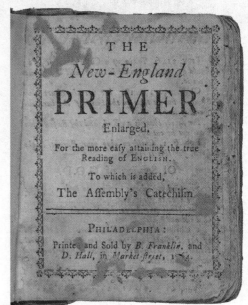

When God gave Moses the Law around 1300–1500 B.C., to be applied by judges and prophets in Israel, the first representative republic on earth was established. This was the pattern our founders were following — God's law as the foundation upon which representatives of the people would adhere. This is "rule of law" — a fixed uniform standard that does not change. It provides for accountability as well. The elected representatives can be un-elected if they fail to rule according to this standard.

A brief look at the first colonial textbooks demonstrates the Christian content imbedded in them. *The New England Primer* was printed in Boston in 1690. It became known as the "Little Bible of New England" and is considered the most influential schoolbook in the history of American education. It was very small — 3x5 inches and 88 pages in length — yet its contents shaped the hearts and minds of those who shaped the nation, printing over three million copies during the late 1600s and early 1700s. All lessons included Scripture truths, including learning the alphabet:

"In Adam's Fall we sinned all

Thy Life to mend, This Book attend [picture of the Bible alongside]

The Cat doth play, and after slay

A Dog will bite a Thief at Night

An Eagle' flight is out of sight

The idle Fool is whipt at School," etc., through the entire alphabet.

Another set of classic textbooks, *McGuffey Readers*, were written by a pastor and designed to build character as well as vocabulary. These books were first published in 1836 and sold more than 122 million copies within 75 years! They are still available today and still just as instructive for building character and vocabulary.

With the Bible at the heart of schooling, early Americans understood the role of government to be a simple one: protect from evildoers the God-given rights to life, liberty, and property. They also understood the role of education as coming to know God and the Scriptures, gaining knowledge about creation, learning what was needed for a productive life and learning to live right by God.

Tragically, public education has become a Godless, monolithic monopoly today, overseen by government bureaucrats rather than parents, with forced, compulsory attendance, and content that is more about teaching students *what* to think, rather than learning *how* to think. It is no longer about character building or Christian principles, but rather strives for uniformity, not achievement, turning out obedient citizens who will do as the government tells them. Indeed, the Bible and prayer were banned from schools by Supreme Court decisions in 1963. What fruit has this netted? Academically, America is near the bottom of science and math scores in developed countries. Even worse, crime and violence have increased dramatically on school campuses in addition to our neighborhoods. How did we lose educational freedom and excellence?

---

9   http://webstersdictionary1828.com/Dictionary/republic

THE DOWNFALL AND RESHAPING OF PUBLIC EDUCATION IN AMERICA

In the midst of this educational liberty that birthed a constitutional republic based on the Bible and the rule of law, "reformers" arose whose stated desire was to destroy the Christian foundations in America. They understood the best vehicle to accomplish this goal was through national public education, usurping parental authority and oversight, and changing the society through the child's training. Robert Owens, one of the more zealous leaders for public schools, believed the "salvation" of the world (which in Owens' mind meant the embracing of socialism) depended upon the eradication of biblical education.[10]

To better understand what these "reformers" had in mind, we need to set out a clear definition of socialism:

> A political movement to establish a system of ownership and operation of the means of production and distribution by society or the community, rather than by private individuals, with all members of society or the community sharing in the work and the products. In Communist doctrine, [Socialism is] the stage of society coming between the capitalist stage and the communist stage, in which *private ownership of the means of production and distribution has been eliminated* (emphasis added).[11]

This form of government which these "reformers" sought to put into place was based upon the "rule of man," which changes according to who is in charge. There is no accountability because it removes the uniform, fixed "rule of law" based on God's laws, upon which our constitutional republic was founded. In other words, their desire was to reshape the entire fabric of America and the family, faith, and freedoms upon which it was based. To achieve such an aggressive goal, a re-education of American youth was essential.

---

10 Blumenfeld, *Is Public Education Necessary?* (Powder Springs, Georgia: American Vision, 2011), pp. 79-80.
11 *Webster's New World Dictionary, College Edition* (Cleveland & New York: The World Publishing Company, 1959), p. 1384.

To the Owenites in 1828 it was clear that national public education was the essential first step on the road to socialism and that this would require a sustained effort of propaganda and political activism over a long period of time.[12]

They understood this was a long-term goal. Indeed, it was not until 1963 — 135 years later — that the Supreme Court began to issue egregious (and unconstitutional) rulings removing the Bible and prayer from public schools. Horace Mann, a contemporary of Owens and fellow "reformer" referred to these new schools as "common schools" in that they would replace the varied and parental educational choices that were in place, creating a supposed Utopia when all had the same government-controlled education.[13]

Where did they get these ideas? From a primary leader in the French Revolution — Jean Jacques Rousseau. His philosophy on raising children reflected a very different worldview from America's founders. He never married, had five illegitimate children, and placed each of them on the day of their birth in the local orphanage for "the state" to raise. He wrote, "*Fathers owe their children to the state*."[14] His belief was clearly that the state replaced the family — a socialist worldview, not a Christian worldview.

Will and Ariel Durant, well-known American historians, summarized this philosophy as it related to education: "Rousseau wanted a system of public instruction by the state . . . [to] withdraw the child as much as possible from parents and relatives."[15]

Rousseau's ideas were adapted by the Prussians when they determined their loss to Napoleon in 1806 was due to soldiers thinking for themselves on the battlefield instead of following orders. They created a new eight-year system of schooling to provide skills needed in the industrial revolution, discipline, respect for authority, but *above all, the ability to follow orders — social obedience through indoctrination*.

This Prussian model was largely developed by German philosopher Johann Gottlieb Fichte who worked with Napoleon. Fichte's desire was to make Germany responsible to carry the French Revolution virtues as espoused by Rousseau into the future. This model included:

- Levying a tax to fund compulsory schooling

- Requiring uniform training of teachers (control the teacher, control the classroom, control the students)

- The civil government is always right — loyalty to the crown and preparation for the battlefield (never question authority)

- Stamp out all independent thinking

- This Prussian system established what to learn, what to think about and how long to think about it. It was an educational system designed for the good of civil government, not the good of society or the children.

Fichte said,

Education should aim at destroying free will so that after pupils are thus schooled they will be incapable throughout the rest of their lives of thinking or acting otherwise than their school masters would have wished. When this technique has been perfected, every government that has long been in charge of education for more than one generation will be able to control its subjects securely without the need of armies or policemen.[16]

12 Samuel L. Blumenfeld, *Is Public Education Necessary*? (Powder Springs, Georgia, American Vision, 2011), pp. 79-80.
13 Ibid.
14 Jean-Jacques Rousseau, *Emile, or Education* (1762), p. 19. https://oll.libertyfund.org/titles/rousseau-emile-or-education
15 Ronald Nash, *Worldviews in Conflict* (Grand Rapids, Michigan: Zondervan Academic, 1992), p. 90.
16 Johann Gottlieb Fichte, *Addresses to the German Nation* (1807), Second Address: "The General Nature of the New Education" (Chicago & London: The Open Court Publishing Company, 1922), p. 20.

It is easy to see why some historians use this philosophy to conclude that Fichte was the father of German Nazi socialism — total control of the training of youth. This type of education was dramatically demonstrated historically by the Hitler "Brown Shirts" — students doing exactly what they were taught to do, with no independent sense of right and wrong involved.

This horrific scheme came to America when Horace Mann traveled to Prussia in the 1830s and became enamored with this educational method of eliminating free thought from his students, and subsequently designed an educational system for Massachusetts directly based on these concepts. The movement quickly spread nationally, not only in primary education but to universities where teachers were taught this methodology, which in essence is brainwashing and indoctrination, not educating.

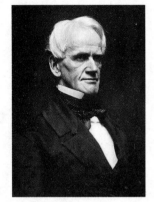

Horace Mann (left), echoing the philosophy of Rousseau, claimed that the state held the responsibility for the education of children. He said, "The State is the true parent of the child. Society in its collective capacity is a real – not a nominal – sponsor and god-father for all the children."[17] This principle is directly contrary to the word of God, the basis for American education, which resulted in the rule of law and free thinking.

Orestes Brownson (right), one of the architects of the public education movement, converted to Christianity and exposed the plot to create a national school system aimed at destroying Christianity. He wrote, "The great object was to get rid of Christianity, and to convert our churches into halls of science. The plan was not to make open attacks on religion, although we might belabor the clergy and bring them into contempt where we could; but to establish a system of state — we said national — schools, from which all religion was to be excluded, in which nothing was to be taught but such knowledge as is verifiable by the senses, and to which all parents were to be compelled by law to send their children."[18]

This desire of 19th-century socialist "reformers" has been accomplished. The public schools have been used by such revolutionaries to completely undercut the constitutional republic our forefathers established. "The public schools would become the chief instrument in implementing the revolution the enemies of Christianity desired. The schools became the new temples of the new religion of Man. The teachers were the new priests. Man, or more precisely, 'humanity' as incorporated in the State, became the new god and has remained so to this day."[19]

John Dewey (1859–1952), known as the father of modern public education, continued to propagate this new socialist, anti-God philosophy. A self-proclaimed atheist and author of the first Humanist Manifesto, he wrote, "There is no God and there is no soul. Hence, there is no need for the props of traditional religion. With dogma and creed excluded, then immutable truth is dead and buried, there is no room for fixed and natural law or permanent moral absolutes."[20] Some historians have also attributed the following quote to Dewey: "The children who know how to think for themselves spoil the harmony of the Collective Society."[21] This is a tenet of socialism-group think: no one should be taught to think independently.

17 R.J. Rushdoony, *Messianic Character of American Education* (Vallecito, California: Ross House Books, 1995), p. 24.
18 Samuel L. Blumenfeld, *Is Public Education Necessary?* (Powder Springs, Georgia: American Vision, 2011), pp. 95–96.
19 J. Steven Wilkins, *America — The First 350 Years* (Monroe, Louisiana: Covenant Publicans, 1988), p. 134.
20 John Dewey, "Soul-Searching," *Teacher Magazine*, September 1933, p. 33.
21 https://www.quotes.net/quote/9541

WHAT DOES HISTORY SHOW US SOCIALISM PRODUCES?

Modern-day political leaders, professors, and their students who promote socialism rely on name-calling and slogans to push their agenda. "Corporate greed" and "worker exploitation" are some of their favorite accusations. Who could possibly support these ideas or men who would practice them? Karl Marx used this slogan to describe Socialism: "From each according to his ability, to each according to his needs."[22] Who could possibly oppose such "fairness"?

To honestly evaluate any political system, straightforward questions need to be asked and answered, especially regarding authority — who is in charge of this system? For example, if socialism (by definition) is . . . a system of ownership and operation of the means of production and distribution by *society or the community, rather than by private individuals*, with all members of society or the community sharing in the work and the products . . . we need to ask the following:

- Who establishes the standard by which this distribution occurs?

- Who decides what house you live in? Who gets the nice one? Who gets the poorly constructed one? Who lives in a multiple-unit apartment complex?

- Who decides what job you have and how much money you make and how many hours you work?

- Who decides what medical care is available and which doctor will perform it?

- Who decides what food will be grown, how much and where, and its cost?

The answer to all the above questions in relation to socialism is the government, or the dictator in charge of the government. If an individual wants to change his job, improve his condition, live in a nicer home, pick his own doctor and medical care, he does not have the freedom to do so. These decisions are all made by the state. In a constitutional republic, individuals are free to make these choices.

True history (not revisionist history) paints a bleak picture of all socialist regimes where "fairness" never enters the equation. Socialist and communist leaders have all ruled as cruel dictators and there are many examples: Stalin, Mao Zedong, Pol Pot, Ho Chi Minh, Kim Jong-il, Hitler, Castro, Ceausescu, Hugo Chavez, Nicolas Maduro, Tito. Look up any of these socialist/communist dictators and you'll find a trail of misery, starvation, and death, not the promised Utopia of "From each according to his ability, to each according to his needs."

Those who still argue for socialism say that the right person has not been in charge yet. However, an honest look at two very different socialist/communist experiments demonstrates that it does not matter who is in charge. Whether socialism is practiced by overt dictators, or men with benevolent desires, the outcome is still starvation and death.

A. Vladimir Lenin

At the beginning of the 20th century, Lenin seized power in Russia through the Bolshevik Revolution. He stated, "The goal of socialism is communism."[23] When the socialistic promises of abundance proved false, the people became disillusioned and disruptive. Fear, chaos, and shortages became everyday life, facilitating Lenin's godless government to maintain power. A similar outcome is seen with Stalin.

22 https://www.brainyquote.com/quotes/karl_marx_136396
23 https://www.brainyquote.com/quotes/vladimir_lenin_136421

B.   Joseph Stalin

Stalin seized power in Russia in 1922 and engineered a famine in 1932–33 that killed millions in his war against the kulaks (self-sufficient farmers). He shipped out all the food from entire districts and deployed an army to prevent the starving peasants from migrating in search of nourishment. An estimated six to seven million people perished in this man-made catastrophe, all for the purpose of creating an absolute dictatorship.

C.   William Bradford and the Pilgrims

Compelled by the contract with their financial backers, the Pilgrims farmed the land communally for their first two years in America. The lack of incentive to work resulted in such a poor crop that the Pilgrims nearly starved during the first two winters. To alleviate this problem, the leaders shifted to an individual enterprise system where every family farmed their own parcel of land and ate the fruit of their own labor. The Pilgrim's leader, Governor Bradford wrote that "this had very good success; for it made all hands very industrious. . . . The women now went willingly into the field and took their little ones with them to set corn, which before [they] would allege weakness and inability."[24] They produced an abundant crop and never lacked for food again.

This historical example of the Pilgrims demonstrates that communal farming with no individual incentive does not even work with Christians who have a common vision, goals, and purposes. The Pilgrims example shows that taking away private property and bringing the community into a common wealth or work station does not make people happy or cause them to flourish. Ownership of their own parcel of land is what motivated them to great levels of production.

A similar outcome occurred in Russia. "When Russia allowed 'each farming family 2–3 acres of ground to operate privately and sell its produce in the local market, these tiny private farm plots produced more meat, vegetables, and fruit than all of the huge government farms combined.' "[25]

These farming practices illustrate differing government philosophies that were learned through education. One philosophy causes people to prosper, the other to starve. Here's a good summary slogan — Capitalism makes. Socialism takes.

Proper education — learning how to think, not being taught what to think — in both history and government will lead students to the principles and choices to bring benefit to them and society. Eliminating the profit motive upon which biblical capitalism is based has failed throughout history. In spite of this, America's classrooms are still promoting the socialism introduced by Horace Mann in the 1800s.

---

24 William Bradford, *Of Plimoth Plantation* (Boston, MA: Wright, 1901), p. 162.
25 Cleon Skousen, *Study Guide to the Making of America* (National Center for Constitutional Studies).

SOCIALISM IDEALS IN AMERICAN TEXTBOOKS

Revisionist history is a plague infecting a number of our history and government textbooks, many of which teach and promote socialist practices and principles as though these are part of America's history. This is not only untrue, but such teaching steers the hearts and minds of American youth away from their heritage of Christian self-government under God. What brought about this terrible shift? Alexander Solzhenitsyn (left), Russian historian and author of *The Gulag Archipelago*, survived years in a communist concentration camp, being found guilty of writing politically incorrect comments against Stalin. He gives us the answer: "A great disaster had befallen Russia: Men have forgotten God; that's why all this has happened."[26]

Solzhenitsyn's statement also points us to the remedy of our current mis-education: Bring God, the Bible and primary sources back to the forefront of education so young people can learn their true history and heritage. But what exactly is a heritage? Karl Marx was an avowed enemy of American thought. His philosophies led men like Stalin, Lenin, and other communist leaders to kill between 85 and 100 million people. That's almost one-fourth or 25 percent of the entire population of America. Marx said, "Take away the heritage of a people and they are easily destroyed." Sounds like it's pretty important to learn what a heritage is if we are to avoid destruction of our way of life.

- Heritage — inheritance; an estate that passes from an ancestor [forefather] to an heir[27]
- Estate — property in general[28]
- Property — exclusive right of ownership[29]
- Most importantly, James Madison, Founding Father and author of the Constitution, said of property: "Conscience is our most sacred property."[30]

Thinking through these definitions we can conclude that a heritage and property are not always tangible. Everyone is a property owner, including young people, because your thoughts are your property. Your conscience — ideals and principles, the idea of what is right and wrong — is part of your property. The way we think and the way parents teach their children to think is the most important part of our heritage.

Going further back still, what heritage did America's forefathers leave us? What were the thoughts of those who established America? What were their concepts of right and wrong? What did they pass on to us? The answers to these questions will lead to the truth of our American heritage and what it means to be an American.

Throughout this course you have learned directly from reading our founding documents that there is a distinct American view of law and government that is written in the Declaration of Independence. These ideas are part of your American heritage:

- There is a God.
- Our rights come from Him.

---

26 Bill Federer's "American Minute – Russia" "Men Have Forgotten God." Stand to Reason. https://www.str.org/blog/men-have-forgotten-god#.XMx_ko5KhPZ
27 http://webstersdictionary1828.com/Dictionary/heritage
28 http://webstersdictionary1828.com/Dictionary/estate
29 http://webstersdictionary1828.com/Dictionary/property
30 This can be found in paragraph 13, line 2 at https://oll.libertyfund.org/titles/madison-the-writings-vol-6-1790-1802/simple#lf1356-06_head_023

- The purpose of government is to protect and secure those God-given rights.

Modern national education standards being put forth "evolved" from teaching these truths found clearly in our founding documents to putting forth the agenda of revisionist historians. Fox News carried the story of a Common Core curriculum worksheet which contained the following statements on an English class worksheet:

- [The President] makes sure the country's laws are fair.

- The wants of an individual are less important than the well being of the nation.

- Government officials' commands must be obeyed by all.[31]

None of these statements are true, and the final one regarding obedience to government officials' commands falls right in line with Rousseau and Fichte's teachings and subsequent American socialist "reformers." ("Education should aim at destroying free will so that after pupils are thus schooled they will be incapable throughout the rest of their lives of thinking or acting otherwise than their school masters would have wished." —Johann Gottlieb Fichte). The final statement also rebuts the very purpose the Declaration of Independence was written, and America's subsequent separation from the tyranny of England's government officials' arbitrary and unlawful commands.

Let's look at an example from public school curriculum that undermines the most basic principles of government set out by the Declaration of Independence which states: "We hold these truths to be self-evident, that all men are created equal [and] are endowed by their Creator with certain unalienable Rights . . . life, liberty and the pursuit of happiness [and that] to secure these rights Governments are instituted among men." Let's first address three basic principles regarding this statement prior to comparing it to modern-day curriculum.

1. Is God mentioned, and if so in what capacity? (Yes, as Creator.)

2. What is the source of the unalienable rights mentioned? (They are a gift given by God, and their unalienable nature means they cannot be taken away.)

3. What is the purpose of government? (To secure those rights.)

Now compare these foundational beliefs and structure of our government to the Ohio Department of Education K–12, 2012 Social Studies Standards [page 24], which instructs teachers to present the following principles: "… service to the nation [military, community, or serving in public office] which guarantees the rights of the people. . . . Individual rights are relative, not absolute. The exercise of rights must be balanced by the rights of others and by the common good."[32] Let's address the same basic questions regarding these statements:

1. Is God mentioned? (No.)

2. What is the source of your rights? (Community or military service; they must be earned.)

3. Are these rights secured/protected by the government or can they be taken away? (They are NOT absolute, and may be removed for the "common good.")

Here is a third example: Massachusetts Institute of Technology (MIT) — a college known for engineering majors, recently entered the publishing world on March 24, 2017, with a book entitled *Communism for Kids*, a fairy tale book for little kids opening with: "Once upon a time people yearned to be free of the misery of capitalism. How could their dream come true?" The book then goes on to teach children how to think about the "miseries of Capitalism" compared to the ideal of communism.[33]

31 "Grade School & Government Worksheet had 'Politically Charged' Examples, https://www.youtube.com/watch?v=_W0R26emaMI.
32 https://www.ohiotestprep.com/ag4-1studyguide.html.
33 Bini Adamczak, *Communism for Kids* (Cambridge and London, The MIT Press, 2017). https://www.amazon.com/Communism-Kids-Press-Bini-Adamczak-ebook/dp/B06XX19G47/ref=sr_1_1?keywords=communism+for+kids&qid=1556897640&s=books&sr=1-1

These are all examples of educational malpractice (revisionist history) at its worst — taking away the heritage of the freedom and responsibility of American ideas and ideals upon which the nation was founded, and replacing it with the tenets of socialism or communism. Such teaching has resulted in more than 75 percent of youth raised in Christian homes losing their faith by the time they graduate from college.[34]

These examples put forth the doctrine of socialism/communism. Socialism appears on the surface to be fair-minded with equality for all, but there is no nation in the world throughout all of history that socialism has succeeded in meeting its lofty goals of egalitarianism. Frederic Bastiat, a 19th-century French statesman, referred to socialism as "legal plunder." Taking money from those who work and giving it to those who do not always degenerates into creating shortages of food and other necessities, hyper-inflation, and ultimate takeover by tyrants of varying degrees of cruelty and greed. Venezuela is the latest example, but history is replete with others, as mentioned earlier.

Other well-respected historical leaders have more accurately summed up socialism and its consequences:

- The problem with socialism is that you eventually run out of other people's money. — Margaret Thatcher[35]

- Socialism is a philosophy of failure, the creed of ignorance and the gospel of envy; its inherent virtue is the equal sharing of misery. — Winston Churchill[36]

Let's look at one more example of education to see the importance of truth and learning how to think through everything you read and see, using your American heritage of God and the Bible as the source of authority and truth as your measuring stick.

EDUCATION HAS CONSEQUENCES — A HISTORICAL CASE STUDY

Charles Darwin was born on February 12, 1809. His theory of evolution claims men were not created, instead they evolved, and all men are not equal as some are more evolved than others. His book, *Origin of Species*, subtitled "The Preservation of Favoured Races in the Struggle for Life," was published in 1859. It was read and re-read by Karl Marx who described himself as a "sincere admirer" of Darwin. Marx wrote, "Darwin's book is very important and serves me as a basis in natural selection for the class struggle in history."[37]

In 1871, Darwin (right) authored *Descent of Man*, in which he wrote:

With savages, the weak in body or mind are soon eliminated… We civilized men, on the other hand…build asylums for the imbecile, the

34 Stephen McDowell, *Biblical Revival and the Transformation of Nations* (Charlottesville, Virginia: Providence Foundation, March 2013), p. 2.
35 https://www.goodreads.com/quotes/138248-the-problem-with-socialism-is-that-you-eventually-run-out
36 https://www.brainyquote.com/quotes/winston_churchill_164131
37 Letter to Lassalle, January 26, 1861, https://answersingenesis.org/charles-darwin/racism/the-darwinian-foundation-of-communism/

maimed and the weak… Thus the weak members propagate their kind. No one who has attended to the breeding of domestic animals will doubt that this must be highly injurious to the race of man… Hardly anyone is so ignorant as to allow his worst animals to breed… Civilized races of man will almost certainly exterminate and replace the savage races throughout the world.[38]

Such arguments came to be known as "Social Darwinism" and were used by Supreme Court Justice Roger Taney (appointed by Democrat President Andrew Jackson) to justify the racist 1857 Supreme Court decision of Dred Scott which stated in part, "Slaves had . . . been regarded as beings of an inferior order . . . so far inferior, that they had no rights which the white man was bound to respect; and that the Negro might justly and lawfully be reduced to slavery for his benefit."[39]

Darwin's theory also influenced Margaret Sanger, who promoted "eugenics" and "forced sterilization" to eliminate inferior races. Sanger founded the organization Planned Parenthood for this purpose, and referred to her plans as the "elimination of 'human weeds' overrunning the human garden."[40] In 1970, Margaret Sanger's Planned Parenthood began receiving federal funding when Republican President Richard Nixon signed the Title X Family Planning Services and Population Research Act.

More than 60 million babies have been aborted since the inception of Planned Parenthood. Darwin's evolutionary lies were embraced and acted upon by both Democrat and Republican presidents. It is not a political party issue. It is a moral issue that had its evil roots in a flawed educational philosophy.

There are many ways that "Social Darwinism" is manifesting in society today, the most disturbing being in the Christian community. Most Christians reject the idea of evolution as a scientific model, believing instead in creationism — that God created everything in this world. This is good. But here's the question we are going to investigate: Can a person REJECT evolution as a *model of origins*, but ACCEPT evolution as a *philosophy or worldview*? To answer this question, we're going to review a test — the PEERS test — that was given to students who identified themselves as Christians.

The PEERS test is a diagnostic tool designed by the Nehemiah Institute, a Christian think-tank, to measure a Christian's worldview. It is not academic, but rather addresses **P**-Politics; **E**-Economics; **E**-Education; **R**-Religion; and **S**-Social Issues. This test consists of a series of statements to which the students rate their level of agreement or disagreement. The choices are: (1) Strongly Agree; (2) Tend to Agree; (3) Neutral; (4) Tend to Disagree; (5) Strongly Disagree.

Here are four statements found in the PEERS test. As you read them, "rank" your own level of agreement or disagreement:

1. The concept of family, traditionally understood as father, mother, and children, needs to be redefined to include other types of committed relationships.

2. Because human nature is constantly changing, values and ethics will also change. Therefore, each generation should be free to adopt moral standards appropriate to their preferences.

3. A primary function of civil government is to enact educational and social programs designed to prevent overpopulation of its land.

4. The State exists to help individuals and businesses who cannot help themselves. When everyone contributes their "fair share" through progressive taxation, society benefits.[41]

38 Darwin, Charles. *The Descent of Man, and Selection in Relation to Sex, Volume 1* (New York: D. Appleton and Company, 1872), pp. 162, 193.
39 "The Case Of Dred Scott In The United States Supreme Court. The Full Opinions Of Chief Justice Taney And Justice Curtis, And Abstracts Of The Opinions Of The Other Judges; With An Analysis Of The Points Ruled, And Some Concluding Observations." (New York: Horace Greeley & Co, 1860), p. 13. https://www.loc.gov/resource/llst.020
40 https://www.stopp.org/pdfs/brochures/whowasmarsan.pdf
41 Daniel J. Smithwick, *Teachers, Curriculum, Control: A World of Difference in Public and Christian Schools* (Lexington, Kentucky: Nehemiah Institute, 1999), pp. 8-9.

How did you do? If you've grasped the material we've taught you throughout this course, we would hope you either "tended to disagree" or "strongly disagreed" with every one of these statements, which would mean you have a biblical worldview, an understanding of the founding of America, our American legal system, and your heritage. However, the 2015 PEERS test showed that 90 percent of the youth from Christian homes *strongly agreed* with these statements.

They believe we should redefine the family. They believe we need to change our moral standards as times change. They believe the government should be involved in controlling supposed "overpopulation." They believe in progressive taxation. Bottom line: These kids love Jesus, but they don't have a clue as to how to apply His principles to life, family, business, or government. They are embracing social Darwinism — an evolutionary, humanistic, relativistic worldview, while calling themselves Christians. Where did they learn this? In their classrooms.

HOW DID THIS HAPPEN? WHAT IS THE SOLUTION? IN CONCLUSION

By and large, Christians must accept the responsibility for this educational disaster. Parents have "surrendered" their children to be "educated" by the government without monitoring their textbooks to discover the transformation that was occurring, the teaching of core values and convictions that are antithetical to their personal beliefs. There was a lack of teaching from America's pulpits either recognizing or standing against this ungodly takeover of education by the state.

But there is a remedy. The good news is that it has never been easier or more cost effective for Americans to take back their educational authority for their children. There is a growing array of options available, ranging from homeschooling materials and parent-led cooperatives, to independent, charter schools, private, online, and Christian schools to suit every need. Virtually every parent can do it.

In addition, the pulpits can be re-ignited to take their place as purveyors of the truth in every area of life, including education. The Reverend Martin Luther King, Jr. (right) said, "The church must be reminded that it is . . . the conscience . . . guide and critic of the state."[42] Churches can be encouraged to start schools, but they must not be driven by national curriculum standards, but rather supported by parents who will also determine the content of the education from biblical and primary sources.

Students such as you can learn your heritage by reading true history written from primary sources, such as this course. We must begin discovering truth through sciences, applying truth through *technology*, interpreting truth through *humanities*, implementing truth through *commerce* and *social action*, transmitting truth through *education* and *arts*, and preserving truth

42 https://kinginstitute.stanford.edu/king-papers/documents/knock-midnight

through *government* and *law*. Above all, parents and children need to work to learn and maintain the ideas and principles that birthed our American heritage of freedom.

Noah Webster spent his entire adult life working to reform America and to provide a foundation of liberty, happiness, and prosperity for all citizens. He understood that *ideas have consequences*, that the battle for the future of our country would be waged in the *marketplace of ideas*, and that those adhering to godly truth must enter into the battle in every conceivable sphere. He understood that what we teach our children is part of the heritage we leave them.

On President Herbert Hoover's 80th birthday, August 10, 1954, he said it best:

> Our Founding Fathers did not invent the priceless boon of individual freedom and respect for the dignity of men. That great gift to mankind sprang from the Creator and not from governments. . . . A nation is strong or weak, it thrives or perishes upon what it believes to be true. If our YOUTH are rightly instructed in the *faith of our fathers* . . . then our power will be stronger. God has blessed us with . . . HERITAGE. The great documents of that heritage are not from Karl Marx. They are from the Bible, the Declaration of Independence, and the Constitution of the United States. Within them alone can the safeguards of freedom survive [emphasis added].[43]

The Hoover men. Herbert Hoover with family (1950).

Who will educate America's children? Parents or government? There are only these two choices. According to our constitutional republic and our biblical foundations, parents are the ones in charge of their children's education and any local school choice. Proper education in faith, family, and freedom was the pathway to America's greatness in the founding era. The path is still there, albeit overgrown with weeds at the moment. The great news is that we have the resources, the power, and the authority to clean it up and make America great again. It begins with you.

LECTURE REVIEWS

1. Complete Lecture Sixteen Review Worksheet.

2. Complete Lecture Sixteen Review Quiz, including True & False Questions.

---

43 https://www.loc.gov/rr/record/pressclub/pdf/HerbertHoover.pdf

CHAPTER SEVENTEEN
PRESIDENT GEORGE WASHINGTON'S FAREWELL ADDRESS (1796)

SPECIFIC OBJECTIVES

At the end of his second term as president, George Washington wrote a powerful message to his fellow citizens. As the first person to serve in this important role, he shared many important insights in his words. As you read it, see if you can determine:

☆ *The main themes of Washington's farewell*

☆ *Common issues the nation may still face today*

☆ *Washington's views on public service and the Office of the President*

You should be able to answer the following questions:

☆ *What important points did Washington feel the need to tell the nation?*

☆ *What were his thoughts on unity of government?*

☆ *What did Washington encourage them to "cherish"?*

☆ *What division among the geography of the states did Washington identify in his speech in terms of varied interests among the two?*

"A man's heart deviseth his way: but the LORD directeth his steps."
—Proverbs 16:9

"...the Constitution is the guide which I never can abandon."[1]
—George Washington

1 https://founders.archives.gov/documents/
   Washington/05-18-02-0305

194

Friends and Fellow Citizens:

1. The period for a new election of a citizen to administer the executive government of the United States being not far distant, and the time actually arrived when your thoughts must be employed in designating the person who is to be clothed with that important trust, it appears to me proper, especially as it may conduce to a more distinct expression of the public voice, that I should now apprise you of the resolution I have formed, to decline being considered among the number of those out of whom a choice is to be made.

2. I beg you, at the same time, to do me the justice to be assured that this resolution has not been taken without a strict regard to all the considerations appertaining to the relation which binds a dutiful citizen to his country; and that in withdrawing the tender of service, which silence in my situation might imply, I am influenced by no diminution of zeal for your future interest, no deficiency of grateful respect for your past kindness, but am supported by a full conviction that the step is compatible with both.

3. The acceptance of, and continuance hitherto in, the office to which your suffrages have twice called me have been a uniform sacrifice of inclination to the opinion of duty and to a deference for what appeared to be your desire. I constantly hoped that it would have been much earlier in my power, consistently with motives which I was not at liberty to disregard, to return to that retirement from which I had been reluctantly drawn. The strength of my inclination to do this, previous to the last election, had even led to the preparation of an address to declare it to you; but mature reflection on the then perplexed and critical posture of our affairs with foreign nations, and the unanimous advice of persons entitled to my confidence, impelled me to abandon the idea.

4. I rejoice that the state of your concerns, external as well as internal, no longer renders the pursuit of inclination incompatible with the sentiment of duty or propriety, and am persuaded, whatever partiality may be retained for my services, that, in the present circumstances of our country, you will not disapprove my determination to retire.

5. The impressions with which I first undertook the arduous trust were explained on the proper occasion. In the discharge of this trust, I will only say that I have, with good intentions, contributed towards the organization and administration of the government the best exertions of which a very fallible judgment was capable. Not unconscious in the outset of the inferiority of my qualifications, experience in my own eyes, perhaps still more in the eyes of others, has strengthened the motives to

diffidence of myself; and every day the increasing weight of years admonishes me more and more that the shade of retirement is as necessary to me as it will be welcome. Satisfied that if any circumstances have given peculiar value to my services, they were temporary, I have the consolation to believe that, while choice and prudence invite me to quit the political scene, patriotism does not forbid it.

Wedding of George Washington and Martha Custis.

that heaven may continue to you the choicest tokens of its beneficence; that your union and brotherly affection may be perpetual; that the free Constitution, which is the work of your hands, may be sacredly maintained; that its administration in every department may be stamped with wisdom and virtue; that, in fine, the happiness of the people of these States, under the auspices of liberty, may be made complete by so careful a preservation and so prudent a use of this blessing as will acquire to them the glory of recommending it to the applause, the affection, and adoption of every nation which is yet a stranger to it.

6. In looking forward to the moment which is intended to terminate the career of my public life, my feelings do not permit me to suspend the deep acknowledgment of that debt of gratitude which I owe to my beloved country for the many honors it has conferred upon me; still more for the steadfast confidence with which it has supported me; and for the opportunities I have thence enjoyed of manifesting my inviolable attachment, by services faithful and persevering, though in usefulness unequal to my zeal. If benefits have resulted to our country from these services, let it always be remembered to your praise, and as an instructive example in our annals, that under circumstances in which the passions, agitated in every direction, were liable to mislead, amidst appearances sometimes dubious, vicissitudes of fortune often discouraging, in situations in which not unfrequently want of success has countenanced the spirit of criticism, the constancy of your support was the essential prop of the efforts, and a guarantee of the plans by which they were effected. Profoundly penetrated with this idea, I shall carry it with me to my grave, as a strong incitement to unceasing vows

7. Here, perhaps, I ought to stop. But a solicitude for your welfare, which cannot end but with my life, and the apprehension of danger, natural to that solicitude, urge me, on an occasion like the present, to offer to your solemn contemplation, and to recommend to your frequent review, some sentiments which are the result of much reflection, of no inconsiderable observation, and which appear to me all-important to the permanency of your felicity as a people. These will be offered to you with the more freedom, as you can only see in them the disinterested warnings of a parting friend, who can possibly have no personal motive to bias his counsel. Nor can I forget, as an encouragement to it, your indulgent reception of my sentiments on a former and not dissimilar occasion.

8. Interwoven as is the love of liberty with every

ligament of your hearts, no recommendation of mine is necessary to fortify or confirm the attachment.

9. The unity of government which constitutes you one people is also now dear to you. It is justly so, for it is a main pillar in the edifice of your real independence, the support of your tranquility at home, your peace abroad; of your safety; of your prosperity; of that very liberty which you so highly prize. But as it is easy to foresee that, from different causes and from different quarters, much pains will be taken, many artifices employed to weaken in your minds the conviction of this truth; as this is the point in your political fortress against which the batteries of internal and external enemies will be most constantly and actively (though often covertly and insidiously) directed, it is of infinite moment that you should properly estimate the immense value of your national union to your collective and individual happiness; that you should cherish a cordial, habitual, and immovable attachment to it; accustoming yourselves to think and speak of it as of the palladium of your political safety and prosperity; watching for its preservation with jealous anxiety; discountenancing whatever may suggest even a suspicion that it can in any event be abandoned; and indignantly frowning upon the first dawning of every attempt to alienate any portion of our country from the rest, or to enfeeble the sacred ties which now link together the various parts.

10. For this you have every inducement of sympathy and interest. Citizens, by birth or choice, of a common country, that country has a right to concentrate your affections. The name of American, which belongs to you in your national capacity, must always exalt the just pride of patriotism more than any appellation derived from local discriminations. With slight shades of difference, you have the same religion, manners,

Early portrait of George Washington wearing his colonel's uniform of the Virginia Regiment from the French and Indian War.

habits, and political principles. You have in a common cause fought and triumphed together; the independence and liberty you possess are the work of joint counsels, and joint efforts of common dangers, sufferings, and successes.

11. But these considerations, however powerfully they address themselves to your sensibility, are greatly outweighed by those which apply more immediately to your interest. Here every portion of our country finds the most commanding motives for carefully guarding and preserving the union of the whole.

12. The North, in an unrestrained intercourse with the South, protected by the equal laws of a common government, finds in the productions of the latter great additional resources of maritime and commercial enterprise and precious materials of manufacturing industry. The South, in the same intercourse, benefiting by the agency of the North, sees its agriculture grow and its commerce expand. Turning partly into its own channels the seamen of the North, it finds its particular navigation invigorated; and, while it contributes, in different ways, to nourish and increase the general mass of the national navigation, it looks forward to the protection of a maritime strength, to which itself is unequally adapted. The East, in a like intercourse with the West, already finds, and in the progressive improvement of interior communications by land and water, will more and more find a valuable vent for the commodities which it brings from abroad, or manufactures at home. The West derives from the East supplies requisite to its growth and comfort, and, what is perhaps of still greater consequence, it must of necessity owe the secure enjoyment of indispensable outlets for its own productions to the weight, influence, and the future maritime strength of the Atlantic side of the Union, directed by an indissoluble community of interest

as one nation. Any other tenure by which the West can hold this essential advantage, whether derived from its own separate strength, or from an apostate and unnatural connection with any foreign power, must be intrinsically precarious.

13. While, then, every part of our country thus feels an immediate and particular interest in union, all the parts combined cannot fail to find in the united mass of means and efforts greater strength, greater resource, proportionably greater security from external danger, a less frequent interruption of their peace by foreign nations; and, what is of inestimable value, they must derive from union an exemption from those broils and wars between themselves, which so frequently afflict neighboring countries not tied together

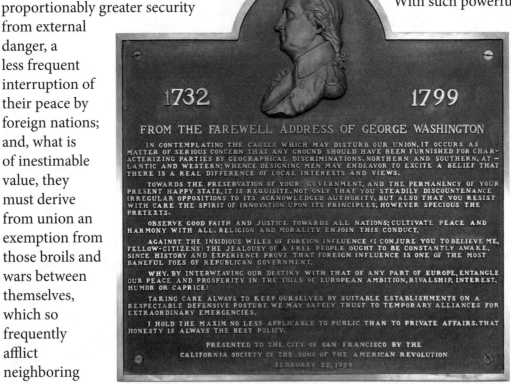

Plaque at city hall in San Francisco, California (CC0 1.0)

by the same governments, which their own rival ships alone would be sufficient to produce, but which opposite foreign alliances, attachments, and intrigues would stimulate and embitter. Hence, likewise, they will avoid the necessity of those overgrown military establishments which, under any form of government, are inauspicious to liberty, and which are to be regarded as particularly hostile to republican liberty. In this sense it is that your union ought to be considered as a main prop of your liberty, and that the love of the one ought to endear to you the preservation of the other.

14. These considerations speak a persuasive language to every reflecting and virtuous mind,

and exhibit the continuance of the Union as a primary object of patriotic desire. Is there a doubt whether a common government can embrace so large a sphere? Let experience solve it. To listen to mere speculation in such a case were criminal. We are authorized to hope that a proper organization of the whole with the auxiliary agency of governments for the respective subdivisions, will afford a happy issue to the experiment. It is well worth a fair and full experiment. With such powerful and obvious motives to union, affecting all parts of our country, while experience shall not have demonstrated its impracticability, there will always be reason to distrust the patriotism of those who in any quarter may endeavor to weaken its bands.

15. In contemplating the causes which may disturb our Union, it occurs as matter of serious concern that any ground should have been furnished for characterizing parties by geographical discriminations, Northern and Southern, Atlantic and Western; whence designing men may endeavor to excite a belief that there is a real difference of local interests and views. One of the expedients of party to acquire influence within particular districts is to misrepresent the opinions and aims of other districts. You cannot shield yourselves too much against the jealousies and heartburnings which spring from these misrepresentations; they tend to render alien to each other those who ought to be bound together by fraternal affection. The inhabitants of our Western country have lately had a useful lesson on this head; they have seen, in the negotiation by the Executive, and in the unani-

mous ratification by the Senate, of the treaty with Spain, and in the universal satisfaction at that event, throughout the United States, a decisive proof how unfounded were the suspicions propagated among them of a policy in the General Government and in the Atlantic States unfriendly to their interests in regard to the Mississippi; they have been witnesses to the formation of two treaties, that with Great Britain, and that with Spain, which secure to them everything they could desire, in respect to our foreign relations, towards confirming their prosperity. Will it not be their wisdom to rely for the preservation of these advantages on the Union by which they were procured? Will they not henceforth be deaf to those advisers, if such there are, who would sever them from their brethren and connect them with aliens?

16. To the efficacy and permanency of your Union, a government for the whole is indispensable. No alliance, however strict, between the parts can be an adequate substitute; they must inevitably experience the infractions and interruptions which all alliances in all times have experienced. Sensible of this momentous truth, you have improved upon your first essay, by the adoption of a constitution of government better calculated than your former for an intimate union, and for the efficacious management of your common concerns. This government, the offspring of our own choice, uninfluenced and unawed, adopted upon full investigation and mature deliberation, completely free in its principles, in the distribution of its powers, uniting security with energy, and containing within itself a provision for its own amendment, has a just claim to your confidence and your support. Respect for its authority, compliance with its laws, acquiescence in its measures, are duties enjoined by the fundamental maxims of true liberty. The basis of our political systems is the right of the people to make and to alter their constitutions of government. But the Constitution which at any time exists, till changed by an explicit and authentic act of the whole people, is sacredly obligatory upon all. The very idea of the power and the right of the people to

establish government presupposes the duty of every individual to obey the established government.

17. All obstructions to the execution of the laws, all combinations and associations, under whatever plausible character, with the real design to direct, control, counteract, or awe the regular deliberation and action of the constituted authorities, are destructive of this fundamental principle, and of fatal tendency. They serve to organize faction, to give it an artificial and extraordinary force; to put, in the place of the delegated will of the nation the will of a party, often a small but artful and enterprising minority of the community; and, according to the alternate triumphs of different parties, to make the public administration the mirror of the ill-concerted and incongruous projects of faction, rather than the organ of consistent and wholesome plans digested by common counsels and modified by mutual interests.

18. However combinations or associations of the above description may now and then answer popular ends, they are likely, in the course of time and things, to become potent engines, by which cunning, ambitious, and unprincipled men will be enabled to subvert the power of the people and to usurp for themselves the reins of government, destroying afterwards the very engines which have lifted them to unjust dominion.

19. Towards the preservation of your government, and the permanency of your present happy state, it is requisite, not only that you steadily discountenance irregular oppositions to its acknowledged authority, but also that you resist with care the spirit of innovation upon its principles, however specious the pretexts. One method of assault may be to effect, in the forms of the Constitution, alterations which will impair the energy of the system, and thus to undermine what cannot be directly overthrown. In all the changes to which you may be invited, remember that time and habit are at least as necessary to fix the true character of governments as of other human institutions; that experience is the surest standard

by which to test the real tendency of the existing constitution of a country; that facility in changes, upon the credit of mere hypothesis and opinion, exposes to perpetual change, from the endless variety of hypothesis and opinion; and remember, especially, that for the efficient management of your common interests, in a country so extensive as ours, a government of as much vigor as is consistent with the perfect security of liberty is indispensable. Liberty itself will find in such a government, with powers properly distributed and adjusted, its surest guardian. It is, indeed, little else than a name, where the government is too feeble to withstand the enterprises of faction, to confine each member of the society within the limits prescribed by the laws, and to maintain all in the secure and tranquil enjoyment of the rights of person and property.

George Washington before the Battle of Trenton

20. I have already intimated to you the danger of parties in the State, with particular reference to the founding of them on geographical discriminations. Let me now take a more comprehensive view, and warn you in the most solemn manner against the baneful effects of the spirit of party generally.

21. This spirit, unfortunately, is inseparable from our nature, having its root in the strongest passions of the human mind. It exists under different shapes in all governments, more or less stifled, controlled, or repressed; but, in those of the popular form, it is seen in its greatest rankness, and is truly their worst enemy.

22. The alternate domination of one faction over another, sharpened by the spirit of revenge, natural to party dissension, which in different ages and countries has perpetrated the most horrid enormities, is itself a frightful despotism. But this leads at length to a more formal and permanent despotism. The disorders and miseries which result gradually incline the minds of men to seek security and repose in the absolute power of an individual; and sooner or later the chief of some prevailing faction, more able or more fortunate than his competitors, turns this disposition to the purposes of his own elevation, on the ruins of public liberty.

23. Without looking forward to an extremity of this kind (which nevertheless ought not to be entirely out of sight), the common and continual mischiefs of the spirit of party are sufficient to make it the interest and duty of a wise people to discourage and restrain it.

24. It serves always to distract the public councils and enfeeble the public administration. It agitates the community with ill-founded jealousies and false alarms, kindles the animosity of one part against another, foments occasionally riot and insurrection. It opens the door to foreign influence and corruption, which finds a facilitated access to the government itself through the channels of party passions. Thus the policy and the will of one country are subjected to the policy and will of another.

25. There is an opinion that parties in free countries are useful checks upon the administration of the government and serve to keep alive the spirit of liberty. This within certain limits is probably true; and in governments of a monarchical cast, patriotism may look with indulgence, if not with favor, upon the spirit of party. But in those of the popular character, in governments purely elective, it is a spirit not to be encouraged. From their natural tendency, it is certain there will always be enough of that spirit for every salutary purpose. And there being constant danger of excess, the effort ought to be by force of public opinion, to mitigate and assuage it.

A fire not to be quenched, it demands a uniform vigilance to prevent its bursting into a flame, lest, instead of warming, it should consume.

26. It is important, likewise, that the habits of thinking in a free country should inspire caution in those entrusted with its administration, to confine themselves within their respective constitutional spheres, avoiding in the exercise of the powers of one department to encroach upon another. The spirit of encroachment tends to consolidate the powers of all the departments in one, and thus to create, whatever the form of government, a real despotism. A just estimate of that love of power, and proneness to abuse it, which predominates in the human heart, is sufficient to satisfy us of the truth of this position. The necessity of reciprocal checks in the exercise of political power, by dividing and distributing it into different depositaries, and constituting each the guardian of the public weal against invasions by the others, has been evinced by experiments ancient and modern; some of them in our country and under our own eyes. To preserve them must be as necessary as to institute them. If, in the opinion of the people, the distribution or modification of the constitutional powers be in any particular wrong, let it be corrected by an amendment in the way which the Constitution designates. But let there be no change by usurpation; for though this, in one instance, may be the instrument of good, it is the customary weapon by which free governments are destroyed. The precedent must always greatly overbalance in permanent evil any partial or transient benefit, which the use can at any time yield.

27. Of all the dispositions and habits which lead to political prosperity, religion and morality are indispensable supports.

In vain would that man claim the tribute of patriotism, who should labor to subvert these great pillars of human happiness, these firmest props of the duties of men and citizens. The mere politician, equally with the pious man, ought to respect and to cherish them. A volume could not trace all their connections with private and public felicity. Let it simply be asked: Where is the security for property, for reputation, for life, if the sense of religious obligation desert the oaths which are the instruments of investigation in courts of justice ? And let us with caution indulge the supposition that morality can be maintained without religion. Whatever may be conceded to the influence of refined education on minds of peculiar structure, reason and experience both forbid us to expect that national morality can prevail in exclusion of religious principle.

28. It is substantially true that virtue or morality is a necessary spring of popular government. The rule, indeed, extends with more or less force to every species of free government. Who that is a sincere friend to it can look with indifference upon attempts to shake the foundation of the fabric?

29. Promote then, as an object of primary importance, institutions for the general diffusion of knowledge. In proportion as the structure of a government gives force to public opinion, it is essential that public opinion should be enlightened.

30. As a very important source of strength and security, cherish public credit. One method of preserving it is to use it as sparingly as possible, avoiding occasions of expense by cultivating peace, but remembering also that timely disbursements to prepare for danger frequently prevent much greater disbursements to repel it, avoiding likewise

the accumulation of debt, not only by shunning occasions of expense, but by vigorous exertion in time of peace to discharge the debts which unavoidable wars may have occasioned, not ungenerously throwing upon posterity the burden which we ourselves ought to bear. The execution of these maxims belongs to your representatives, but it is necessary that public opinion should co-operate. To facilitate to them the performance of their duty, it is essential that you should practically bear in mind that towards the payment of debts there must be revenue; that to have revenue there must be taxes; that no taxes can be devised which are not more or less inconvenient and unpleasant; that the intrinsic embarrassment, inseparable from the selection of the proper objects (which is always a choice of difficulties), ought to be a decisive motive for a candid construction of the conduct of the government in making it, and for a spirit of acquiescence in the measures for obtaining revenue, which the public exigencies may at any time dictate.

President George Washington

31. Observe good faith and justice towards all nations; cultivate peace and harmony with all. Religion and morality enjoin this conduct; and can it be, that good policy does not equally enjoin it? It will be worthy of a free, enlightened, and at no distant period, a great nation, to give to mankind the magnanimous and too novel example of a people always guided by an exalted justice and benevolence. Who can doubt that, in the course of time and things, the fruits of such a plan would richly repay any temporary advantages which might be lost by a steady adherence to it? Can it be that Providence has not connected the permanent felicity of a nation with its virtue? The experiment, at least, is recommended by every sentiment which ennobles human nature. Alas! is it rendered impossible by its vices?

32. In the execution of such a plan, nothing is more essential than that permanent, inveterate antipathies against particular nations, and passionate attachments for others, should be excluded; and that, in place of them, just and amicable feelings towards all should be cultivated. The nation which indulges towards another a habitual hatred or a habitual fondness is in some degree a slave. It is a slave to its animosity or to its affection, either of which is sufficient to lead it astray from its duty and its interest. Antipathy in one nation against another disposes each more readily to offer insult and injury, to lay hold of slight causes of umbrage, and to be haughty and intractable, when accidental or trifling occasions of dispute occur. Hence, frequent collisions, obstinate, envenomed, and bloody contests. The nation, prompted by ill-will and resentment, sometimes impels to war the government, contrary to the best calculations of policy. The government sometimes participates in the national propensity, and adopts through passion what reason would reject; at other times it makes the animosity of the nation subservient to projects of hostility instigated by pride, ambition, and other sinister and pernicious motives. The peace often, sometimes perhaps the liberty, of nations, has been the victim.

33. So likewise, a passionate attachment of one nation for another produces a variety of evils. Sympathy for the favorite nation, facilitating the illusion of an imaginary common interest in cases where no real common interest exists, and infusing into one the enmities of the other, betrays the former into a participation in the quarrels and wars of the latter without adequate inducement or justification. It leads also to concessions to the favorite nation of privileges denied to others which is apt doubly to injure the nation making the concessions; by unnecessarily parting with what ought to have been retained, and by exciting jealousy, ill-will, and a disposition to retaliate, in the parties from whom equal privileges are

withheld. And it gives to ambitious, corrupted, or deluded citizens (who devote themselves to the favorite nation), facility to betray or sacrifice the interests of their own country, without odium, sometimes even with popularity; gilding, with the appearances of a virtuous sense of obligation, a commendable deference for public opinion, or a laudable zeal for public good, the base or foolish compliances of ambition, corruption, or infatuation.

George Washington at Mt. Vernon with workers harvesting grain.

34. As avenues to foreign influence in innumerable ways, such attachments are particularly alarming to the truly enlightened and independent patriot. How many opportunities do they afford to tamper with domestic factions, to practice the arts of seduction, to mislead public opinion, to influence or awe the public councils? Such an attachment of a small or weak towards a great and powerful nation dooms the former to be the satellite of the latter.

35. Against the insidious wiles of foreign influence (I conjure you to believe me, fellow-citizens) the jealousy of a free people ought to be constantly awake, since history and experience prove that foreign influence is one of the most baneful foes of republican government. But that jealousy to be useful must be impartial; else it becomes the instrument of the very influence to be avoided, instead of a defense against it. Excessive partiality for one foreign nation and excessive dislike of another cause those whom they actuate to see danger only on one side, and serve to veil and even second the arts of influence on the other. Real patriots who may resist the intrigues of the favorite are liable to become suspected and odious, while its tools and dupes usurp the applause and confidence of the people, to surrender their interests.

36. The great rule of conduct for us in regard to foreign nations is in extending our commercial relations, to have with them as little political connection as possible. So far as we have already formed engagements, let them be fulfilled with perfect good faith. Here let us stop. Europe has a set of primary interests which to us have none; or a very remote relation. Hence she must be engaged in frequent controversies, the causes of which are essentially foreign to our concerns. Hence, therefore, it must be unwise in us to implicate ourselves by artificial ties in the ordinary vicissitudes of her politics, or the ordinary combinations and collisions of her friendships or enmities.

37. Our detached and distant situation invites and enables us to pursue a different course. If we remain one people under an efficient government. the period is not far off when we may defy material injury from external annoyance; when we may take such an attitude as will cause the neutrality we may at any time resolve upon to be scrupulously respected; when belligerent nations, under the impossibility of making acquisitions upon us, will not lightly hazard the giving us provocation; when we may choose peace or war, as our interest, guided by justice, shall counsel.

38. Why forego the advantages of so peculiar a situation? Why quit our own to stand upon foreign ground? Why, by interweaving our destiny with that of any part of Europe, entangle our peace and prosperity in the toils of European ambition, rivalship, interest, humor or caprice?

It is our true policy to steer clear of permanent alliances with any portion of the foreign world; so far, I mean, as we are now at liberty to do it; for let me not be understood as capable of patronizing infidelity to existing engagements. I hold the maxim no less applicable to public than to private affairs, that honesty is always the best policy. I repeat it, therefore, let those engagements be observed in their genuine sense. But, in my opinion, it is unnecessary and would be unwise to extend them.

39. Taking care always to keep ourselves by suitable establishments on a respectable defensive posture, we may safely trust to temporary alliances for extraordinary emergencies.

40. Harmony, liberal intercourse with all nations, are recommended by policy, humanity, and interest. But even our commercial policy should hold an equal

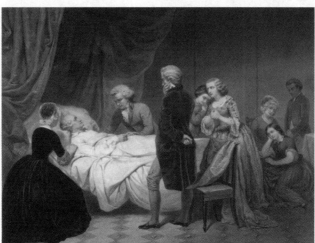

George Washington on his death-bed

and impartial hand; neither seeking nor granting exclusive favors or preferences; consulting the natural course of things; diffusing and diversifying by gentle means the streams of commerce, but forcing nothing; establishing (with powers so disposed, in order to give trade a stable course, to define the rights of our merchants, and to enable the government to support them) conventional rules of intercourse, the best that present circumstances and mutual opinion will permit, but temporary, and liable to be from time to time abandoned or varied, as experience and circumstances shall dictate; constantly keeping in view that it is folly in one nation to look for disinterested favors from another; that it must pay with a portion of its independence for whatever it may accept under that character; that, by such acceptance, it may place itself in the condition of having given equivalents for nominal favors, and yet of being reproached with ingratitude for not

giving more. There can be no greater error than to expect or calculate upon real favors from nation to nation. It is an illusion, which experience must cure, which a just pride ought to discard.

41. In offering to you, my countrymen, these counsels of an old and affectionate friend, I dare not hope they will make the strong and lasting impression I could wish; that they will control the usual current of the passions, or prevent our nation from running the course which has hitherto marked the destiny of nations. But, if I may even flatter myself that they may be productive of some partial benefit, some occasional good; that they may now and then recur to moderate the fury of party spirit, to warn against the mischiefs of foreign intrigue, to guard against the impostures of pretended patriotism; this hope will be a full recompense for the solicitude for your welfare, by which they have been dictated.

42. How far in the discharge of my official duties I have been guided by the principles which have been delineated, the public records and other evidences of my conduct must witness to you and to the world. To myself, the assurance of my own conscience is, that I have at least believed myself to be guided by them.

43. In relation to the still subsisting war in Europe, my proclamation of the twenty-second of April, 1793, is the index of my plan. Sanctioned by your approving voice, and by that of your representatives in both houses of Congress, the spirit of that measure has continually governed me, uninfluenced by any attempts to deter or divert me from it.

44. After deliberate examination, with the aid of the best lights I could obtain, I was well satisfied that our country, under all the circumstances of the case, had a right to take, and was bound

in duty and interest to take, a neutral position. Having taken it, I determined, as far as should depend upon me, to maintain it, with moderation, perseverance, and firmness.

45. The considerations which respect the right to hold this conduct, it is not necessary on this occasion to detail. I will only observe that, according to my understanding of the matter, that right, so far from being denied by any of the belligerent powers, has been virtually admitted by all.

46. The duty of holding a neutral conduct may be inferred, without anything more, from the obligation which justice and humanity impose on every nation, in cases in which it is free to act, to maintain inviolate the relations of peace and amity towards other nations.

George Washington's tomb, Mount Vernon, Virginia
(between 1919 and 1929, LOC)

47. The inducements of interest for observing that conduct will best be referred to your own reflections and experience. With me a predominant motive has been to endeavor to gain time to our country to settle and mature its yet recent institutions, and to progress without interruption to that degree of strength and consistency which is necessary to give it, humanly speaking, the command of its own fortunes.

48. Though, in reviewing the incidents of my administration, I am unconscious of intentional error, I am nevertheless too sensible of my defects not to think it probable that I may have committed many errors. Whatever they may be, I fervently beseech the Almighty to avert or mitigate the evils to which they may tend. I shall also carry with me the hope that my country will never cease to view them with indulgence; and that, after forty five years of my life dedicated to its service with an upright zeal, the faults of incompetent abilities will be consigned to oblivion, as myself must soon be to the mansions of rest.

49. Relying on its kindness in this as in other things, and actuated by that fervent love towards it, which is so natural to a man who views in it the native soil of himself and his progenitors for several generations, I anticipate with pleasing expectation that retreat in which I promise myself to realize, without alloy, the sweet enjoyment of partaking, in the midst of my fellow-citizens, the benign influence of good laws under a free government, the ever-favorite object of my heart, and the happy reward, as I trust, of our mutual cares, labors, and dangers.

United States

19th September, 1796

Geo. Washington

LECTURE REVIEWS

1. Complete Lecture Seventeen Review Worksheet.

2. Complete Lecture Seventeen Review Quiz, including True & False Questions.

CHAPTER EIGHTEEN
RECLAIMING THE CONSTITUTION:
HOW DO WE APPROACH THE RESTORATION OF THE AMERICAN CONSTITUTIONAL REPUBLIC?

GENERAL OBJECTIVES

You should understand, embrace, and impart to others that there is a specific view of Law and Government that is distinctively American in nature. We call this The American View of Law and Government, and it is based on a biblical worldview.

SPECIFIC OBJECTIVES

☆ *Share your knowledge with other students.*

☆ *Develop a passion for understanding and voting in defense of the Constitution.*

☆ *Take an interest in elections at all levels, seeking to support candidates that support constitutional processes.*

☆ *Consider how you can serve your nation, state, and community.*

"My people are destroyed for lack of knowledge: because thou hast rejected knowledge, I will also reject thee, that thou shalt be no priest to me: seeing thou hast forgotten the law of thy God, I will also forget thy children."
    —Hosea 4:6

"History fails to record a single precedent in which nations subject to moral decay have not passed into political and economic decline. There has been either a spiritual awakening to overcome the moral lapse, or a progressive deterioration leading to ultimate national disaster."
    —General Douglas MacArthur

"If the foundations be destroyed, what can the righteous do?"
    —Psalm 11:3

Watch Video Lecture

▶ **Lecture Fifteen:** Reclaiming the Constitution: How Do We Approach the Restoration of the American Constitutional Republic? Follow along with the notes in the following section.

IS THE SITUATION HOPELESS? CAN OUR CONSTITUTIONAL REPUBLIC BE RESTORED?

Here are some actions we can take:

A. Make sure our own faith is based on the Solid Rock, the Lord Jesus Christ and His revealed Word, and live a life of integrity consistent with that profession. The basic building stones of a nation are families and individuals of solid character.

"Our Constitution was made only for a moral and religious people. It is wholly inadequate for the government of any other."[1]

– John Adams

B. Build a base of citizens who understand constitutional principles of government and who will not elect anyone to public office who does not respect those principles.

1. Alexis de Tocqueville, 1835, after noting American ignorance about European affairs: *"But if you question (the average American) respecting his own country, the cloud that dimmed his intelligence will immediately disperse; his language will become as clear and precise as his thoughts. He will inform you what his rights are and by what means he exercises them; he will be able to point out customs which obtain the political world. You will find that he is well acquainted with the rules of the administration, and that he is familiar with the mechanism of the laws. The citizen of the United States does not acquire his practical science and his positive notions from books; the instructions he has acquired may have prepared him for receiving those ideas, but it did not furnish them. The American learns to know the laws by participating in the act of legislation; and he takes a lesson in the forms of government from governing. The great work of society is ever going on before his eyes and, as it were, under his hands."*[2]

2. By contrast:

   a. Americans apparently know more about *The Simpsons* than they do about the First Amendment. Only one in four Americans can name more than one of the five freedoms guaranteed by the First Amendment. But more than half can name at least two members of the cartoon family, according to a survey. —Associated Press March 1, 2006.

   b. The goals of the Communist Manifesto have become the operational objectives of American Government today.

3. Karl Marx in creating the Communist Manifesto designed these planks AS A TEST to determine whether a society has become communist or not. If they are all in effect and in force, then the people ARE practicing communists.

   Communism by any other name is still communism. The Ten Planks of Communism stated in the Communist Manifesto and some of their American counterparts are as follows:

---

1 From John Adams to Massachusetts Militia, 11 October 1798." https://founders.archives.gov/documents/Adams/99-02-02-3102
2 Tocqueville, A., Reeve, H. and Bigelow, J. Democracy in America. (New York: D. Appleton and Company, 1904), p. 343.

a. Abolition of private property and the application of all rents of land to public purposes.

b. A heavy progressive or graduated income tax.

c. Abolition of all rights of inheritance.

d. Confiscation of the property of all emigrants and rebels.

e. Centralization of credit in the hands of the state, by means of a national bank with State capital and an exclusive monopoly.

f. Extension of factories and instruments of production owned by the State, the bringing into cultivation of waste lands, and the improvement of the soil generally in accordance with a common plan.

g. Equal liability of all to labor. Establishment of industrial armies, especially for agriculture.

h. Combination of agriculture with manufacturing industries, gradual abolition of the distinction between town and country, by a more equitable distribution of population over the country.

i. Free education for all children in public schools. Abolition of children's factory labor in its present form. Combination of education with industrial production.

C. Is your elected representative competent? Below are some questions you can ask a current office seeker or office holder to determine their competency:

1. Do you believe our Constitution is a "living document?" If so, what does that mean?

2. What is the purpose of civil government?

3. Do you believe the Bible has a proper role in the formulation of law and policy? If so, how?

4. Do you believe the Constitution should be construed according to the intent of the Framers?[3]

D. The church is the sleeping giant of America with huge numbers of people that need to be taught the biblical principles of government, such as:

1. The Bible deals with law and government.

2. Colonial preachers used to preach "election sermons."

3. Evaluate the character qualifications by the standard of 1 Timothy 3:1-7:

This is a true saying, if a man desire the office of a bishop, he desireth a good work. A bishop then must be blameless, the husband of one wife, vigilant, sober, of good behaviour, given to hospitality, apt to teach; Not given to wine, no striker, not greedy of filthy lucre; but patient, not a brawler, not covetous; One that ruleth well his own house, having his children in subjection with all gravity; (For if a man know not how to rule his own house, how shall he take care of the church of God?) Not a novice, lest being lifted up with pride he fall into the condemnation of the devil. Moreover he must have a good report of them which are without; lest he fall into reproach and the snare of the devil.

4. Coordinate the presentation of one of the many *Institute on the Constitution* courses or opportunities for networking.

   a. Various educational programs for school-aged youth through adults; pastors and community leaders; law enforcement personnel.

   b. Webcasts on various government principles.

   c. Connections to Host/Leaders within your State.

5. Become informed.

E. Help judges, lawyers and law students understand constitutional principles:

1. Law affects all of us, is made by all of us, and is too important to be left only to the law profession.

2. Support lawyers who defend the rights of Christians, such as Liberty Counsel, Alliance Defending Freedom, the Rutherford Institute, and others.

3. Support groups working to promote understanding of our constitutional heritage, such as Institute on the Constitution, Plymouth Rock Foundation, Wallbuilders, Foundation for American Christian Education (F.A.C.E.), Foundation for Moral Law, and others.

4. Share the *Institute on the Constitution* with your lawyer. Consider becoming a lawyer or paralegal.

F. Take a firm stand for jurisprudence of Original Intent, and resist the concept of a "living Constitution." Definitions:

1. Original Intent: The Constitution should be interpreted as written according to the intent of the Framers.

---

3   More Candidate questions can be found at TheAmericanView.com, under *Constitution Course Supplemental Assignments.*

2. Living Constitution: The meaning of the Constitution changes and evolves with time.

3. Reasons for jurisprudence of Original Intent:

   a. Original Intent applies in virtually every other field of law; interpretation of statutes, interpretation of contracts, interpretation of wills and trusts.

   b. The Framers, believing in absolute truth, clearly assumed Original Intent would be the guiding principle. (See Lecture Fourteen.)

   c. Millions of Americans swear to uphold the Constitution when they enter the armed forces or other public office.

   d. The Constitution is entitled to greater deference than court decisions or statutes.

   e. Original Intent can be determined, in most cases, by studying the Framers and the original documents, particularly the Federalist papers.

   f. Original Intent does not preclude flexibility in application. (Can apply as principle.)

   g. If change is necessary, the Constitution can and should be amended, not misinterpreted and stretched beyond recognition.

   h. Even those who reject Original Intent nevertheless quote the Framers when it suits their purposes – e.g., Jefferson's *"wall of separation between church and state."*

   i. Eliminating Original Intent leads to many dangers; erosion of constitutional limitations, judicial usurpation of power, insecurity of human rights. (See Lecture Fourteen.)

   j. Thomas Jefferson, 1823: *"On every question of construction, (let us) carry ourselves back to the time when the Constitution was adopted, recollect the spirit manifested in the debates, and instead of trying what meaning may be squeezed out of the text, or invented against it, conform to the probable one in which it was passed."*

G. Work for the election or appointment of judges (at all levels) who understand and believe in Original Intent, Strict Construction, and Judicial Restraint. What is needed: A systematic method of evaluating judges so voters can know whether to vote for them.

H. Work for the election of a President who recognizes his proper role in the constitutional system and who will appoint Federal judges and justices who hold sound constitutional principles.

I. Work to bring Congress back to sound constitutional principles. Write letters. Make phone calls. Show up at their offices. Begin with your own representatives. If their thinking and voting are sound, work to re-elect them; if not, work to replace them with those who will:

   1. Resist the growth of administrative law – government by unelected administrative agencies which make their own regulations, and which are, in practice, responsible to virtually no one but themselves.

   2. Cut down the size of government – even if your "pet" programs are affected.

3. In accordance with Article III, Section 2, support efforts to limit the Federal courts' Jurisdiction such as the Constitutional Restoration Act. This is a check on the judiciary which the Framers placed in the Constitution, but which has not been used in over 100 years.

J. Support "Tenth Amendment Resolutions" in state legislatures. These resolutions, already passed in several states, declare that Federal mandates which lack specific constitutional authority will be considered invalid. State legislators can be natural allies on this issue since they don't like Federal encroachments on their authority, particularly unfunded Federal mandates.

K. Speak out! Make your views known to your friends, your community, and your elected representatives.

LEARN AND LIVE LIBERTY

GET INVOLVED – While no one can do everything, everyone can do SOMETHING. Don't let your constitutional rights or knowledge atrophy for lack of use. Find your passion and begin!
Some suggestions:

A. Use educational materials available at the *Institute on the Constitution* to reach your church, civic groups and neighborhoods:[4]

1. Host this 12-week Constitution course or volunteer to support anyone who does, helping with classes, presentations or administrative details.

2. Speak to your Pastor, church, or civic leaders about our One-Day Seminar — *The Truth of America's Founding — Your Heritage & Mine.*[5]

3. Help start an American Club at your local high school, college or homeschool co-op. Pass the "Liberty Baton."

4. Learn about *Liberty Camp for Kids* and share the information with local church youth leaders. Another way to pass the "Liberty Baton"!

5. *The Duty of the Jury* – a course which brings out the astonishing truth that the jury is to judge the law as well as the facts in order to defend our constitutional republic.

6. All law enforcement officers take an oath to uphold the Constitution, but few have studied it. Let them know about *The Sheriff & the Citizen* course and your commitment to support them constitutionally.

B. Speak to your pastor about adding primary source referenced material regarding America's founding to the Church library — DVDs, books, pamphlets — to educate the church on their civil duties as Christians.

C. Work with local, state or national organizations that hold a **constitutional** position on the issues, not just "conservative" opinions. Or join "conservative" groups and begin to insert constitutional ideas into their discussions and policies.

D. Attend local meetings – City Council, Township Trustees or County Commission. Unmask "Regional Planning" as unconstitutional and promoting violations of private property rights.

---

4 Details and materials can be viewed at www.theamericanview.com
5 https://www.instituteontheconstitution.com/truth-of-americas-founding

E. Attend school board meetings, or run for school board, to bring our schools out of unconstitutional federal control and back to local control.

F. Consider running for office yourself and/or work with others to identify qualified individuals (especially within your church) and encourage them and help them to run for office, particularly local offices like Precinct Committees, Trustees, Commissioners.[6]

Acknowledge God

Recognize, Rebuild, Repair, Restore or Reaffirm yourself, Family and Church Governments

A. **PRAY** for our constitutional republic, our country's elected officials, our Church leaders, our families and friends, and for freedom-loving people everywhere!

B. **REPENT** of your individual sin, followed by requests for repentance of our country and Jesus Christ's Church.

C. **STUDY** Scripture by reading God's Holy Word, the Bible, every day.

D. **REPEAT** these steps daily or as required with a special supplication for Revival in the Church.

---

6   For more ideas, including a Suggested Reading list, go to Constitution Course Supplemental Assignments found at TheAmericanView.com.

"If my people, which are called by my name, shall humble themselves, and pray, and seek my face, and turn from their wicked ways; then will I hear from heaven, and will forgive their sin, and will heal their land."
–2 Chronicles 7:14

"Except the LORD build the house, they labour in vain that build it: except the LORD keep the city, the watchman waketh but in vain."
–Psalm 127:1

"Posterity! you will never know how much it cost the present generation to preserve your freedom! I hope you will make a good use of it. If you do not, I shall repent in Heaven that I ever took half the pains to preserve it."[7]
–John Adams in a letter to Abigail Adams; Philadelphia, Saturday evening, April 26, 1777

"It does not take a majority to prevail...but rather an irate, tireless minority, keen on setting brushfires of freedom in the minds of men."[8]
–Samuel Adams, known as the Father of the American Revolution

That's you — a *tireless minority setting brushfires of freedom in people's minds.* You now know the truth of America's founding documents. Spread it. Educate to activate! Together, we CAN make a brighter future for ourselves, and one day, our children and grandchildren!

7 https://founders.archives.gov/documents/Adams/04-02-02-0169
8 https://www.brainyquote.com/quotes/samuel_adams_392728

Constitution High Points

Article I – Legislative – Key Point: All legislative authority rests with Congress. Section 8 lists 18 specific areas within which they can make law – NO OTHERS.

Article II – Executive – Key Point: Executive Orders are NOT law.

Article III – Judicial – Key Point: Court decisions are NOT the law of the land (i.e. Roe v. Wade). Decision applies ONLY to the parties of the case decided. This nation was founded under rule of law, not case law.

Article IV: Republican form of government guaranteed to all states.

Article V – Amendment Procedure: No Article V Convention/ConCon!

Article VI – Debts, Treaties & Oaths – Key Points: Treaties are pursuant to (must AGREE with) the Constitution and do NOT overrule it. Also, all elected representatives are BOUND BY OATH to support this Constitution.

Article VII: Ratification declaration of this Constitution – September 17, 1787

Important Definitions

Power – force or strength (*Webster's 1828 Dictionary*)

Authority – legal power (*Webster's 1828 Dictionary*)

Legal – according to the laws of nature and of nature's God (*Webster's 1828 Dictionary*)

The Laws of Nature's God – the moral law…contained in the …10 commandments written by the finger of God. (*Webster's 1828 Dictionary*)

Laws of nature – a rule of conduct…established by the Creator… prior to any [written] precept. (*Webster's 1828 Dictionary*) [Comment: The laws of nature are intuitively and instinctively known to man. They are in his God-given conscience.]

Pretended legislation – Any "laws" passed that are outside the boundaries of the Laws of Nature and Nature's God. [See Declaration of Independence Grievances #13 and #19.]

Tyranny – arbitrary or despotic exercise of power; the exercise of power over others with a rigor not authorized by law. (*Webster's 1828 Dictionary*)

Interposition – The action of a state while exercising its sovereignty in rejecting a federal mandate that it believes is unconstitutional or overreaching. (*Black's Law Dictionary*)

Nullification – the act of making something void; the action of a state in abrogating a federal law on the basis of state sovereignty. (*Black's Law Dictionary*)

Politics - the science of government; that part of ethics which consists in the regulation and government of a nation or state for the preservation of its safety, peace and prosperity…also for the protection of its citizens in their rights, with the preservation and improvement of their morals. (*Webster's 1828 Dictionary*)

Property – The exclusive right of possessing, enjoying and disposing of a thing; ownership. In the beginning of the world, the Creator gave to man dominion over the earth, over the fish of the sea and the fowls of the air, and over every living thing. This is the foundation of man's property in the earth and in all its productions… The labor of inventing, making or producing anything constitutes one of the highest and most indefeasible titles to property. (*Webster's 1828 Dictionary*)

LECTURE REVIEWS

1. Complete Lecture Eighteen Review Worksheet.

2. Complete Lecture Eighteen Review Quiz, including True & False Questions.

Appendix A
The Mayflower Compact

NOVEMBER 11, 1620

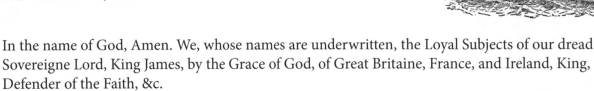

In the name of God, Amen. We, whose names are underwritten, the Loyal Subjects of our dread Sovereigne Lord, King James, by the Grace of God, of Great Britaine, France, and Ireland, King, Defender of the Faith, &c.

Having undertaken for the Glory of God, and Advancement of the Christian Faith, and the Honour of our King and Country, a Voyage to plant the first colony in the Northerne Parts of Virginia; doe, by these Presents, solemnly and mutually in the Presence of God and one of another, covenant and combine ourselves together into a civill Body Politick, for our better Ordering and Preservation, and Furtherance of the Ends aforesaid; And by Virtue hereof do enact, constitute, and frame, such just and equall Laws, Ordinances, Acts, Constitutions, and Offices, from time to time, as shall be thought most meete and convenient for the Generall Good of the Colonie; unto which we promise all due Submission and Obedience.

In Witness whereof we have hereunto subscribed our names at Cape Cod the eleventh of November, in the Raigne of our Sovereigne Lord, King James of England, France, and Ireland, the eighteenth, and of Scotland, the fiftie-fourth, Anno. Domini, 1620.

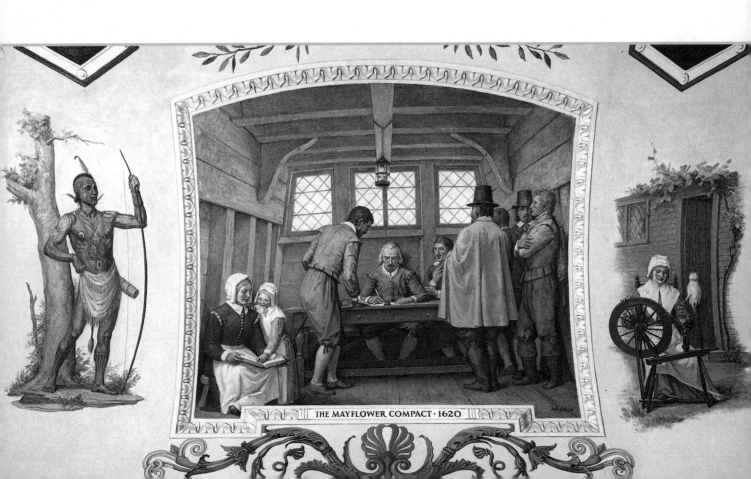

THE MAYFLOWER COMPACT · 1620

Mr. John Carver

Mr. Stephen Hopkins

Mr. William Bradford

Digery Priest

Mr. Edward Winslow

Thomas Williams

Mr. William Brewster

Gilbert Winslow

Isaac Allerton

Edmund Margesson

Miles Standish

Peter Brown

John Alden

Richard Bitteridge

John Turner

George Soule

Francis Eaton

Edward Tilly

James Chilton

John Tilly

John Craxton

Francis Cooke

John Billington

Thomas Rogers

Joses Fletcher

Thomas Tinker

John Goodman

John Ridgate

Mr. Samuel Fuller

Edward Fuller

Mr. Christopher Martin

Richard Clark

Mr. William Mullins

Richard Gardiner

Mr. William White

Mr. John Allerton

Mr. Richard Warren

Thomas English

John Howland

Edward Doten

Edward Liester

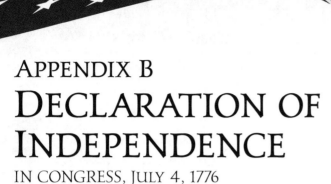

APPENDIX B
DECLARATION OF INDEPENDENCE
IN CONGRESS, JULY 4, 1776

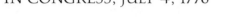
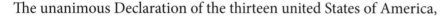

The unanimous Declaration of the thirteen united States of America,

When in the Course of human events, it becomes necessary for one people to dissolve the political bands which have connected them with another, and to assume among the powers of the earth, the separate and equal station to which the Laws of Nature and of Nature's God entitle them, a decent respect to the opinions of mankind requires that they should declare the causes which impel them to the separation.

We hold these truths to be self-evident, that all men are created equal, that they are endowed by their Creator with certain unalienable Rights, that among these are Life, Liberty and the pursuit of Happiness.—That to secure these rights, Governments are instituted among Men, deriving their just powers from the consent of the governed, —That whenever any Form of Government becomes destructive of these ends, it is the Right of the People to alter or to abolish it, and to institute new Government, laying its foundation on such principles and organizing its powers in such form, as to them shall seem most likely to effect their Safety and Happiness. Prudence, indeed, will dictate that Governments long established should not be changed for light and transient causes; and accordingly all experience hath shewn, that mankind are more disposed to suffer, while evils are sufferable, than to right themselves by abolishing the forms to which they are accustomed. But when a long train of abuses and usurpations, pursuing invariably the same Object evinces a design to reduce them under absolute Despotism, it is their right, it is their duty, to throw off such Government, and to provide new Guards for their future security.—Such has been the patient sufferance of these Colonies; and such is now the necessity which constrains them to alter their former Systems of Government.

The history of the present King of Great Britain is a history of repeated injuries and usurpations, all having in direct object the establishment of an absolute tyranny over these States. To prove this, let facts be submitted to a candid world.

1. He has refused his assent to laws, the most wholesome and necessary for the public good.

2. He has forbidden his Governors to pass laws of immediate and pressing importance, unless suspended in their operation till his assent should be obtained; and when so suspended, he has utterly neglected to attend to them.

3. He has refused to pass other laws for the accommodation of large districts of people, unless those people would relinquish the right of representation in the legislature, a right inestimable to them and formidable to tyrants only.

4. He has called together legislative bodies at places unusual, uncomfortable, and distant from the depository of their public records, for the sole purpose of fatiguing them into compliance with his measures.

5. He has dissolved representative houses repeatedly, for opposing with manly firmness his invasions on the rights of the people.

6. He has refused for a long time, after such dissolutions, to cause others to be elected; whereby the legislative powers, incapable of annihilation, have returned to the people at large for their exercise; the state remaining in the mean time exposed to all the dangers of invasion from without, and convulsions within.

7. He has endeavoured to prevent the population of these States; for that purpose obstructing the laws for naturalization of foreigners; refusing to pass others to encourage their migrations hither, and raising the conditions of new appropriations of lands.

8. He has obstructed the administration of justice, by refusing his assent to laws for establishing judiciary powers.

9. He has made judges dependent on his will alone, for the tenure of their offices, and the amount and payment of their salaries.

10. He has erected a multitude of new offices, and sent hither swarms of Officers to harass our people, and eat out their substance.

11. He has kept among us, in times of peace, standing armies without the consent of our legislatures.

12. He has affected to render the military independent of and superior to the civil power.

13. He has combined with others to subject us to a jurisdiction foreign to our constitution, and unacknowledged by our laws; giving his assent to their acts of pretended legislation: —

14. For quartering large bodies of armed troops among us:

15. For protecting them, by a mock trial, from punishment for any murders which they should commit on the inhabitants of these states:

16. For cutting off our trade with all parts of the world:

17. For imposing taxes on us without our consent:

18. For depriving us in many cases, of the benefits of trial by jury:

19. For transporting us beyond seas to be tried for pretended offences:

20. For abolishing the free System of English Laws in a neighbouring province, establishing therein an arbitrary government, and enlarging its boundaries so as to render it at once an example and fit instrument for introducing the same absolute rule into these colonies:

21. For taking away our charters, abolishing our most valuable Laws, and altering fundamentally the forms of our governments:

22. For suspending our own legislatures, and declaring themselves invested with power to legislate for us in all cases whatsoever.

23. He has abdicated government here, by declaring us out of his protection and waging war against us.

24. He has plundered our seas, ravaged our coasts, burnt our towns, and destroyed the lives of our people.

25. He is at this time transporting large Armies of foreign mercenaries to compleat(sic) the works of death, desolation and tyranny, already begun with circumstances of cruelty & perfidy scarcely paralleled in the most barbarous ages, and totally unworthy the head of a civilized nation.

26. He has constrained our fellow citizens taken captive on the high seas to bear arms against their country, to become the executioners of their friends and brethren, or to fall themselves by their hands.

27. He has excited domestic insurrections amongst us, and has endeavoured to bring on the inhabitants of our frontiers, the merciless Indian savages, whose known rule of warfare, is an undistinguished destruction of all ages, sexes and conditions.[1]

In every stage of these Oppressions We have Petitioned for Redress in the most humble terms: Our repeated Petitions have been answered only by repeated injury. A Prince whose character is thus marked by every act which may define a Tyrant, is unfit to be the ruler of a free people.

Nor have We been wanting in attentions to our British brethren. We have warned them from time to time of attempts by their legislature to extend an unwarrantable jurisdiction over us. We have reminded them of the circumstances of our emigration and settlement here. We have appealed to their native justice and magnanimity, and we have conjured them by the ties of our common kindred to disavow these usurpations, which, would inevitably interrupt our connections and correspondence. They too have been deaf to the voice of justice and of consanguinity. We must, therefore, acquiesce in the necessity, which denounces our Separation, and hold them, as we hold the rest of mankind, Enemies in War, in Peace Friends.

We, therefore, the Representatives of the united States of America, in General Congress, Assembled, appealing to the Supreme Judge of the world for the rectitude of our intentions, do, in the Name, and by Authority of the good People of these Colonies, solemnly publish and declare, That these United Colonies are, and of Right ought to be Free and Independent States; that they are Absolved from all Allegiance to the British Crown, and that all political connection between them and the State of Great Britain, is and ought to be totally dissolved; and that as Free and Independent States, they have full Power to levy War, conclude Peace, contract Alliances, establish Commerce, and to do all other Acts and Things which Independent States may of right do. And for the support of this Declaration, with a firm reliance on the protection of divine Providence, we mutually pledge to each other our Lives, our Fortunes and our sacred Honor.

---

1 Numbers 1-27 beside each grievance were added for educational purposes. These numbers do not appear in the original document.

Georgia:

Button Gwinnett

Lyman Hall

George Walton

North Carolina:

William Hooper

Joseph Hewes

John Penn

South Carolina:

Edward Rutledge

Thomas Heyward, Jr.

Thomas Lynch, Jr.

Arthur Middleton

Maryland:

Samuel Chase

William Paca

Thomas Stone

Charles Carroll of Carrollton

Virginia:

George Wythe

Richard Henry Lee

Thomas Jefferson

Benjamin Harrison

Thomas Nelson, Jr.

Francis Lightfoot Lee

Carter Braxton

Pennsylvania:

Robert Morris

Benjamin Rush

Benjamin Franklin

John Morton

George Clymer

James Smith

George Taylor

James Wilson

George Ross

Delaware:

Caesar Rodney

George Read

Thomas McKean

New York:

William Floyd

Philip Livingston

Francis Lewis

Lewis Morris

New Jersey:

Richard Stockton

John Witherspoon

Francis Hopkinson

John Hart

Abraham Clark

New Hampshire:

Josiah Bartlett

William Whipple

Massachusetts:

John Hancock

Samuel Adams

John Adams

Robert Treat Paine

Elbridge Gerry

Rhode Island:

Stephen Hopkins

William Ellery

Connecticut:

Roger Sherman

Samuel Huntington

William Williams

Oliver Wolcott

New Hampshire:

Matthew Thornton

APPENDIX C
THE UNITED STATES CONSTITUTION

We the People of the United States, in Order to form a more perfect Union, establish Justice, insure domestic Tranquility, provide for the common defence, promote the general Welfare, and secure the Blessings of Liberty to ourselves and our Posterity, do ordain and establish this Constitution for the United States of America.

Article I.

Section 1.

All legislative Powers herein granted shall be vested in a Congress of the United States, which shall consist of a Senate and House of Representatives.

Section 2.

The House of Representatives shall be composed of Members chosen every second Year by the People of the several States, and the Electors in each State shall have the Qualifications requisite for Electors of the most numerous Branch of the State Legislature.

No Person shall be a Representative who shall not have attained to the Age of twenty five Years, and been seven Years a Citizen of the United States, and who shall not, when elected, be an Inhabitant of that State in which he shall be chosen.

Representatives and direct Taxes shall be apportioned among the several States which may be included within this Union, according to their respective Numbers, which shall be determined by adding to the whole Number of free Persons, including those bound to Service for a Term of Years, and excluding Indians not taxed, three fifths of all other Persons. The actual Enumeration shall be made within three Years after the first Meeting of the Congress of the United States, and within every subsequent Term of ten Years, in such Manner as they shall by Law direct. The Number of Representatives shall not exceed one for every thirty Thousand, but each State shall have at Least one Representative; and until such enumeration shall be made, the State of New Hampshire shall be entitled to chuse[1] three, Massachusetts eight, Rhode-Island and Providence Plantations one, Connecticut five, New-York six, New Jersey four, Pennsylvania eight, Delaware one, Maryland six, Virginia ten, North Carolina five, South Carolina five, and Georgia three.

When vacancies happen in the Representation from any State, the Executive Authority thereof shall issue Writs of Election to fill such Vacancies.

The House of Representatives shall chuse their Speaker and other Officers; and shall have the sole Power of Impeachment.

1 This is an alternate spelling of the word "choose" that was used at this time. There are other misspellings in the documents as well as British spellings.

Section 3.

The Senate of the United States shall be composed of two Senators from each State, chosen by the Legislature thereof for six Years; and each Senator shall have one Vote.

Immediately after they shall be assembled in Consequence of the first Election, they shall be divided as equally as may be into three Classes. The Seats of the Senators of the first Class shall be vacated at the Expiration of the second Year, of the second Class at the Expiration of the fourth Year, and of the third Class at the Expiration of the sixth Year, so that one third may be chosen every second Year; and if Vacancies happen by Resignation, or otherwise, during the Recess of the Legislature of any State, the Executive thereof may make temporary Appointments until the next Meeting of the Legislature, which shall then fill such Vacancies.

No Person shall be a Senator who shall not have attained to the Age of thirty Years, and been nine Years a Citizen of the United States, and who shall not, when elected, be an Inhabitant of that State for which he shall be chosen.

The Vice-President of the United States shall be President of the Senate, but shall have no Vote, unless they be equally divided.

The Senate shall chuse their other Officers, and also a President pro tempore, in the Absence of the Vice-President, or when he shall exercise the Office of President of the United States.

The Senate shall have the sole Power to try all Impeachments. When sitting for that Purpose, they shall be on Oath or Affirmation. When the President of the United States is tried, the Chief Justice shall preside: And no Person shall be convicted without the Concurrence of two thirds of the Members present.

Judgment in Cases of Impeachment shall not extend further than to removal from Office, and disqualification to hold and enjoy any Office of honor, Trust or Profit under the United States: but the Party convicted shall nevertheless be liable and subject to Indictment, Trial, Judgment and Punishment, according to Law.

Section 4.

The Times, Places and Manner of holding Elections for Senators and Representatives, shall be prescribed in each State by the Legislature thereof; but the Congress may at any time by Law make or alter such Regulations, except as to the Places of chusing Senators.

The Congress shall assemble at least once in every Year, and such Meeting shall be on the first Monday in December, unless they shall by Law appoint a different Day.

Section 5.

The Times, Places and Manner of holding Elections for Senators and Representatives, shall be prescribed in each State by the Legislature thereof; but the Congress may at any time by Law make or alter such Regulations, except as to the Places of chusing Senators.

Attendance of absent Members, in such Manner, and under such Penalties as each House may provide.

Each House may determine the Rules of its Proceedings, punish its Members for disorderly Behaviour, and, with the Concurrence of two thirds, expel a Member.

Each House shall keep a Journal of its Proceedings, and from time to time publish the same, excepting such Parts as may in their Judgment require Secrecy; and the Yeas and Nays of the Members of either House on any question shall, at the Desire of one fifth of those Present, be entered on the Journal.

Neither House, during the Session of Congress, shall, without the Consent of the other, adjourn for more than three days, nor to any other Place than that in which the two Houses shall be sitting.

Section 6.

The Senators and Representatives shall receive a Compensation for their Services, to be ascertained by Law, and paid out of the Treasury of the United States. They shall in all Cases, except Treason, Felony and Breach of the Peace, be privileged from Arrest during their Attendance at the Session of their respective Houses, and in going to and returning from the same; and for any Speech or Debate in either House, they shall not be questioned in any other Place.

No Senator or Representative shall, during the Time for which he was elected, be appointed to any civil Office under the Authority of the United States, which shall have been created, or the Emoluments whereof shall have been encreased during such time; and no Person holding any Office under the United States, shall be a Member of either House during his Continuance in Office.

Section 7.

All Bills for raising Revenue shall originate in the House of Representatives; but the Senate may propose or concur with Amendments as on other Bills.

Every Bill which shall have passed the House of Representatives and the Senate, shall, before it become a Law, be presented to the President of the United States: If he approve he shall sign it, but if not he shall return it, with his Objections to that House in which it shall have originated, who shall enter the Objections at large on their Journal, and proceed to reconsider it. If after such Reconsideration two thirds of that House shall agree to pass the Bill, it shall be sent, together with the Objections, to the other House, by which it shall likewise be reconsidered, and if approved by two thirds of that House, it shall become a Law. But in all such Cases the Votes of both Houses shall be determined by yeas and Nays, and the Names of the Persons voting for and against the Bill shall be entered on the Journal of each House respectively. If any Bill shall not be returned by the President within ten Days (Sundays excepted) after it shall have been presented to him, the Same shall be a Law, in like Manner as if he had signed it, unless the Congress by their Adjournment prevent its Return, in which Case it shall not be a Law.

Every Order, Resolution, or Vote to which the Concurrence of the Senate and House of Representatives may be necessary (except on a question of Adjournment) shall be presented to the President of the United States; and before the Same shall take Effect, shall be approved by him, or being disapproved by him, shall be repassed by two thirds of the Senate and House of Representatives, according to the Rules and Limitations prescribed in the Case of a Bill.

Section 8.

1. The Congress shall have Power To lay and collect Taxes, Duties, Imposts and Excises, to pay the Debts and provide for the common Defense and general Welfare of the United States; but all Duties, Imposts and Excises shall be uniform throughout the United States;

2. To borrow Money on the credit of the United States;

3. To regulate Commerce with foreign Nations, and among the several States, and with the Indian Tribes;

4. To establish an uniform Rule of Naturalization, and uniform Laws on the subject of Bankruptcies throughout the United States;

5. To coin Money, regulate the Value thereof, and of foreign Coin, and fix the Standard of Weights and Measures;

6. To provide for the Punishment of counterfeiting the Securities and current Coin of the United States;

7. To establish Post Offices and post Roads;

8. To promote the Progress of Science and useful Arts, by securing for limited Times to Authors and Inventors the exclusive Right to their respective Writings and Discoveries;

9. To constitute Tribunals inferior to the supreme Court;

10. To define and punish Piracies and Felonies committed on the high Seas, and Offences against the Law of Nations;

11. To declare War, grant Letters of Marque and Reprisal, and make Rules concerning Captures on Land and Water;

12. To raise and support Armies, but no Appropriation of Money to that Use shall be for a longer Term than two Years;

13. To provide and maintain a Navy;

14. To make Rules for the Government and Regulation of the land and naval Forces;

15. To provide for calling forth the Militia to execute the Laws of the Union, suppress Insurrections and repel Invasions;

16. To provide for organizing, arming, and disciplining, the Militia, and for governing such Part of them as may be employed in the Service of the United States, reserving to the States respectively, the Appointment of the Officers, and the Authority of training the Militia according to the discipline prescribed by Congress;

17. To exercise exclusive Legislation in all Cases whatsoever, over such District (not exceeding ten Miles square) as may, by Cession of particular States, and the Acceptance of Congress, become the Seat of the Government of the United States, and to exercise like Authority over all Places purchased by the Consent of the Legislature of the State in which the Same shall be, for the Erection of Forts, Magazines, Arsenals, dock-Yards, and other needful Buildings;—And

18. To make all Laws which shall be necessary and proper for carrying into Execution the foregoing Powers, and all other Powers vested by this Constitution in the Government of the United States, or in any Department or Officer thereof.[2]

Section 9.

The Migration or Importation of such Persons as any of the States now existing shall think proper to admit, shall not be prohibited by the Congress prior to the Year one thousand eight hundred and eight, but a Tax or duty may be imposed on such Importation, not exceeding ten dollars for each Person.

The Privilege of the Writ of Habeas Corpus shall not be suspended, unless when in Cases of Rebellion or Invasion the public Safety may require it.

No Bill of Attainder or ex post facto Law shall be passed.

No Capitation, or other direct, Tax shall be laid, unless in Proportion to the Census or enumeration herein before directed to be taken.

No Tax or Duty shall be laid on Articles exported from any State.

---

2   Numbers 1-18 in Article I, Section 8 were added for educational purposes. These numbers do not appear in the original document.

No Preference shall be given by any Regulation of Commerce or Revenue to the Ports of one State over those of another; nor shall Vessels bound to, or from, one State, be obliged to enter, clear, or pay Duties in another.

No Money shall be drawn from the Treasury, but in Consequence of Appropriations made by Law; and a regular Statement and Account of the Receipts and Expenditures of all public Money shall be published from time to time.

No Title of Nobility shall be granted by the United States: And no Person holding any Office of Profit or Trust under them, shall, without the Consent of the Congress, accept of any present, Emolument, Office, or Title, of any kind whatever, from any King, Prince, or foreign State.

Section 10.

No State shall enter into any Treaty, Alliance, or Confederation; grant Letters of Marque and Reprisal; coin Money; emit Bills of Credit; make any Thing but gold and silver Coin a Tender in Payment of Debts; pass any Bill of Attainder, ex post facto Law, or Law impairing the Obligation of Contracts, or grant any Title of Nobility.

No State shall, without the Consent of the Congress, lay any Imposts or Duties on Imports or Exports, except what may be absolutely necessary for executing it's inspection Laws: and the net Produce of all Duties and Imposts, laid by any State on Imports or Exports, shall be for the Use of the Treasury of the United States; and all such Laws shall be subject to the Revision and Controul of the Congress.

No State shall, without the Consent of Congress, lay any Duty of Tonnage, keep Troops, or Ships of War in time of Peace, enter into any Agreement or Compact with another State, or with a foreign Power, or engage in War, unless actually invaded, or in such imminent Danger as will not admit of delay.

Article II.

Section 1.

The executive Power shall be vested in a President of the United States of America. He shall hold his Office during the Term of four Years, and, together with the Vice-President, chosen for the same Term, be elected, as follows:

Each State shall appoint, in such Manner as the Legislature thereof may direct, a Number of Electors, equal to the whole Number of Senators and Representatives to which the State may be entitled in the Congress: but no Senator or Representative, or Person holding an Office of Trust or Profit under the United States, shall be appointed an Elector.

The Electors shall meet in their respective States, and vote by Ballot for two Persons, of whom one at least shall not be an Inhabitant of the same State with themselves. And they shall make a List of all the Persons voted for, and of the Number of Votes for each; which List they shall sign and certify, and transmit sealed to the Seat of the Government of the United States, directed to the President of the Senate. The President of the Senate shall, in the Presence of the Senate and House of Representatives, open all the Certificates, and the Votes shall then be counted. The Person having the greatest Number of Votes shall be the President, if such Number be a Majority of the whole Number of Electors appointed; and if there be more than one who have such Majority, and have an equal Number of Votes, then the House of Representatives shall immediately chuse by Ballot one of them for President; and if no Person have a Majority, then from the five highest on the List the said House shall in like Manner chuse the President. But in chusing the President, the Votes shall be taken by States, the Representation from each State having one Vote; A quorum for this purpose shall consist of a Member or Members from two thirds of the States, and a Majority of all the States shall be necessary to a Choice. In every Case, after the Choice of the President, the Person having the greatest Number of Votes of the Electors shall be the Vice-President. But if there should remain two or more who have equal Votes, the Senate shall chuse from them by Ballot the Vice-President.

The Congress may determine the Time of chusing the Electors, and the Day on which they shall give their Votes; which Day shall be the same throughout the United States.

No Person except a natural born Citizen, or a Citizen of the United States, at the time of the Adoption of this Constitution, shall be eligible to the Office of President; neither shall any Person be eligible to that Office who shall not have attained to the Age of thirty five Years, and been fourteen Years a Resident within the United States.

In Case of the Removal of the President from Office, or of his Death, Resignation, or Inability to discharge the Powers and Duties of the said Office, the Same shall devolve on the Vice-President, and the Congress may by Law provide for the Case of Removal, Death, Resignation or Inability, both of the President and Vice-President, declaring what Officer shall then act as President, and such Officer shall act accordingly, until the Disability be removed, or a President shall be elected.

The President shall, at stated Times, receive for his Services, a Compensation, which shall neither be increased nor diminished during the Period for which he shall have been elected, and he shall not receive within that Period any other Emolument from the United States, or any of them.

Before he enter on the Execution of his Office, he shall take the following Oath or Affirmation:—"I do solemnly swear (or affirm) that I will faithfully execute the Office of President of the United States, and will to the best of my Ability, preserve, protect and defend the Constitution of the United States."

Section 2.

The President shall be Commander in Chief of the Army and Navy of the United States, and of the Militia of the several States, when called into the actual Service of the United States; he may require the Opinion, in writing, of the principal Officer in each of the executive Departments, upon any Subject relating to the Duties of their respective Offices, and he shall have Power to grant Reprieves and Pardons for Offences against the United States, except in Cases of Impeachment.

He shall have Power, by and with the Advice and Consent of the Senate, to make Treaties, provided two thirds of the Senators present concur; and he shall nominate, and by and with the Advice and Consent of the Senate, shall appoint Ambassadors, other public Ministers and Consuls, Judges of the supreme Court, and all other Officers of the United States, whose Appointments are not herein otherwise provided for, and which shall be established by Law: but the Congress may by Law vest the Appointment of such inferior Officers, as they think proper, in the President alone, in the Courts of Law, or in the Heads of Departments.

The President shall have Power to fill up all Vacancies that may happen during the Recess of the Senate, by granting Commissions which shall expire at the End of their next Session.

Section 3.

He shall from time to time give to the Congress Information of the State of the Union, and recommend to their Consideration such Measures as he shall judge necessary and expedient; he may, on extraordinary Occasions, convene both Houses, or either of them, and in Case of Disagreement between them, with Respect to the Time of Adjournment, he may adjourn them to such Time as he shall think proper; he shall receive Ambassadors and other public Ministers; he shall take Care that the Laws be faithfully executed, and shall Commission all the Officers of the United States.

Section 4.

The President, Vice-President and all civil Officers of the United States, shall be removed from Office on Impeachment for, and Conviction of, Treason, Bribery, or other high Crimes and Misdemeanors.

Article III.

Section 1.

The judicial Power of the United States shall be vested in one supreme Court, and in such inferior Courts as the Congress may from time to time ordain and establish. The Judges, both of the supreme and inferior Courts, shall hold their Offices during good Behaviour, and shall, at stated Times, receive for their Services a Compensation, which shall not be diminished during their Continuance in Office.

Section 2.

The judicial Power shall extend to all Cases, in Law and Equity, arising under this Constitution, the Laws of the United States, and Treaties made, or which shall be made, under their Authority;—to all Cases affecting Ambassadors, other public Ministers and Consuls;—to all Cases of admiralty and maritime Jurisdiction;—to Controversies to which the United States shall be a Party;—to Controversies between two or more States;— between a State and Citizens of another State,—between Citizens of different States,—between Citizens of the same State claiming Lands under Grants of different States, and between a State, or the Citizens thereof, and foreign States, Citizens or Subjects.

In all Cases affecting Ambassadors, other public Ministers and Consuls, and those in which a State shall be Party, the supreme Court shall have original Jurisdiction. In all the other Cases before mentioned, the supreme Court shall have appellate Jurisdiction, both as to Law and Fact, with such Exceptions, and under such Regulations as the Congress shall make.

The Trial of all Crimes, except in Cases of Impeachment, shall be by Jury; and such Trial shall be held in the State where the said Crimes shall have been committed; but when not committed within any State, the Trial shall be at such Place or Places as the Congress may by Law have directed.

Section 3.

Treason against the United States, shall consist only in levying War against them, or in adhering to their Enemies, giving them Aid and Comfort. No Person shall be convicted of Treason unless on the Testimony of two Witnesses to the same overt Act, or on Confession in open Court.

The Congress shall have Power to declare the Punishment of Treason, but no Attainder of Treason shall work Corruption of Blood, or Forfeiture except during the Life of the Person attainted.

Article IV.

Section 1.

Full Faith and Credit shall be given in each State to the public Acts, Records, and judicial Proceedings of every other State. And the Congress may by general Laws prescribe the Manner in which such Acts, Records and Proceedings shall be proved, and the Effect thereof.

Section 2.

The Citizens of each State shall be entitled to all Privileges and Immunities of Citizens in the several States.

A Person charged in any State with Treason, Felony, or other Crime, who shall flee from Justice, and be found in another State, shall on Demand of the executive Authority of the State from which he fled, be delivered up, to be removed to the State having Jurisdiction of the Crime.

No Person held to Service or Labour in one State, under the Laws thereof, escaping into another, shall, in Consequence of any Law or Regulation therein, be discharged from such Service or Labour, but shall be delivered up on Claim of the Party to whom such Service or Labour may be due.

Section 3.

New States may be admitted by the Congress into this Union; but no new State shall be formed or erected within the Jurisdiction of any other State; nor any State be formed by the Junction of two or more States, or Parts of States, without the Consent of the Legislatures of the States concerned as well as of the Congress.

The Congress shall have Power to dispose of and make all needful Rules and Regulations respecting the Territory or other Property belonging to the United States; and nothing in this Constitution shall be so construed as to Prejudice any Claims of the United States, or of any particular State.

Section 4.

The United States shall guarantee to every State in this Union a Republican Form of Government, and shall protect each of them against Invasion; and on Application of the Legislature, or of the Executive (when the Legislature cannot be convened), against domestic Violence.

Article V.

The Congress, whenever two thirds of both Houses shall deem it necessary, shall propose Amendments to this Constitution, or, on the Application of the Legislatures of two thirds of the several States, shall call a Convention for proposing Amendments, which, in either Case, shall be valid to all Intents and Purposes, as Part of this Constitution, when ratified by the Legislatures of three fourths of the several States, or by Conventions in three fourths thereof, as the one or the other Mode of Ratification may be proposed by the Congress; Provided that no Amendment which may be made prior to the Year One thousand eight hundred and eight shall in any Manner affect the first and fourth Clauses in the Ninth Section of the first Article; and that no State, without its Consent, shall be deprived of its equal Suffrage in the Senate.

Article VI.

All Debts contracted and Engagements entered into, before the Adoption of this Constitution, shall be as valid against the United States under this Constitution, as under the Confederation.

This Constitution, and the Laws of the United States which shall be made in Pursuance thereof; and all Treaties made, or which shall be made, under the Authority of the United States, shall be the supreme Law of the Land; and the Judges in every State shall be bound thereby, any Thing in the Constitution or Laws of any State to the Contrary notwithstanding.

The Senators and Representatives before mentioned, and the Members of the several State Legislatures, and all executive and judicial Officers, both of the United States and of the several States, shall be bound by Oath or Affirmation, to support this Constitution; but no religious Test shall ever be required as a Qualification to any Office or public Trust under the United States.

Article VII.

The Ratification of the Conventions of nine States, shall be sufficient for the Establishment of this Constitution between the States so ratifying the Same.

The Word, "the," being interlined between the seventh and eighth Lines of the first Page, the Word "Thirty" being partly written on an Erazure in the fifteenth Line of the first Page, The Words "is tried" being interlined between the thirty second and thirty third Lines of the first Page and the Word "the" being interlined between the forty third and forty fourth Lines of the second Page.

Attest William Jackson Secretary

Done in Convention by the Unanimous Consent of the States present the Seventeenth Day of September in the Year of our Lord one thousand seven hundred and Eighty seven and of the Independence of the United States of America the Twelfth In witness whereof We have hereunto subscribed our Names,

G. Washington- Presidt. and deputy from Virginia

New Hampshire: John Langdon, Nicholas Gilman

Massachusetts: Nathaniel Gorham, Rufus King

Connecticut: Wm. Saml. Johnson, Roger Sherman

New York: Alexander Hamilton

New Jersey: Wil. Livingston, David Brearly, Wm. Paterson, Jona. Dayton

Pennsylvania: B. Franklin, Thomas Mifflin, Robt. Morris, Geo. Clymer, Thos. FitzSimons, Jared Ingersoll, James Wilson, Gouverneur Morris

Delaware: Geo. Read, Gunning Bedford jun, John Dickinson, Richard Bassett, Jaco. Broom

Maryland: James McHenry, Dan of St Thos. Jenifer, Danl Carroll

Virginia: John Blair, James Madison Jr.

North Carolina: Wm. Blount, Richd. Dobbs Spaight, Hu Williamson

South Carolina: J. Rutledge, Charles Cotesworth Pinckney, Charles Pinckney, Pierce Butler

Georgia: William Few, Abr Baldwin

Image of the U.S. Constitution.

AMENDMENTS TO THE CONSTITUTION OF THE UNITED STATES

Bill of Rights 1791

THE Conventions of a number of the States, having at the time of their adopting the Constitution, expressed a desire, in order to prevent misconstruction or abuse of its powers, that further declaratory and restrictive clauses should be added: And as extending the ground of public confidence in the Government, will best ensure the beneficent ends of its institution.

RESOLVED by the Senate and House of Representatives of the United States of America, in Congress assembled, two thirds of both Houses concurring, that the following Articles be proposed to the Legislatures of the several States, as amendments to the Constitution of the United States, all, or any of which Articles, when ratified by three fourths of the said Legislatures, to be valid to all intents and purposes, as part of the said Constitution; viz.

ARTICLES in addition to, and Amendment of the Constitution of the United States of America, proposed by Congress, and ratified by the Legislatures of the several States, pursuant to the fifth Article of the original Constitution.*

Amendment I

Congress shall make no law respecting an establishment of religion, or prohibiting the free exercise thereof; or abridging the freedom of speech, or of the press; or the right of the people peaceably to assemble, and to petition the government for a redress of grievances.

Amendment II

A well regulated militia, being necessary to the security of a free state, the right of the people to keep and bear arms, shall not be infringed.

Amendment III

No soldier shall, in time of peace be quartered in any house, without the consent of the owner, nor in time of war, but in a manner to be prescribed by law.

---

*The first ten amendments to the Constitution are known as the Bill of Rights. They were approved by the 1st Congress and ratified in 1791.

Amendment IV

The right of the people to be secure in their persons, houses, papers, and effects, against unreasonable searches and seizures, shall not be violated, and no warrants shall issue, but upon probable cause, supported by oath or affirmation, and particularly describing the place to be searched, and the persons or things to be seized.

Amendment V

No person shall be held to answer for a capital, or otherwise infamous crime, unless on a presentment or indictment of a grand jury, except in cases arising in the land or naval forces, or in the militia, when in actual service in time of war or public danger; nor shall any person be subject for the same offense to be twice put in jeopardy of life or limb; nor shall be compelled in any criminal case to be a witness against himself, nor be deprived of life, liberty, or property, without due process of law; nor shall private property be taken for public use, without just compensation.

Amendment VI

In all criminal prosecutions, the accused shall enjoy the right to a speedy and public trial, by an impartial jury of the state and district wherein the crime shall have been committed, which district shall have been previously ascertained by law, and to be informed of the nature and cause of the accusation; to be confronted with the witnesses against him; to have compulsory process for obtaining witnesses in his favor, and to have the assistance of counsel for his defense.

Amendment VII

In suits at common law, where the value in controversy shall exceed twenty dollars, the right of trial by jury shall be preserved, and no fact tried by a jury, shall be otherwise reexamined in any court of the United States, than according to the rules of the common law.

Amendment VIII

Excessive bail shall not be required, nor excessive fines imposed, nor cruel and unusual punishments inflicted.

Amendment IX

The enumeration in the Constitution, of certain rights, shall not be construed to deny or disparage others retained by the people.

Amendment X

The powers not delegated to the United States by the Constitution, nor prohibited by it to the states, are reserved to the states respectively, or to the people.

Amendment XI (1795)

The judicial power of the United States shall not be construed to extend to any suit in law or equity, commenced or prosecuted against one of the United States by citizens of another state, or by citizens or subjects of any foreign state.

Amendment XII (1804)

The electors shall meet in their respective states and vote by ballot for President and Vice-President, one of whom, at least, shall not be an inhabitant of the same state with themselves; they shall name in their ballots the person voted for as President, and in distinct ballots the person voted for as Vice-President, and they shall make distinct lists of all persons voted for as President, and of all persons voted for as Vice-President, and of the number of votes for each, which lists they shall sign and certify, and transmit sealed to the seat of the government of the United States, directed to the President of the Senate;—The President of the Senate shall, in the presence of the Senate and House of Representatives, open all the certificates and the votes shall then be counted;—the person having the greatest number of votes for President, shall be the President, if such number be a majority of the whole number of electors appointed; and if no person have such majority, then from the persons having the highest numbers not exceeding three on the list of those voted for as President, the House of Representatives shall choose immediately, by ballot, the President. But in choosing the President, the votes shall be taken by states, the representation from each state having one vote; a quorum for this purpose shall consist of a member or members from two-thirds of the states, and a majority of all the states shall be necessary to a choice. And if the House of Representatives shall not choose a President whenever the right of choice shall devolve upon them, before the fourth day of March next following, then the Vice-President shall act as President, as in the case of the death or other constitutional disability of the President. The person having the greatest number of votes as Vice-President, shall be the Vice-President, if such number be a majority of the whole number of electors appointed, and if no person have a majority, then from the two highest numbers on the list, the Senate shall choose the Vice-President; a quorum for the purpose shall consist of two-thirds of the whole number of Senators, and a majority of the whole number shall be necessary to a choice. But no person constitutionally ineligible to the office of President shall be eligible to that of Vice-President of the United States.

Amendment XIII (1865)

Section 1. Neither slavery nor involuntary servitude, except as a punishment for crime whereof the party shall have been duly convicted, shall exist within the United States, or any place subject to their jurisdiction.

Section 2. Congress shall have power to enforce this article by appropriate legislation.

Amendment XIV (1868)

Section 1. All persons born or naturalized in the United States, and subject to the jurisdiction thereof, are citizens of the United States and of the state wherein they reside. No state shall make or enforce any law which shall abridge the privileges or immunities of citizens of the United States; nor shall any state deprive any person of life, liberty, or property, without due process of law; nor deny to any person within its jurisdiction the equal protection of the laws.

Section 2. Representatives shall be apportioned among the several states according to their respective numbers, counting the whole number of persons in each state, excluding Indians not taxed. But when the right to vote at any election for the choice of electors for President and Vice President of the United States, Representatives in Congress, the executive and judicial officers of a state, or the members of the legislature thereof, is denied to any of the male inhabitants of such state, being twenty-one years of age, and citizens of the United States, or in any way abridged, except for participation in rebellion, or other crime, the basis of representation therein shall be reduced in the proportion which the number of such male citizens shall bear to the whole number of male citizens twenty-one years of age in such state.

Section 3. No person shall be a Senator or Representative in Congress, or elector of President and Vice President, or hold any office, civil or military, under the United States, or under any state, who, having previously taken an oath, as a member of Congress, or as an officer of the United States, or as a member of any state legislature, or as an executive or judicial officer of any state, to support the Constitution of the United States, shall have engaged in insurrection or rebellion against the same, or given aid or comfort to the enemies thereof. But Congress may by a vote of two-thirds of each House, remove such disability.

Section 4. The validity of the public debt of the United States, authorized by law, including debts incurred for payment of pensions and bounties for services in suppressing insurrection or rebellion, shall not be questioned. But neither the United States nor any state shall assume or pay any debt or obligation incurred in aid of insurrection or rebellion against the United States, or any claim for the loss or emancipation of any slave; but all such debts, obligations and claims shall be held illegal and void.

Section 5. The Congress shall have power to enforce, by appropriate legislation, the provisions of this article.

Amendment XV (1870)

Section 1. The right of citizens of the United States to vote shall not be denied or abridged by the United States or by any state on account of race, color, or previous condition of servitude.

Section 2. The Congress shall have power to enforce this article by appropriate legislation.

Amendment XVI (1913)

The Congress shall have power to lay and collect taxes on incomes, from whatever source derived, without apportionment among the several states, and without regard to any census of enumeration.

Amendment XVII (1913)

The Senate of the United States shall be composed of two Senators from each state, elected by the people thereof, for six years; and each Senator shall have one vote. The electors in each state shall have the qualifications requisite for electors of the most numerous branch of the state legislatures. When vacancies happen in the representation of any state in the Senate, the executive authority of such state shall issue writs of election to fill such vacancies: Provided, that the legislature of any state may empower the executive thereof to make temporary appointments until the people fill the vacancies by election as the legislature may direct.

This amendment shall not be so construed as to affect the election or term of any Senator chosen before it becomes valid as part of the Constitution.

Amendment XVIII (1919)

Section 1. After one year from the ratification of this article the manufacture, sale, or transportation of intoxicating liquors within, the importation thereof into, or the exportation thereof from the United States and all territory subject to the jurisdiction thereof for beverage purposes is hereby prohibited.

Section 2. The Congress and the several states shall have concurrent power to enforce this article by appropriate legislation.

Section 3. This article shall be inoperative unless it shall have been ratified as an amendment to the Constitution by the legislatures of the several states, as provided in the Constitution, within seven years from the date of the submission hereof to the states by the Congress.

Amendment XIX (1920)

The right of citizens of the United States to vote shall not be denied or abridged by the United States or by any state on account of sex.

Congress shall have power to enforce this article by appropriate legislation.

Amendment XX (1933)

Section 1. The terms of the President and Vice President shall end at noon on the 20th day of January, and the terms of Senators and Representatives at noon on the 3d day of January, of the years in which such terms would have ended if this article had not been ratified; and the terms of their successors shall then begin.

Section 2. The Congress shall assemble at least once in every year, and such meeting shall begin at noon on the 3d day of January, unless they shall by law appoint a different day.

Section 3. If, at the time fixed for the beginning of the term of the President, the President elect shall have died, the Vice President elect shall become President. If a President shall not have been chosen before the time fixed for the beginning of his term, or if the President elect shall have failed to qualify, then the Vice President elect shall act as President until a President shall have qualified; and the Congress may by law provide for the case wherein neither a President elect nor a Vice President elect shall have qualified, declaring who shall then act as President, or the manner in which one who is to act shall be selected, and such person shall act accordingly until a President or Vice President shall have qualified.

Section 4. The Congress may by law provide for the case of the death of any of the persons from whom the House of Representatives may choose a President whenever the right of choice shall have devolved upon them, and for the case of the death of any of the persons from whom the Senate may choose a Vice President whenever the right of choice shall have devolved upon them.

Section 5. Sections 1 and 2 shall take effect on the 15th day of October following the ratification of this article.

Section 6. This article shall be inoperative unless it shall have been ratified as an amendment to the Constitution by the legislatures of three-fourths of the several states within seven years from the date of its submission.

Amendment XXI (1933)

Section 1. The eighteenth article of amendment to the Constitution of the United States is hereby repealed.

Section 2. The transportation or importation into any state, territory, or possession of the United States for delivery or use therein of intoxicating liquors, in violation of the laws thereof, is hereby prohibited.

Section 3. This article shall be inoperative unless it shall have been ratified as an amendment to the Constitution by conventions in the several states, as provided in the Constitution, within seven years from the date of the submission hereof to the states by the Congress.

Amendment XXII (1951)

Section 1. No person shall be elected to the office of the President more than twice, and no person who has held the office of President, or acted as President, for more than two years of a term to which some other person was elected President shall be elected to the office of the President more than once. But this article shall not apply to any person holding the office of President when this article was proposed by the Congress, and shall not prevent any person who may be holding the office of President, or acting as President, during the term within which this article becomes operative from holding the office of President or acting as President during the remainder of such term.

Section 2. This article shall be inoperative unless it shall have been ratified as an amendment to the Constitution by the legislatures of three-fourths of the several states within seven years from the date of its submission to the states by the Congress.

Amendment XXIII (1961)

Section 1. The District constituting the seat of government of the United States shall appoint in such manner as the Congress may direct:

A number of electors of President and Vice President equal to the whole number of Senators and Representatives in Congress to which the District would be entitled if it were a state, but in no event more than the least populous state; they shall be in addition to those appointed by the states, but they shall be considered, for the purposes of the election of President and Vice President, to be electors appointed by a state; and they shall meet in the District and perform such duties as provided by the twelfth article of amendment.

Section 2. The Congress shall have power to enforce this article by appropriate legislation.

Amendment XXIV (1964)

Section 1. The right of citizens of the United States to vote in any primary or other election for President or Vice President, for electors for President or Vice President, or for Senator or Representative in Congress, shall not be denied or abridged by the United States or any state by reason of failure to pay any poll tax or other tax.

Section 2. The Congress shall have power to enforce this article by appropriate legislation.

Amendment XXV (1967)

Section 1. In case of the removal of the President from office or of his death or resignation, the Vice President shall become President.

Section 2. Whenever there is a vacancy in the office of the Vice President, the President shall nominate a Vice President who shall take office upon confirmation by a majority vote of both Houses of Congress.

Section 3. Whenever the President transmits to the President pro tempore of the Senate and the Speaker of the House of Representatives his written declaration that he is unable to discharge the powers and duties of his office, and until he transmits to them a written declaration to the contrary, such powers and duties shall be discharged by the Vice President as Acting President.

Section 4. Whenever the Vice President and a majority of either the principal officers of the executive departments or of such other body as Congress may by law provide, transmit to the President pro tempore of the Senate and the Speaker of the House of Representatives their written declaration that the President is unable to discharge the powers and duties of his office, the Vice President shall immediately assume the powers and duties of the office as Acting President.

Thereafter, when the President transmits to the President pro tempore of the Senate and the Speaker of the House of Representatives his written declaration that no inability exists, he shall resume the powers and duties of his office unless the Vice President and a majority of either the principal officers of the executive department or of such other body as Congress may by law provide, transmit within four days to the President pro tempore of the Senate and the Speaker of the House of Representatives their written declaration that the President is unable to discharge the powers and duties of his office. Thereupon Congress shall decide the issue, assembling within forty-eight hours for that purpose if not in session. If the Congress, within twenty-one days after receipt of the latter written declaration, or, if Congress is not in session, within twenty-one days after Congress is required to assemble, determines by two-thirds vote of both Houses that the President is unable to discharge the powers and duties of his office, the Vice President shall continue to discharge the same as Acting President; otherwise, the President shall resume the powers and duties of his office.

Amendment XXVI (1971)

Section 1. The right of citizens of the United States, who are 18 years of age or older, to vote, shall not be denied or abridged by the United States or any state on account of age.

Section 2. The Congress shall have the power to enforce this article by appropriate legislation.

Amendment XXVII (1992)

No law varying the compensation for the services of the Senators and Representatives shall take effect until an election of Representatives shall have intervened.

Bill of Rights

Congress of the United States,

begun and held at the City of, New York, on
Wednesday, the fourth of March, one thousand and seven hundred and eighty nine.

The Conventions of a number of the States having, at the time of their adopting the Constitution, expressed a desire, in order to prevent misconstruction or abuse of its powers, that further declaratory and restrictive clauses should be added: And as extending the ground of public confidence in the Government, will best insure the beneficent ends of its institution:

Resolved, by the SENATE and HOUSE of REPRESENTATIVES of the UNITED STATES of AMERICA in Congress assembled, two thirds of both Houses concurring. That the following Articles be proposed to the Legislatures of the several States, as Amendments to the Constitution of the United States; all, or any of which articles, when ratified by three fourths of the said Legislatures, to be valid to all intents and purposes, as part of the said Constitution, viz.

Articles in addition to, and Amendment of the Constitution of the United States of America, proposed by Congress, and ratified by the Legislatures of the several States, pursuant to the fifth Article of the Original Constitution.

Article the first ...... After the first enumeration required by the first Article of the Constitution, there shall be one Representative for every thirty thousand, until the number shall amount to one hundred, after which, the proportion shall be so regulated by Congress, that there shall be not less than one hundred Representatives, nor less than one Representative for every forty thousand persons, until the number of Representatives shall amount to two hundred, after which, the proportion shall be so regulated by Congress, that there shall not be less than two hundred Representatives, nor more than one Representative for every fifty thousand persons. [Not Ratified]

Article the second .... No law, varying the compensation for the services of the Senators and Representatives, shall take effect, until an election of Representatives shall have intervened. [Not Ratified]

Article the third .... Congress shall make no law respecting an establishment of religion, or prohibiting the free exercise thereof; or abridging the freedom of speech, or of the press; or the right of the people peaceably to assemble, and to petition the Government for a redress of grievances.

Article the fourth ..... A well regulated Militia, being necessary to the security of a free State, the right of the people to keep and bear Arms, shall not be infringed.

Article the fifth .... No Soldier shall, in time of peace, be quartered in any house, without the consent of the owner, nor in time of war, but in a manner to be prescribed by law.

Article the sixth ...... The right of the people to be secure in their persons, houses, papers, and effects, against unreasonable searches and seizures, shall not be violated, and no Warrants shall issue but upon probable cause, supported by oath or affirmation, and particularly describing the place to be searched, and the persons or things to be seized.

Article the seventh ... No person shall be held to answer for a capital, or otherwise infamous crime, unless on a presentment or indictment of a grand jury, except in cases arising in the land or Naval forces, or in the Militia, when in actual service in time of War or public danger; nor shall any person be subject for the same offence to be twice put in jeopardy of life or limb; nor shall be compelled in any criminal case, to be a witness against himself, nor be deprived of life, liberty, or property, without due process of law; nor shall private property be taken for public use without just compensation.

Article the eighth ..... In all criminal prosecutions, the accused shall enjoy the right to a speedy and public trial by an impartial jury of the State and district wherein the crime shall have been committed, which district shall have been previously ascertained by law, and to be informed of the nature and cause of the accusation; to be confronted with the witnesses against him; to have compulsory process for obtaining witnesses in his favor, and to have the assistance of counsel for his defence.

Article the ninth ...... In suits at common law, where the value in controversy shall exceed twenty dollars, the right of trial by jury shall be preserved, and no fact, tried by a jury, shall be otherwise re-examined in any Court of the United States, than according to the rules of the common law.

Article the tenth ...... Excessive bail shall not be required, nor excessive fines imposed, nor cruel and unusual punishments inflicted.

Article the eleventh .. The enumeration in the Constitution, of certain rights, shall not be construed to deny or disparage others retained by the people.

Article the twelfth .... The powers not delegated to the United States by the Constitution, nor prohibited by it to the States, are reserved to the States respectively, or to the people.

Frederick Augustus Muhlenberg Speaker of the House of Representatives.

John Adams, Vice President of the United States, and President of the Senate.

ATTEST,

John Beckley, Clerk of the House of Representatives

Sam. A. Otis Secretary of the Senate.

Image of the Bill of Rights.

How Tyranny Came to America[1]

By Joseph Sobran © 2005 (Note: This excellent article will give you an important perspective on what has happened to the Constitution in our land.)

One of the great goals of education is to initiate the young into the conversation of their ancestors; to enable them to understand the language of that conversation, in all its subtlety, and maybe even, in their maturity, to add to it some wisdom of their own.

The modern American educational system no longer teaches us the political language of our ancestors. In fact, our schooling helps widen the gulf of time between our ancestors and ourselves, because much of what we are taught in the name of civics, political science, or American history is really modern liberal propaganda. Sometimes this is deliberate. Worse yet, sometimes it isn't. Our ancestral voices have come to sound alien to us, and therefore our own moral and political language is impoverished. It's as if the people of England could no longer understand Shakespeare, or Germans couldn't comprehend Mozart and Beethoven.

So, to most Americans, even those who feel oppressed by what they call big government, it must sound strange to hear it said, in the past tense, that tyranny "came" to America. After all, we have a constitution, don't we? We've abolished slavery and segregation. We won two world wars and the Cold War. We still congratulate ourselves before every ballgame on being the Land of the Free. And we aren't ruled by some fanatic with a funny mustache who likes big parades with thousands of soldiers goose-stepping past huge pictures of himself.

For all that, we no longer fully have what our ancestors, who framed and ratified our Constitution, thought of as freedom — a careful division of power that prevents power from becoming concentrated and unlimited. The word they usually used for concentrated power was consolidated — a rough synonym for fascist. And the words they used for any excessive powers claimed or exercised by the state were usurped and tyrannical. They would consider the modern "liberal" state tyrannical in principle; they would see in it not the opposite of the fascist, communist, and socialist states, but their sister.

If Washington and Jefferson, Madison, and Hamilton could come back, the first thing they'd notice would be that the Federal government now routinely assumes thousands of powers never assigned to it — powers never granted, never delegated, never enumerated. These were the words they used, and it's a good idea for us to learn their language. They would say that we no longer live under the Constitution they wrote. And the Americans of a much later era — the period from Cleveland to Coolidge, for example — would say we no longer live even under the Constitution they inherited and amended.

I call the present system "Post–Constitutional America." As I sometimes put it, the U.S. Constitution poses no serious threat to our form of government.

What's worse is that our constitutional illiteracy cuts us off from our own national heritage. And so our politics degenerates into increasingly bitter and unprincipled quarrels about who is going to bear the burdens of war and welfare.

I don't want to sound like an oracle on this subject. As a typical victim

---

of modern public education and a disinformed citizen of this media-ridden country, I took a long time — an embarrassingly long time — to learn what I'm passing on. It was like studying geometry in old age, and discovering how simple the basic principles of space really are. It was the old story: In order to learn, first I had to unlearn. Most of what I'd been taught and told about the Constitution was misguided or even false. And I'd never been told some of the most elementary things, which would have saved me a tremendous amount of confusion.

The Constitution does two things. First, it delegates certain enumerated powers to the Federal government. Second, it separates those powers among the three branches. Most people understand the secondary principle of the separation of powers. But they don't grasp the primary idea of delegated and enumerated powers.

Consider this. We have recently had a big national debate over national health care. Advocates and opponents argued long and loud over whether it could work, what was fair, how to pay for it, and so forth. But almost nobody raised the basic issue: Where does the Federal government get the power to legislate in this area? The answer is: Nowhere. The Constitution lists 18 specific legislative powers of Congress, and not a one of them covers national health care.

As a matter of fact, none of the delegated powers of Congress — and delegated is always the key word — covers Social Security, or Medicaid, or Medicare, or Federal aid to education, or most of what are now miscalled "civil rights," or countless public works projects, or equally countless regulations of business, large and small, or the space program, or farm subsidies, or research grants, or subsidies to the arts and humanities, or ... well, you name it, chances are it's unconstitutional. Even the most cynical opponents of the Constitution would be dumbfounded to learn that the Federal government now tells us where we can smoke. We are less free, more heavily taxed, and worse governed than our ancestors under British rule. Sometimes this government makes me wonder: Was George III really all that bad?

Let's be clear about one thing. Constitutional and unconstitutional aren't just simple terms of approval and disapproval. A bad law may be perfectly constitutional. A wise and humane law may be unconstitutional. But what is almost certainly bad is a constant disposition to thwart or disregard the Constitution.

It's not just a matter of what is sometimes called the "original intent" of the authors of the Constitution. What really matters is the common, explicit, unchallenged understanding of the Constitution, on all sides, over several generations. There was no mystery about it.

The logic of the Constitution was so elegantly simple that a foreign observer could explain it to his countrymen in two sentences. Alexis de Tocqueville wrote that "the attributes of the Federal government were carefully defined [in the Constitution], and all that was not included among them was declared to remain to the governments of the individual states. Thus the government of the states remained the rule, and that of the Federal government the exception."

The Declaration of Independence, which underlies the Constitution, holds that the rights of the people come from God, and that the powers of the government come from the people. Let me repeat that: According to the Declaration of Independence, the rights of the people come from God, and the powers of the government come from the people. Unless you grasp this basic order of things, you'll have a hard time understanding the Constitution.

The Constitution was the instrument by which the American people granted, or delegated, certain specific powers to the Federal government. Any power not delegated was withheld, or "reserved." As we'll see later, these principles are expressed particularly in the Ninth and Tenth Amendments, two crucial but neglected provisions of the Constitution.

Let me say it yet again: The rights of the people come from God. The powers of government come from the people. The American people delegated the specific powers they wanted the Federal government to have through the Constitution. And any additional powers they wanted to grant were supposed to be added by amendment.

It's largely because we've forgotten these simple principles that the country is in so much trouble. The powers of the Federal government have multiplied madly, with only the vaguest justifications and on the most slippery pretexts. Its chief business now is not defending our rights but taking and redistributing our wealth. It has even created its own economy, the tax economy, which is parasitical on the basic and productive voluntary economy. Even much of what passes for "national defense" is a kind of hidden entitlement program, as was illustrated when President George Bush warned some states during the 1992 campaign that Bill Clinton would destroy jobs by closing down military bases. Well, if those bases aren't necessary for our defense, they should be closed down.

Now of course nobody in American politics, not even the most fanatical liberal, will admit openly that he doesn't care what the Constitution says and isn't going to let it interfere with his agenda. Everyone professes to respect it — even the Supreme Court.

That's the problem. The U.S. Constitution serves the same function as the British royal family: it offers a comforting symbol of tradition and continuity, thereby masking a radical change in the actual system of power.

So the people who mean to do without the Constitution have come up with a slogan to keep up appearances: they say the Constitution is a "living document," which sounds like a compliment. They say it has "evolved" in response to "changing circumstances," etc. They sneer at the idea that such a mystic document could still have the same meanings it had two centuries ago, or even, I guess, sixty years ago, just before the evolutionary process started accelerating with fantastic velocity. These people, who tend with suspicious consistency to be liberals, have discovered that the Constitution, whatever it may have meant in the past, now means — again, with suspicious consistency — whatever suits their present convenience.

Do liberals want big Federal entitlement programs? Lo, the Interstate Commerce Clause turns out to mean that the big Federal programs are constitutional! Do liberals oppose capital punishment? Lo, the ban on "cruel and unusual punishment" turns out to mean that capital punishment is unconstitutional! Do liberals want abortion on demand? Lo, the Ninth and Fourteenth Amendments, plus their emanations and penumbras, turn out to mean that abortion is nothing less than a woman's constitutional right!

Can all this be blind evolution? If liberals were more religious, they might suspect the hand of Providence behind it! This marvelous "living document" never seems to impede the liberal agenda in any way. On the contrary: it always seems to demand, by a wonderful coincidence, just what liberals are prescribing on other grounds.

Take abortion. Set aside your own views and feelings about it. Is it really possible that, as the Supreme Court in effect said, all the abortion laws of all 50 states — no matter how restrictive, no matter how permissive — had always been unconstitutional? Not only that, but no previous

Court, no justice on any Court in all our history — not Marshall, not Story, not Taney, not Holmes, not Hughes, not Frankfurter, not even Warren — had ever been recorded as doubting the constitutionality of those laws. Everyone had always taken it for granted that the states had every right to enact them.

Are we supposed to believe, in all seriousness, that the Court's ruling in Roe v. Wade was a response to the text of the Constitution, the discernment of a meaning that had eluded all its predecessors, rather than an enactment of the current liberal agenda? Come now and notice that the parts of this "living document" don't develop equally or consistently. The Court has expanded the meaning of some of liberalism's pet rights, such as freedom of speech, to absurd lengths; but it has neglected or even contracted other rights, such as property rights, which liberalism is hostile to.

In order to appreciate what has happened, you have to stand back from all the details and look at the outline. What follows is a thumbnail history of the Constitution.

In the beginning the states were independent and sovereign. That is why they were called "states": a state was not yet thought of as a mere subdivision of a larger unit, as is the case now. The universal understanding was that in ratifying the Constitution, the 13 states yielded a very little of their sovereignty, but kept most of it.

Those who were reluctant to ratify generally didn't object to the powers the Constitution delegated to the Federal government. But they were suspicious: they wanted assurance that if those few powers were granted, other powers, never granted, wouldn't be seized too. In The Federalist, Hamilton and Madison argued at some length that under the proposed distribution of power the Federal government would never be able to "usurp," as they put it, those other powers. Madison wrote soothingly in Federalist No. 45 that the powers of the Federal government would be "few and defined," relating mostly to war and foreign policy, while those remaining with the states would be "numerous and indefinite," and would have to do with the everyday domestic life of the country. The word "usurpation" occurs numberless times in the ratification debates, reflecting the chief anxiety the champions of the Constitution had to allay. And as a final assurance, the Tenth Amendment stipulated that the powers not "delegated" to the Federal government were "reserved" to the separate states and to the people.

But this wasn't enough to satisfy everyone. Well-grounded fears persisted. And during the first half of the nineteenth century, nearly every president, in his inaugural message, felt it appropriate to renew the promise that the powers of the Federal government would not be exceeded, nor the reserved powers of the states transgressed. The Federal government was to remain truly Federal, with only a few specified powers, rather than "consolidated," with unlimited powers.

The Civil War, or the War Between the States if you like, resulted from the suspicion that the North meant to use the power of the Union to destroy the sovereignty of the Southern states. Whether or not that suspicion was justified, the war itself produced that very result. The South was subjugated and occupied like a conquered country. Its institutions were profoundly remade by the Federal government; the United States of America was taking on the character of an extensive, and highly centralized, empire. Similar processes were underway in Europe, as small states were consolidated into large ones, setting the stage for the tyrannies and gigantic wars of the twentieth century.

Even so, the three constitutional amendments ratified after the war contain a significant clause: "Congress shall have power to enforce this article by appropriate legislation."

Why is this significant? Because it shows that even the conquerors still understood that a new power of Congress required a constitutional amendment. It couldn't just be taken by majority vote, as it would be today. If the Congress then had wanted a national health plan, it would have begun by asking the people for an amendment to the Constitution authorizing it to legislate in the area of health care. The immediate purpose of the Fourteenth Amendment was to provide a constitutional basis for a proposed civil rights act.

But the Supreme Court soon found other uses for the Fourteenth Amendment. It began striking down state laws as unconstitutional. This was an important new twist in American constitutional law. Hamilton, in arguing for judicial review in Federalist No. 78, had envisioned the Court as a check on Congress, resisting the illicit consolidation or centralization of power. And our civics books still describe the function of checks and balances in terms of the three branches of the Federal government mutually controlling each other. But in fact, the Court was now countermanding the state legislatures, where the principle of checks and balances had no meaning, since those state legislatures had no reciprocal control on the Court. This development eventually set the stage for the convulsive Supreme Court rulings of the late twentieth century, from Brown v. Board of Education to Roe v. Wade.

The big thing to recognize here is that the Court had become the very opposite of the institution Hamilton and others had had in mind. Instead of blocking the centralization of power in the Federal government, the Court was assisting it.

The original point of the Federal system was that the Federal government would have very little to say about the internal affairs of the states. But the result of the Civil War was that the Federal government had a great deal to say about those affairs — in Northern as well as Southern states.

Note that this trend toward centralization was occurring largely under Republican presidents. The Democrat Grover Cleveland was one of the last great spokesmen for Federalism. He once vetoed a modest $10,000 Federal grant for drought relief on grounds that there was no constitutional power to do it. If that sounds archaic, remember that the Federal principle remained strong long enough that during the 1950s, the Federal highway program had to be called a "defense" measure in order to win approval, and Federal loans to college students in the 1960s were absurdly called "defense" loans for the same reason. The Tenth Amendment is a refined taste, but it has always had a few devotees.

But Federalism suffered some serious wounds during the presidency of Woodrow Wilson. First came the income tax, its constitutionality established by the Sixteenth Amendment; this meant that every U.S. citizen was now, for the first time, directly accountable to the Federal government. Then the Seventeenth Amendment required that senators be elected by popular vote rather than chosen by state legislators; this meant that the states no longer had their own representation in Congress, so that they now lost their remaining control over the Federal government. The Eighteenth Amendment, establishing Prohibition, gave the Federal government even greater powers over the country's internal affairs. All these amendments were ominous signs that Federalism was losing its traditional place in the hearts, and perhaps the minds, of Americans.

But again, notice that these expansions of Federal power were at least achieved by amending the Constitution, as the Constitution itself requires. The Constitution doesn't claim to be a "living document." It is written on paper, not rubber.

In fact, the radicals of the early twentieth century despaired of achieving socialism or communism as long as the Constitution remained. They regarded it as the critical obstacle to their plans, and thought a revolution would be necessary to remove it. As The New Republic wrote: "To have a socialist society we must have a new Constitution." That's laying it on the line!

Unfortunately, the next generation of collectivists would be less candid in their contempt for the Federal system. Once they learned to feign devotion to the Constitution they secretly regarded

as obsolete, the laborious formality of amendment would no longer be necessary. They could merely pretend that the Constitution was on their side. After Franklin Roosevelt restaffed the Supreme Court with his compliant cronies, the Federal government would be free to make up its own powers as it went along, thanks to the notion that the Constitution was a malleable "living document," whose central meaning could be changed, and even reversed, by ingenious interpretation.

Roosevelt's New Deal brought fascist-style central planning to America — what some call the "mixed economy" but Hilaire Belloc called the Servile State — and his highhanded approach to governance soon led to conflict with the Court, which found several of his chief measures unconstitutional. Early in his second term, as you know, Roosevelt retaliated by trying to "pack" the Court by increasing the number of seats. This power play alienated even many of his allies, but it turned out not to be necessary. After 1937 the Court began seeing things Roosevelt's way. It voted as he wished; several members obligingly retired; and soon he had appointed a majority of the justices. The country virtually got a new Constitution.

Roosevelt's Court soon decided that the Tenth Amendment was a "truism," of no real force. This meant that almost any Federal act was ipso facto constitutional, and the powers "reserved" to the states and the people were just leftovers the Federal government didn't want, like the meal left for the jackals by the satisfied lion. There was almost no limit, now, on what the Federal government could do. In effect, the powers of the Federal government no longer had to come from the people by constitutional delegation: they could be created by simple political power.

Roosevelt also set the baneful precedent of using entitlement programs, such as Social Security, to buy some people's votes with other people's money. It was both a fatal corruption of democracy and the realization of the Servile State in America. The class of voting parasites has been swelling ever since.

So, the New Deal didn't just expand the power of the Federal government; that had been done before. The New Deal did much deeper mischief: it struck at the whole principle of constitutional resistance to Federal expansion. Congress didn't need any constitutional amendment to increase its powers; it could increase its own powers ad hoc, at any time, by simple majority vote.

All this, of course, would have seemed monstrous to our ancestors. Even Alexander Hamilton, who favored a relatively strong central government in his time, never dreamed of a government so powerful.

The Court suffered a bloody defeat at Roosevelt's hands, and since his time it has never found a major act of Congress unconstitutional. This has allowed the power of the Federal government to grow without restraint. At the Federal level, "checks and balances" has ceased to include judicial review.

This is a startling fact, flying as it does in the face of the familiar conservative complaints about the Court's "activism." When it comes to Congress, the Court has been absolutely passive. As if to compensate for its habit of capitulation to Congress, the Court's post–World War II "activism" has been directed entirely against the states, whose laws it has struck down in areas that used to be considered their settled and exclusive provinces. Time after time, it has found "unconstitutional" laws whose legitimacy had stood unquestioned throughout the history of the Republic.

Notice how total the reversal of the Court's role has been. It began with the duty, according to Hamilton, of striking down new seizures of power by Congress. Now it finds constitutional virtually everything Congress chooses to do. The Federal government has assumed myriad new powers nowhere mentioned or implied in the Constitution, yet the Court has never seriously impeded this expansion, or rather explosion, of novel claims of power. What it finds unconstitutional are the traditional powers of the states.

The postwar Court has done pioneering work in one notable area: the separation of church and state. I said "pioneering," not praiseworthy. The Court has consistently imposed an understanding of the First Amendment that is not only exaggerated but unprecedented — most notoriously in its 1962 ruling that prayer in public schools amounts to an "establishment of religion." This interpretation of the Establishment Clause has always been to the disadvantage of Christianity and of any law with roots in Christian morality. And it's impossible to doubt that the justices who voted for this interpretation were voting their predilections.

Maybe that's the point. I've never heard it put quite this way, but the Court's boldest rulings showed something less innocent than a series of honest mistakes. Studying these cases and others of the Court's liberal heyday, one never gets the sense that the majority was suppressing its own preferences; it was clearly enacting them. Those rulings can be described as wishful thinking run amok, and touched with more than a little arrogance. All in all, the Court displayed the opposite of the restrained and impartial temperament one expects even of a traffic-court judge, let alone a Supreme Court.

It's ironic to recall Hamilton's assurance that the Supreme Court would be "the least dangerous" of the three branches of the Federal government. But Hamilton did give us a shrewd warning about what would happen if the Court were ever corrupted: in Federalist No. 78 he wrote that "liberty can have nothing to fear from the judiciary alone, but would have everything to fear from its union with either of the other [branches]." Since Franklin Roosevelt, as I've said, the judiciary has in effect formed a union with the other two branches to aggrandize the power of the Federal government at the expense of the states and the people.

This, in outline, is the constitutional history of the United States. You won't find it in the textbooks, which are required to be optimistic, to present degeneration as development, and to treat the successive pronouncements of the Supreme Court as so many oracular revelations of constitutional meaning. A leading liberal scholar, Leonard Levy, has gone so far as to say that what matters is not what the Constitution says, but what the Court has said about the Constitution in more than 400 volumes of commentary.

This can only mean that the commentary has displaced the original text, and that "We the People" have been supplanted by "We the Lawyers." We the People can't read and understand our own Constitution. We have to have it explained to us by the professionals. Moreover, if the Court enjoys oracular status, it can't really be criticized, because it can do no wrong. We may dislike its results, but future rulings will have to be derived from them as precedents, rather than from the text and logic of the Constitution. And notice that the "conservative" justices appointed by Republican presidents have by and large upheld not the original Constitution, but the most liberal interpretations of the Court itself — notably on the subject of abortion, which I'll return to in a minute.

To sum up this little constitutional history. The history of the Constitution is the story of its inversion. The original understanding of the Constitution has been reversed. The Constitution creates a presumption against any power not plainly delegated to the Federal government and a corresponding presumption in favor of the rights and powers of the states and the people. But we now have a sloppy presumption in favor of Federal power. Most people assume the Federal government can do anything it isn't plainly forbidden to do.

The Ninth and Tenth Amendments were adopted to make the principle of the Constitution as clear as possible. Hamilton, you know, argued against adding a Bill of Rights, on grounds that it would be redundant and confusing. He thought it would seem to imply that the Federal government had more powers than it had been given. Why say, he asked, that the freedom of

the press shall not be infringed, when the Federal government would have no power by which it could be infringed? And you can even make the case that he was exactly right. He understood, at any rate, that our freedom is safer if we think of the Constitution as a list of powers rather than as a list of rights.

Be that as it may, the Bill of Rights was adopted, but it was designed to meet his objection. The Ninth Amendment says: "The enumeration in the Constitution of certain rights shall not be construed to deny or disparage others retained by the people." The Tenth says: "The powers not delegated to the United States by the Constitution, nor prohibited by it to the States, are reserved to the States respectively, or to the people."

Now what these two provisions mean is pretty simple. The Ninth means that the list of the people's rights in the Constitution is not meant to be complete — that they still have many other rights, like the right to travel or to marry, which may deserve just as much respect as the right not to have soldiers quartered in one's home in peacetime. The Tenth, on the other hand, means that the list of powers "delegated" to the Federal government is complete — and that any other powers the government assumed would be, in the Framers' habitual word, "usurped."

As I said earlier, the Founders believed that our rights come from God, and the government's powers come from us. So the Constitution can't list all our rights, but it can and does list all the Federal government's powers.

You can think of the Constitution as a sort of antitrust act for government, with the Ninth and Tenth Amendments at its core. It's remarkable that the same liberals who think business monopolies are sinister think monopolies of political power are progressive. When they can't pass their programs because of the constitutional safeguards, they complain about "gridlock" — a cliché that shows they miss the whole point of the enumeration and separation of powers.

Well, I don't have to tell you that this way of thinking is absolutely alien to that of today's politicians and pundits. Can you imagine Al Gore, Dan Rostenkowski, or Tom Brokaw having a conversation about political principles with any of the Founding Fathers? If you can, you must have a vivid fantasy life.

And the result of the loss of our original political idiom has been, as I say, to invert the original presumptions. The average American, whether he has had high-school civics or a degree in political science, is apt to assume that the Constitution somehow empowers the government to do nearly anything, while implicitly limiting our rights by listing them. Not that anyone would say it this way. But it's as if the Bill of Rights had said that the enumeration of the Federal government's powers in the Constitution is not meant to deny or disparage any other powers it may choose to claim, while the rights not given to the people in the Constitution are reserved to the Federal government to give or withhold, and the states may be progressively stripped of their original powers.

What it comes to is that we don't really have an operative Constitution anymore. The Federal government defines its own powers day by day. It's limited not by the list of its powers in the Constitution, but by whatever it can get away with politically. Just as the president can now send troops abroad to fight without a declaration of war.

Congress can pass a national health care program without a constitutional delegation of power. The only restraint left is political opposition.

If you suspect I'm overstating the change from our original principles, I give you the late Justice Hugo Black. In a 1965 case called Griswold v. Connecticut, the Court struck down a law forbidding the sale of contraceptives on grounds that it violated a right of "privacy." (This supposed right, of course, became the basis for the Court's even more radical 1973 ruling in Roe v. Wade, but that's another story.) Justice Black dissented in the Griswold case on the following ground: "I like my privacy as well as the next [man]," he wrote, "but I am nevertheless compelled to admit that government has a right to invade it unless prohibited by some specific constitutional provision." What a hopelessly muddled — and really sinister — misconception of the relation between the individual and the state: government has a right to invade our privacy, unless prohibited by the Constitution. You don't have to share the Court's twisted view of the right of privacy in order to be shocked that one of its members takes this view of the "right" of government to invade privacy.

It gets crazier. In 1993 the Court handed down one of the most bizarre decisions of all time. For two decades, enemies of legal abortion had been supporting Republican candidates in the hope of filling the Court with appointees who would review Roe v. Wade. In Planned Parenthood v. Casey, the Court finally did so. But even with eight Republican appointees on the Court, the result was not what the conservatives had hoped for. The Court reaffirmed Roe.

Its reasoning was amazing. A plurality opinion — a majority of the five-justice majority in the case — admitted that the Court's previous ruling in Roe might be logically and historically vulnerable. But it held that the paramount consideration was that the Court be consistent, and not appear to be yielding to public pressure, lest it lose the respect of the public. Therefore, the Court allowed Roe to stand.

Among many things that might be said about this ruling, the most basic is this: The Court in effect declared itself a third party to the controversy, and then, setting aside the merits of the two principals' claims, ruled in its own interest! It was as if the referee in a prize fight had declared himself the winner. Cynics had always suspected that the Court did not forget its self-interest in its decisions, but they never expected to hear it say so.

The three justices who signed that opinion evidently didn't realize what they were saying. A distinguished veteran Court-watcher (who approved of Roe, by the way) told me he had never seen anything like it. The Court was actually telling us that it put its own welfare ahead of the merits of the arguments before it. In its confusion, it was blurting out the truth.

But by then very few Americans could even remember the original constitutional plan. The original plan was as Madison and Tocqueville described it: State government was to be the rule, Federal government the exception. The states' powers were to be "numerous and indefinite," Federal powers "few and defined." This is a matter not only of history, but of iron logic: The Constitution doesn't make sense when read any other way. As Madison asked, why bother listing particular Federal powers unless unlisted powers are withheld?

The unchecked Federal government has not only overflowed its banks; it has even created its own economy. Thanks to its exercise of myriad unwarranted powers, it can claim tens of millions of dependents, at least part of whose income is due to the abuse of the taxing and spending powers for their benefit: government employees, retirees, farmers, contractors, teachers, artists, even soldiers. Large numbers of these people are paid much more than their market value because the taxpayer is forced to subsidize them. By the same token, most taxpayers would instantly be better off if the Federal government simply ceased to exist — or if it suddenly returned to its constitutional functions.

Can we restore the Constitution and recover our freedom? I have no doubt that we can. Like all great reforms, it will take an intelligent, determined effort by many people. I don't want to sow false optimism.

But the time is ripe for a constitutional counter revolution. Discontent with the ruling system, as the 1992 Perot vote showed, is deep and widespread among several classes of people: Christians, conservatives, gun owners, taxpayers, and simple believers in honest government

all have their reasons. The rulers lack legitimacy and don't believe in their own power strongly enough to defend it.

The beauty of it is that the people don't have to invent a new system of government in order to get rid of this one. They only have to restore the one described in the Constitution — the system our government already professes to be upholding. Taken seriously, the Constitution would pose a serious threat to our form of government.

And for just that reason, the ruling parties will be finished as soon as the American people rediscover and awaken their dormant Constitution.

The Law

By Frédéric Bastiat, 1850 (Bastiat was a French author and economist. The following is an English translation from the original French. The original pamphlet was first published in 1850.)

The Law

The law perverted! And the police powers of the state perverted along with it! The law, I say, not only turned from its proper purpose but made to follow an entirely contrary purpose! The law become the weapon of every kind of greed! Instead of checking crime, the law itself guilty of the evils it is supposed to punish!

If this is true, it is a serious fact, and moral duty requires me to call the attention of my fellow-citizens to it.

Life Is a Gift from God

We hold from God the gift which includes all others. This gift is life — physical, intellectual, and moral life.

But life cannot maintain itself alone. The Creator of life has entrusted us with the responsibility of preserving, developing, and perfecting it. In order that we may accomplish this, He has provided us with a collection of marvelous faculties. And He has put us in the midst of a variety of natural resources. By the application of our faculties to these natural resources we convert them into products, and use them. This process is necessary in order that life may run its appointed course.

Life, faculties, production — in other words, individuality, liberty, property — this is man. And in spite of the cunning of artful political leaders, these three gifts from God precede all human legislation, and are superior to it.

Life, liberty, and property do not exist because men have made laws. On the contrary, it was the fact that life, liberty, and property existed beforehand that caused men to make laws in the first place.

What Is Law?

What, then, is law? It is the collective organization of the individual right to lawful defense.

Each of us has a natural right — from God — to defend his person, his liberty, and his property. These are the three basic requirements of life, and the preservation of any one of them is completely dependent upon the preservation of the other two. For what are our faculties but the extension of our individuality? And what is property but an extension of our faculties?

If every person has the right to defend — even by force — his person, his liberty, and his property, then it follows that a group of men have the right to organize and support a common force to protect these rights constantly. Thus the principle of collective right — its reason for existing, its lawfulness — is based on individual right. And the common force that protects this collective right cannot logically have any other purpose or any other mission than that for which it acts as a substitute. Thus, since an individual cannot lawfully use force against the person, liberty, or property of another individual, then the common force — for the same reason — cannot lawfully be used to destroy the person, liberty, or property of individuals or groups.

Such a perversion of force would be, in both cases, contrary to our premise. Force has

SPECIAL READING

been given to us to defend our own individual rights. Who will dare to say that force has been given to us to destroy the equal rights of our brothers? Since no individual acting separately can lawfully use force to destroy the rights of others, does it not logically follow that the same principle also applies to the common force that is nothing more than the organized combination of the individual forces?

If this is true, then nothing can be more evident than this: The law is the organization of the natural right of lawful defense. It is the substitution of a common force for individual forces. And this common force is to do only what the individual forces have a natural and lawful right to do: to protect persons, liberties, and properties; to maintain the right of each, and to cause justice to reign over us all.

A Just and Enduring Government

If a nation were founded on this basis, it seems to me that order would prevail among the people, in thought as well as in deed. It seems to me that such a nation would have the most simple, easy to accept, economical, limited, nonoppressive, just, and enduring government imaginable — whatever its political form might be.

Under such an administration, everyone would understand that he possessed all the privileges as well as all the responsibilities of his existence. No one would have any argument with government, provided that his person was respected, his labor was free, and the fruits of his labor were protected against all unjust attack. When successful, we would not have to thank the state for our success. And, conversely, when unsuccessful, we would no more think of blaming the state for our misfortune than would the farmers

blame the state because of hail or frost. The state would be felt only by the invaluable blessings of safety provided by this concept of government.

It can be further stated that, thanks to the non-intervention of the state in private affairs, our wants and their satisfactions would develop themselves in a logical manner. We would not see poor families seeking literary instruction before they have bread. We would not see cities populated at the expense of rural districts, nor rural districts at the expense of cities. We would not see the great displacements of capital, labor, and population that are caused by legislative decisions.

The sources of our existence are made uncertain and precarious by these state-created displacements. And, furthermore, these acts burden the government with increased responsibilities.

The Complete Perversion of the Law

But, unfortunately, law by no means confines itself to its proper functions. And when it has exceeded its proper functions, it has not done so merely in some inconsequential and debatable matters. The law has gone further than this; it has acted in direct opposition to its own purpose. The law has been used to destroy its own objective: It has been applied to annihilating the justice that it was supposed to maintain; to limiting and destroying rights which its real purpose was to respect. The law has placed the collective force at the disposal of the unscrupulous who wish, without risk,

to exploit the person, liberty, and property of others. It has converted plunder into a right, in order to protect plunder. And it has converted lawful defense into a crime, in order to punish lawful defense.

How has this perversion of the law been accomplished? And what have been the results?

The law has been perverted by the influence of two entirely different causes: stupid greed and false philanthropy. Let us speak of the first.

A Fatal Tendency of Mankind

Self-preservation and self-development are common aspirations among all people. And if everyone enjoyed the unrestricted use of his faculties and the free disposition of the fruits of his labor, social progress would be ceaseless, uninterrupted, and unfailing.

But there is also another tendency that is common among people. When they can, they wish to live and prosper at the expense of others. This is no rash accusation. Nor does it come from a gloomy and uncharitable spirit. The annals of history bear witness to the truth of it: the incessant wars, mass migrations, religious persecutions, universal slavery, dishonesty in commerce, and monopolies. This fatal desire has its origin in the very nature of man — in that primitive, universal, and insuppressible instinct that impels him to satisfy his desires with the least possible pain.

Property and Plunder

Man can live and satisfy his wants only by ceaseless labor; by the ceaseless application of his faculties to natural resources. This process is the origin of property.

But it is also true that a man may live and satisfy his wants by seizing and consuming the products of the labor of others. This process is the origin of plunder.

Now since man is naturally inclined to avoid pain — and since labor is pain in itself — it follows that men will resort to plunder whenever plunder is easier than work. History shows this quite clearly. And under these conditions, neither religion nor morality can stop it.

When, then, does plunder stop? It stops when it becomes more painful and more dangerous than labor.

It is evident, then, that the proper purpose of law is to use the power of its collective force to stop this fatal tendency to plunder instead of to work. All the measures of the law should protect property and punish plunder.

But, generally, the law is made by one man or one class of men. And since law cannot operate without the sanction and support of a dominating force, this force must be entrusted to those who make the laws.

This fact, combined with the fatal tendency that exists in the heart of man to satisfy his wants with the least possible effort, explains the almost universal perversion of the law. Thus it is easy to understand how law, instead of checking injustice, becomes the invincible weapon of injustice. It is easy to understand why the law is used by the legislator to destroy in varying degrees among the rest of the people, their personal independence by slavery, their liberty by oppression, and their property by plunder. This is done for the benefit of the person who makes the law, and in proportion to the power that he holds.

Victims of Lawful Plunder

Men naturally rebel against the injustice of which they are victims. Thus, when plunder is organized by law for the profit of those who make the law, all the plundered classes try somehow to enter — by peaceful or revolutionary means — into the making of laws. According to their degree of enlightenment, these plundered classes may propose one of two entirely different purposes when they attempt to attain political power: Either they may wish to stop lawful plunder, or they may wish to share in it.

Woe to the nation when this latter purpose prevails among the mass victims of lawful

plunder when they, in turn, seize the power to make laws!

Until that happens, the few practice lawful plunder upon the many, a common practice where the right to participate in the making of law is limited to a few persons. But then, participation in the making of law becomes universal. And then, men seek to balance their conflicting interests by universal plunder. Instead of rooting out the injustices found in society, they make these injustices general. As soon as the plundered classes gain political power, they establish a system of reprisals against other classes. They do not abolish legal plunder. (This objective would demand more enlightenment than they possess.) Instead, they emulate their evil predecessors by participating in this legal plunder, even though it is against their own interests.

It is as if it were necessary, before a reign of justice appears, for everyone to suffer a cruel retribution — some for their evilness, and some for their lack of understanding.

The Results of Legal Plunder

It is impossible to introduce into society a greater change and a greater evil than this: the conversion of the law into an instrument of plunder.

What are the consequences of such a perversion? It would require volumes to describe them all. Thus we must content ourselves with pointing out the most striking.

In the first place, it erases from everyone's conscience the distinction between justice and injustice.

No society can exist unless the laws are respected to a certain degree. The safest way to make laws respected is to make them respectable. When law and morality contradict each other, the citizen has the cruel alternative of either losing his moral sense or losing his respect for the law. These two evils are of equal consequence, and it would be difficult for a person to choose between them. The nature of law is to maintain justice. This is so much the case that, in the minds of the people, law and justice are one and the same thing. There is in all of us a strong disposition to believe that anything lawful is also legitimate. This belief is so widespread that many persons have erroneously held that things are "just" because law makes them so. Thus, in order to make plunder appear just and sacred to many consciences, it is only necessary for the law to decree and sanction it. Slavery, restrictions, and monopoly find defenders not only among those who profit from them but also among those who suffer from them.

The Fate of Non-Conformists

If you suggest a doubt as to the morality of these institutions, it is boldly said that "You are a dangerous innovator, a utopian, a theorist, a subversive; you would shatter the foundation upon which society rests."

If you lecture upon morality or upon political science, there will be found official organizations petitioning the government in this vein of thought: "That science no longer be taught exclusively from the point of view of free trade (of liberty, of property, and of justice) as has been the case until now, but also, in the future, science is to be especially taught from the viewpoint of the facts and laws that regulate French industry (facts and laws which are contrary to liberty, to property, and to justice). That, in government-endowed teaching positions, the professor rigorously refrain from endangering in the slightest degree the respect due to the laws now in force."*

General Council of Manufacturers, Agriculture, and Commerce, May 6, 1850.

Thus, if there exists a law which sanctions

slavery or monopoly, oppression or robbery, in any form whatever, it must not even be mentioned. For how can it be mentioned without damaging the respect which it inspires? Still further, morality and political economy must be taught from the point of view of this law; from the supposition that it must be a just law merely because it is a law.

Another effect of this tragic perversion of the law is that it gives an exaggerated importance to political passions and conflicts, and to politics in general.

I could prove this assertion in a thousand ways. But, by way of illustration, I shall limit myself to a subject that has lately occupied the minds of everyone: universal suffrage.

Who Shall Judge?

The followers of Rousseau's school of thought — who consider themselves far advanced, but whom I consider twenty centuries behind the times — will not agree with me on this. But universal suffrage — using the word in its strictest sense — is not one of those sacred dogmas which it is a crime to examine or doubt. In fact, serious objections may be made to universal suffrage.

In the first place, the word universal conceals a gross fallacy. For example, there are 36 million people in France. Thus, to make the right of suffrage universal, there should be 36 million voters. But the most extended system permits only 9 million people to vote. Three persons out of four are excluded. And more than this, they are excluded by the fourth. This fourth person advances the principle of incapacity as his reason for excluding the others.

Universal suffrage means, then, universal suffrage for those who are capable. But there remains this question of fact: Who is capable? Are minors, females, insane persons, and persons who have committed certain major crimes the only ones to be determined incapable?

The Reason Why Voting Is Restricted

A closer examination of the subject shows us the motive which causes the right of suffrage to be based upon the supposition of incapacity. The motive is that the elector or voter does not exercise this right for himself alone, but for everybody.

The most extended elective system and the most restricted elective system are alike in this respect. They differ only in respect to what constitutes incapacity. It is not a difference of principle, but merely a difference of degree.

If, as the republicans of our present-day Greek and Roman schools of thought pretend, the right of suffrage arrives with one's birth, it would be an injustice for adults to prevent women and children from voting. Why are they prevented? Because they are presumed to be incapable. And why is incapacity a motive for exclusion? Because it is not the voter alone who suffers the consequences of his vote; because each vote touches and affects everyone in the entire community; because the people in the community have a right to demand some safeguards concerning the acts upon which their welfare and existence depend.

The Answer Is to Restrict the Law

I know what might be said in answer to this; what the objections might be. But this is not the place to exhaust a controversy of this nature. I wish merely to observe here that this controversy over universal suffrage (as well as most other political questions) which agitates, excites, and overthrows nations, would lose nearly all of its importance if the law had always been what it ought to be.

In fact, if law were restricted to protecting all persons, all liberties, and all properties; if law were nothing more than the organized combination of the individual's right to self defense; if law were the obstacle, the check, the punisher of all oppression and plunder — is it likely that we citizens would then argue much about the extent of the franchise?

Under these circumstances, is it likely that the extent of the right to vote would endanger that supreme good, the public peace? Is it likely that the excluded classes would refuse to peaceably await the coming of their right to vote? Is it likely that those who had the right to vote would jealously defend their privilege?

If the law were confined to its proper functions, everyone's interest in the law would be the same. Is it not clear that, under these circumstances, those who voted could not inconvenience those who did not vote?

The Fatal Idea of Legal Plunder

But on the other hand, imagine that this fatal principle has been introduced: Under the pretense of organization, regulation, protection, or encouragement, the law takes property from one person and gives it to another; the law takes the wealth of all and gives it to a few — whether farmers, manufacturers, ship owners, artists, or comedians. Under these circumstances, then certainly every class will aspire to grasp the law, and logically so.

The excluded classes will furiously demand their right to vote — and will overthrow society rather than not to obtain it. Even beggars and vagabonds will then prove to you that they also have an incontestable title to vote. They will say to you: "We cannot buy wine, tobacco, or salt without paying the tax. And a part of the tax that we pay is given by law — in privileges and subsidies — to men who are richer than we are. Others use the law to raise the prices of bread, meat, iron, or cloth. Thus, since everyone else uses the law for his own profit, we also would like to use the law for our own profit. We demand from the law the right to relief, which is the poor man's plunder. To obtain this right, we also should be voters and legislators in order that we may organize Beggary on a grand scale for our own class, as you have organized Protection on a grand scale for your class. Now don't tell us beggars that you will act for us, and then toss us, as Mr. Mimerel proposes, 600,000 francs to keep us quiet, like throwing us a bone to gnaw. We have other claims. And anyway, we wish to bargain for ourselves as other classes have bargained for themselves!"

And what can you say to answer that argument!

Perverted Law Causes Conflict

As long as it is admitted that the law may be diverted from its true purpose — that it may violate property instead of protecting it — then everyone will want to participate in making the law, either to protect himself against plunder or to use it for plunder. Political questions will always be prejudicial, dominant, and all-absorbing. There will be fighting at the door of the Legislative Palace, and the struggle within will be no less furious. To know this, it is hardly necessary to examine what transpires in the French and English legislatures; merely to understand the issue is to know the answer.

Is there any need to offer proof that this odious perversion of the law is a perpetual source of hatred and discord; that it tends to destroy society itself? If such proof is needed, look at the United States [in 1850]. There is no country in the world where the law is kept more within its proper domain: the protection of every person's liberty and property. As a consequence of this, there appears to be no country in the world where the social order rests on a firmer foundation.

But even in the United States, there are two issues — and only two — that have always endangered the public peace.

Slavery and Tariffs Are Plunder

What are these two issues? They are slavery and tariffs. These are the only two issues where, contrary to the general spirit of the republic of the United States, law has assumed the character of plunder.

Slavery is a violation, by law, of liberty. The protective tariff is a violation, by law, of property.

It is a most remarkable fact that this double legal crime — a sorrowful inheritance of the Old World — should be the only issue which can, and perhaps will, lead to the ruin of the Union. It is indeed impossible to imagine, at the very heart of a society, a more astounding fact than this: The law has come to be an instrument of injustice. And if this fact brings terrible consequences to the United States — where only in the instance of slavery and tariffs — what must be the consequences in Europe, where the perversion of law is a principle; a system?

Two Kinds of Plunder

Mr. de Montalembert [politician and writer] adopting the thought contained in a famous proclamation by Mr. Carlier, has said: "We must make war against socialism." According to the definition of socialism advanced by Mr. Charles Dupin, he meant: "We must make war against plunder."

But of what plunder was he speaking? For there are two kinds of plunder: legal and illegal.

I do not think that illegal plunder, such as theft or swindling — which the penal code defines, anticipates, and punishes — can be called socialism. It is not this kind of plunder that systematically threatens the foundations of society. Anyway, the war against this kind of plunder has not waited for the command of these gentlemen. The war against illegal plunder has been fought since the beginning of the world. Long before the Revolution of February 1848 — long before the appearance even of socialism itself — France had provided police, judges, gendarmes, prisons, dungeons, and scaffolds for the purpose of fighting illegal plunder. The law itself conducts this war, and it is my wish and opinion that the law should always maintain this attitude toward plunder.

The Law Defends Plunder

But it does not always do this. Sometimes the law defends plunder and participates in it. Thus the beneficiaries are spared the shame, danger, and scruple which their acts would otherwise involve. Sometimes the law places the whole apparatus of judges, police, prisons, and gendarmes at the service of the plunderers, and treats the victim — when he defends himself — as a criminal. In short, there is a legal plunder, and it is of this, no doubt, that Mr. de Montalembert speaks.

This legal plunder may be only an isolated stain among the legislative measures of the people. If so, it is best to wipe it out with a minimum of speeches and denunciations — and in spite of the uproar of the vested interests.

How to Identify Legal Plunder

But how is this legal plunder to be identified? Quite simply. See if the law takes from some persons what belongs to them, and gives it to other persons to whom it does not belong. See

if the law benefits one citizen at the expense of another by doing what the citizen himself cannot do without committing a crime.

Then abolish this law without delay, for it is not only an evil itself, but also it is a fertile source for further evils because it invites reprisals. If such a law — which may be an isolated case — is not abolished immediately, it will spread, multiply, and develop into a system.

The person who profits from this law will complain bitterly, defending his acquired rights. He will claim that the state is obligated to protect and encourage his particular industry; that this procedure enriches the state because the protected industry is thus able to spend more and to pay higher wages to the poor workingmen. Do not listen to this sophistry by vested interests. The acceptance of these arguments will build legal plunder into a whole system. In fact, this has already occurred. The present-day delusion is an attempt to enrich everyone at the expense of everyone else; to make plunder universal under the pretense of organizing it.

Legal Plunder Has Many Names

Now, legal plunder can be committed in an infinite number of ways. Thus we have an infinite number of plans for organizing it: tariffs, protection, benefits, subsidies, encouragements, progressive taxation, public schools, guaranteed jobs, guaranteed profits, minimum wages, a right to relief, a right to the tools of labor, free credit, and so on, and so on. All these plans as a whole — with their common aim of legal plunder — constitute socialism.

Now, since under this definition socialism is a body of doctrine, what attack can be made against it other than a war of doctrine? If you find this socialistic doctrine to be false, absurd, and evil, then refute it. And the more false, the more absurd, and the more evil it is, the easier it will be to refute. Above all, if you wish to be strong, begin by rooting out every particle of socialism that may have crept into your legislation. This will be no light task.

Socialism Is Legal Plunder

Mr. de Montalembert has been accused of desiring to fight socialism by the use of brute force. He ought to be exonerated from this accusation, for he has plainly said: "The war that we must fight against socialism must be in harmony with law, honor, and justice."

But why does not Mr. de Montalembert see that he has placed himself in a vicious circle? You would use the law to oppose socialism? But it is upon the law that socialism itself relies. Socialists desire to practice legal plunder, not illegal plunder. Socialists, like all other monopolists, desire to make the law their own weapon. And when once the law is on the side of socialism, how can it be used against socialism? For when plunder is abetted by the law, it does not fear your courts, your gendarmes, and your prisons. Rather, it may call upon them for help.

To prevent this, you would exclude socialism from entering into the making of laws? You would prevent socialists from entering the Legislative Palace? You shall not succeed, I predict, so long as legal plunder continues to be the main business of the legislature. It is illogical — in fact, absurd — to assume otherwise.

The Choice Before Us

This question of legal plunder must be settled once and for all, and there are only three ways to settle it:

1. The few plunder the many.
2. Everybody plunders everybody.
3. Nobody plunders anybody.

We must make our choice among limited plunder, universal plunder, and no plunder. The law can follow only one of these three.

Limited legal plunder: This system prevailed when the right to vote was restricted. One would turn back to this system to prevent the invasion of socialism.

Universal legal plunder: We have been threatened with this system since the franchise was made universal. The newly enfranchised majority has decided to formulate law on the same principle of legal plunder that was used by their predecessors when the vote was limited.

No legal plunder: This is the principle of justice, peace, order, stability, harmony, and logic. Until the day of my death, I shall proclaim this principle with all the force of my lungs (which alas! is all too inadequate).*

*Translator's note: At the time this was written, Mr. Bastiat knew that he was dying of tuberculosis. Within a year, he was dead.

The Proper Function of the Law

And, in all sincerity, can anything more than the absence of plunder be required of the law? Can the law — which necessarily requires the use of force — rationally be used for anything except protecting the rights of everyone? I defy anyone to extend it beyond this purpose without perverting it and, consequently, turning might against right. This is the most fatal and most illogical social perversion that can possibly be imagined. It must be admitted that the true solution — so long searched for in the area of social relationships — is contained in these simple words: Law is organized justice.

Now this must be said: When justice is organized by law — that is, by force — this excludes the idea of using law (force) to organize any human activity whatever, whether it be labor, charity, agriculture, commerce, industry, education, art, or religion. The organizing by law of any one of these would inevitably destroy the essential organization — justice. For truly, how can we imagine force being used against the liberty of citizens without it also being used against justice, and thus acting against its proper purpose?

The Seductive Lure of Socialism

Here I encounter the most popular fallacy of our times. It is not considered sufficient that the law should be just; it must be philanthropic. Nor is it sufficient that the law should guarantee to every citizen the free and inoffensive use of his faculties for physical, intellectual, and moral self-improvement. Instead, it is demanded that the law should directly extend welfare, education, and morality throughout the nation.

This is the seductive lure of socialism. And I repeat again: These two uses of the law are in direct contradiction to each other. We must choose between them. A citizen cannot at the same time be free and not free.

Enforced Fraternity Destroys Liberty

Mr. de Lamartine once wrote to me thusly: "Your doctrine is only the half of my program. You have stopped at liberty; I go on to fraternity." I answered him: "The second half of your program will destroy the first."

In fact, it is impossible for me to separate the word fraternity from the word voluntary. I cannot possibly understand how fraternity can be legally enforced without liberty being legally destroyed, and thus justice being legally trampled underfoot.

Legal plunder has two roots: One of them, as I have said before, is in human greed; the other is in false philanthropy. At this point, I think that I should explain exactly what I mean by the word plunder.*

Translator's note: The French word used by Mr. Bastiat is spoliation.

Plunder Violates Ownership

I do not, as is often done, use the word in any vague, uncertain, approximate, or metaphorical sense. I use it in its scientific acceptance — as expressing the idea opposite to that of property [wages, land, money, or whatever]. When a portion of wealth is transferred from the person who owns it — without his consent and without compensation, and whether by force or by fraud — to anyone who does not own it, then I say that property is violated; that an act of plunder is committed.

I say that this act is exactly what the law is supposed to suppress, always and everywhere. When the law itself commits this act that it is supposed to suppress, I say that plunder is still committed, and I add that from the point of view of society and welfare, this aggression against rights is even worse. In this case of legal plunder, however, the person who receives the benefits is not responsible for the act of plundering. The responsibility for this legal plunder rests with the law, the legislator, and society itself. Therein lies the political danger.

It is to be regretted that the word plunder is offensive. I have tried in vain to find an inoffensive word, for I would not at any time — especially now — wish to add an irritating word to our dissentions. Thus, whether I am believed or not, I declare that I do not mean to attack the intentions or the morality of anyone. Rather, I am attacking an idea which I believe to be false; a system which appears to me to be unjust; an injustice so independent of personal intentions that each of us profits from it without wishing to do so, and suffers from it without knowing the cause of the suffering.

Three Systems of Plunder

The sincerity of those who advocate protectionism, socialism, and communism is not here questioned. Any writer who would do that must be influenced by a political spirit or a political fear. It is to be pointed out, however, that protectionism, socialism, and communism are basically the same plant in three different stages of its growth. All that can be said is that legal plunder is more visible in communism because it is complete plunder; and in protectionism because the plunder is limited to specific groups and industries.* Thus it follows that, of the three systems, socialism is the vaguest, the most indecisive, and, consequently, the most sincere stage of development.

If the special privilege of government protection against competition — a monopoly — were granted only to one group in France, *the iron workers, for instance, this act would so obviously be legal plunder that it could not last for long. It is for this reason that we see all the protected trades combined into a common cause. They even organize themselves in such a manner as to appear to represent all persons who labor. Instinctively, they feel that legal plunder is concealed by generalizing it.*

But sincere or insincere, the intentions of persons are not here under question. In fact, I have already said that legal plunder is based partially on philanthropy, even though it is a false philanthropy.

With this explanation, let us examine the value — the origin and the tendency — of this popular aspiration which claims to accomplish the general welfare by general plunder.

Law Is Force

Since the law organizes justice, the socialists ask why the law should not also organize labor, education, and religion.

Why should not law be used for these purposes? Because it could not organize labor, education, and religion without destroying justice. We must remember that law is force, and that, consequently, the proper functions of the law cannot lawfully extend beyond the proper functions of force.

When law and force keep a person within the bounds of justice, they impose nothing but a mere negation. They oblige him only to abstain from harming others. They violate neither his personality, his liberty, nor his property. They safeguard all of these. They are defensive; they defend equally the rights of all.

Law Is a Negative Concept

The harmlessness of the mission performed by law and lawful defense is self-evident; the usefulness is obvious; and the legitimacy cannot be disputed.

As a friend of mine once remarked, this negative concept of law is so true that the statement, the purpose of the law is to cause justice to reign, is not a rigorously accurate statement. It ought to be stated that the purpose of the law is to prevent injustice from reigning. In fact, it is injustice, instead of justice, that has an existence of its own. Justice is achieved only when injustice is absent.

But when the law, by means of its necessary agent, force, imposes upon men a regulation of labor, a method or a subject of education, a religious faith or creed — then the law is no longer negative; it acts positively upon people. It substitutes the will of the legislator for their own wills; the initiative of the legislator for their own initiatives. When this happens, the people no longer need to discuss, to compare, to plan ahead; the law does all this for them. Intelligence becomes a useless prop for the people; they cease to be men; they lose their personality, their liberty, their property.

Try to imagine a regulation of labor imposed by force that is not a violation of liberty; a transfer of wealth imposed by force that is not a violation of property. If you cannot reconcile these contradictions, then you must conclude that the law cannot organize labor and industry without organizing injustice.

The Political Approach

When a politician views society from the seclusion of his office, he is struck by the spectacle of the inequality that he sees. He deplores the deprivations which are the lot of so many of our brothers, deprivations which appear to be even sadder when contrasted with luxury and wealth.

Perhaps the politician should ask himself whether this state of affairs has not been caused by old conquests and lootings, and by more recent legal plunder. Perhaps he should consider this proposition: Since all persons seek well-being and perfection, would not a condition of justice be sufficient to cause the greatest efforts toward progress, and the greatest possible equality that is compatible with individual responsibility? Would not this be in accord with the concept of individual responsibility which God has willed in order that mankind may have the choice between vice and virtue, and the resulting punishment and reward?

But the politician never gives this a thought. His mind turns to organizations, combinations, and arrangements — legal or apparently legal. He attempts to remedy the evil by increasing and perpetuating the very thing that caused the evil in the first place:

legal plunder. We have seen that justice is a negative concept. Is there even one of these positive legal actions that does not contain the principle of plunder?

The Law and Charity

You say: "There are persons who have no money," and you turn to the law. But the law is not a breast that fills itself with milk. Nor are the lacteal veins of the law supplied with milk from a source outside the society. Nothing can enter the public treasury for the benefit of one citizen or one class unless other citizens and other classes have been forced to send it in. If every person draws from the treasury the amount that he has put in it, it is true that the law then plunders nobody. But this procedure does nothing for the persons who have no money. It does not promote equality of income. The law can be an instrument of equalization only as it takes from some persons and gives to other persons. When the law does this, it is an instrument of plunder.

With this in mind, examine the protective tariffs, subsidies, guaranteed profits, guaranteed jobs, relief and welfare schemes, public education, progressive taxation, free credit, and public works. You will find that they are always based on legal plunder, organized injustice.

The Law and Education

You say: "There are persons who lack education," and you turn to the law. But the law is not, in itself, a torch of learning which shines its light abroad. The law extends over a society where some persons have knowledge and others do not; where some citizens need to learn, and others can teach. In this matter of education, the law has only two alternatives: It can permit this transaction of teaching-and-learning to operate freely and without the use of force, or it can force human wills in this matter by taking from some of them enough to pay the teachers who are appointed by government to instruct others, without charge. But in this second case, the law commits legal plunder by violating liberty and property.

The Law and Morals

You say: "Here are persons who are lacking in morality or religion," and you turn to the law. But law is force. And need I point out what a violent and futile effort it is to use force in the matters of morality and religion?

It would seem that socialists, however self-complacent, could not avoid seeing this monstrous legal plunder that results from such systems and such efforts. But what do the socialists do? They cleverly disguise this legal plunder from others — and even from themselves — under the seductive names of fraternity, unity, organization, and association. Because we ask so little from the law — only justice — the socialists thereby assume that we reject fraternity, unity, organization, and association. The socialists brand us with the name individualist.

But we assure the socialists that we repudiate only forced organization, not natural organization. We repudiate the forms of association that are forced upon us, not free association. We repudiate forced fraternity, not true fraternity. We repudiate the artificial unity that does nothing more than deprive persons of individual responsibility. We do not repudiate the natural unity of mankind under Providence.

A Confusion of Terms

Socialism, like the ancient ideas from which it springs, confuses the distinction between government and society. As a result of this, every time we object to a thing being done by government, the socialists conclude that we object to its being done at all.

We disapprove of state education. Then the socialists say that we are opposed to any education. We object to a state religion. Then the socialists say that we want no religion at all. We object to a state-enforced equality. Then they say that we are against equality. And so on, and so on. It is as if the socialists were to accuse us of not wanting persons to eat because we do not want the state to raise grain.

The Influence of Socialist Writers

How did politicians ever come to believe this weird idea that the law could be made to produce what it does not contain — the wealth, science, and religion that, in a positive sense, constitute prosperity? Is it due to the influence of our modern writers on public affairs?

Present-day writers — especially those of the socialist school of thought — base their various theories upon one common hypothesis: They divide mankind into two parts. People in general — with the exception of the writer himself — from the first group. The writer, all alone, forms the second and most important group. Surely this is the weirdest and most conceited notion that ever entered a human brain!

In fact, these writers on public affairs begin by supposing that people have within themselves no means of discernment; no motivation to action. The writers assume that people are inert matter, passive particles, motionless atoms, at best a kind of vegetation indifferent to its own manner of existence. They assume that people are susceptible to being shaped — by the will and hand of another person — into an infinite variety of forms, more or less symmetrical, artistic, and perfected. Moreover, not one of these writers on governmental affairs hesitates to imagine that he himself — under the title of organizer, discoverer, legislator, or founder — is this will and hand, this universal motivating force, this creative power whose sublime mission is to mold these scattered materials — persons — into a society.

These socialist writers look upon people in the same manner that the gardener views his trees. Just as the gardener capriciously shapes the trees into pyramids, parasols, cubes, vases, fans, and other forms, just so does the socialist writer whimsically shape human beings into groups, series, centers, sub-centers, honeycombs, labor corps, and other variations. And just as the gardener needs axes, pruning hooks, saws, and shears to shape his trees, just so does the socialist writer need the force that he can find only in law to shape human beings. For this purpose, he devises tariff laws, tax laws, relief laws, and school laws.

The Socialists Wish to Play God

Socialists look upon people as raw material to be formed into social combinations. This is so true that, if by chance, the socialists have any doubts about the success of these combinations, they will demand that a small portion of mankind be set aside to experiment upon. The popular idea of trying all systems is well known. And one socialist leader has been known seriously to demand that the Constituent Assembly give him a small district with all its inhabitants, to try his experiments upon.

In the same manner, an inventor makes a model before he constructs the full-sized machine; the chemist wastes some chemicals — the farmer wastes some seeds and land — to try out an idea.

263

But what a difference there is between the gardener and his trees, between the inventor and his machine, between the chemist and his elements, between the farmer and his seeds! And in all sincerity, the socialist thinks that there is the same difference between him and mankind!

It is no wonder that the writers of the nineteenth century look upon society as an artificial creation of the legislator's genius. This idea — the fruit of classical education — has taken possession of all the intellectuals and famous writers of our country. To these intellectuals and writers, the relationship between persons and the legislator appears to be the same as the relationship between the clay and the potter.

Moreover, even where they have consented to recognize a principle of action in the heart of man — and a principle of discernment in man's intellect — they have considered these gifts from God to be fatal gifts. They have thought that persons, under the impulse of these two gifts, would fatally tend to ruin themselves. They assume that if the legislators left persons free to follow their own inclinations, they would arrive at atheism instead of religion, ignorance instead of knowledge, poverty instead of production and exchange.

The Socialists Despise Mankind

According to these writers, it is indeed fortunate that Heaven has bestowed upon certain men — governors and legislators — the exact opposite inclinations, not only for their own sake but also for the sake of the rest of the world! While mankind tends toward evil, the legislators yearn for good; while mankind advances toward darkness, the legislators aspire for enlightenment; while mankind is drawn toward vice, the legislators are attracted toward virtue. Since they have decided that this is the true state of affairs, they then demand the use of force in order to substitute their own inclinations for those of the human race.

Open at random any book on philosophy, politics, or history, and you will probably see how deeply rooted in our country is this idea — the child of classical studies, the mother of socialism. In all of them, you will probably find this idea that mankind is merely inert matter, receiving life, organization, morality, and prosperity from the power of the state. And even worse, it will be stated that mankind tends toward degeneration, and is stopped from this downward course only by the mysterious hand of the legislator. Conventional classical thought everywhere says that behind passive society there is a concealed power called law or legislator (or called by some other terminology that designates some unnamed person or persons of undisputed influence and authority) which moves, controls, benefits, and improves mankind.

A Defense of Compulsory Labor

Let us first consider a quotation from Bossuet [tutor to the Dauphin in the Court of Louis XIV]:*

"One of the things most strongly impressed (by whom?) upon the minds of the Egyptians was patriotism.... No one was permitted to be useless to the state. The law assigned to each one his work, which was handed down from father to son. No one was permitted to have two professions. Nor could a person change from one job to another.... But there was one task to which all were forced to conform: the study of the laws and of wisdom. Ignorance of religion and of the political regulations of the country was not excused under any circumstances. Moreover, each occupation was assigned (by whom?) to a certain

district.... Among the good laws, one of the best was that everyone was trained (by whom?) to obey them. As a result of this, Egypt was filled with wonderful inventions, and nothing was neglected that could make life easy and quiet."

*Translator's note: The parenthetical expressions and the italicized words throughout this book were supplied by Mr. Bastiat. All subheads and bracketed material were supplied by the translator.

Thus, according to Bossuet, persons derive nothing from themselves. Patriotism, prosperity, inventions, husbandry, science — all of these are given to the people by the operation of the laws, the rulers. All that the people have to do is to bow to leadership.

A Defense of Paternal Government

Bossuet carries this idea of the state as the source of all progress even so far as to defend the Egyptians against the charge that they rejected wrestling and music. He said:

> "How is that possible? These arts were invented by Trismegistus [who was alleged to have been Chancellor to the Egyptian god Osiris]."

And again among the Persians, Bossuet claims that all comes from above:

> *"One of the first responsibilities of the prince was to encourage agriculture.... Just as there were offices established for the regulation of armies, just so were there offices for the direction of farm work.... The Persian people were inspired with an overwhelming respect for royal authority."*

And according to Bossuet, the Greek people, although exceedingly intelligent, had no sense of personal responsibility; like dogs and horses, they themselves could not have invented the most simple games:

> *"The Greeks, naturally intelligent and courageous, had been early cultivated by the kings and settlers who had come from Egypt. From these Egyptian rulers, the Greek people had learned bodily exercises, foot races, and horse and chariot races.... But the best thing that the Egyptians had taught the Greeks was to become docile, and to permit themselves to be formed by the law for the public good."*

The Idea of Passive Mankind

It cannot be disputed that these classical theories [advanced by these latter-day teachers, writers, legislators, economists, and philosophers] held that everything came to the people from a source outside themselves. As another example, take Fenelon [archbishop, author, and instructor to the Duke of Burgundy].

He was a witness to the power of Louis XIV. This, plus the fact that he was nurtured in the classical studies and the admiration of antiquity, naturally caused Fenelon to accept the idea that mankind should be passive; that the misfortunes and the prosperity — vices and virtues — of people are caused by the external influence exercised upon them by the law and the legislators. Thus, in his Utopia of Salentum,

he puts men — with all their interests, faculties, desires, and possessions — under the absolute discretion of the legislator. Whatever the issue may be, persons do not decide it for themselves; the prince decides for them. The prince is depicted as the soul of this shapeless mass of people who form the nation. In the prince resides the thought, the foresight, all progress, and the principle of all organization. Thus all responsibility rests with him.

The whole of the tenth book of Fenelon's Telemachus proves this. I refer the reader to it, and content myself with quoting at random from this celebrated work to which, in every other respect, I am the first to pay homage.

SPECIAL READING

Socialists Ignore Reason and Facts

With the amazing credulity which is typical of the classicists, Fenelon ignores the authority of reason and facts when he attributes the general happiness of the Egyptians, not to their own wisdom but to the wisdom of their kings:

"We could not turn our eyes to either shore without seeing rich towns and country estates most agreeably located; fields, never fallowed, covered with golden crops every year; meadows full of flocks; workers bending under the weight of the fruit which the earth lavished upon its cultivators; shepherds who made the echoes resound with the soft notes from their pipes and flutes. "Happy," said Mentor, "is the people governed by a wise king. . ."

Later, Mentor desired that I observe the contentment and abundance which covered all Egypt, where twenty-two thousand cities could be counted. He admired the good police regulations in the cities; the justice rendered in favor of the poor against the rich; the sound education of the children in obedience, labor, sobriety, and the love of the arts and letters; the exactness with which all religious ceremonies were performed; the unselfishness, the high regard for honor, the faithfulness to men, and the fear of the gods which every father taught his children. He never stopped admiring the prosperity of the country. "Happy," said he, "is the people ruled by a wise king in such a manner."

Socialists Want to Regiment People

Fenelon's idyll on Crete is even more alluring. Mentor is made to say:

"All that you see in this wonderful island results from the laws of Minos. The education which he ordained for the children makes their bodies strong and robust. From the very beginning, one accustoms the children to a life of frugality and labor, because one assumes that all pleasures of the senses weaken both body and mind. Thus one allows them no pleasure except that of becoming invincible by virtue, and of acquiring glory.... Here one punishes three vices that go unpunished among other people: ingratitude, hypocrisy, and greed. There

is no need to punish persons for pomp and dissipation, for they are unknown in Crete.... No costly furniture, no magnificent clothing, no delicious feasts, no gilded palaces are permitted."

Thus does Mentor prepare his student to mold and to manipulate — doubtless with the best of intentions — the people of Ithaca. And to convince the student of the wisdom of these ideas, Mentor recites to him the example of Salentum.

It is from this sort of philosophy that we receive our first political ideas! We are taught to treat persons much as an instructor in agriculture teaches farmers to prepare and tend the soil.

A Famous Name and an Evil Idea

Now listen to the great Montesquieu on this same subject:

"To maintain the spirit of commerce, it is necessary that all the laws must favor it. These laws, by proportionately dividing up the fortunes as they are made in commerce,

should provide every poor citizen with sufficiently easy circumstances to enable him to work like the others. These same laws should put every rich citizen in such lowered circumstances as to force him to work in order to keep or to gain."

Thus the laws are to dispose of all fortunes!

Although real equality is the soul of the state in a democracy, yet this is so difficult to establish that an extreme precision in this matter would not always be desirable. It is sufficient that there be established a census to reduce or fix these differences in wealth within a certain limit. After this is done, it remains for specific laws to equalize inequality by imposing burdens upon the rich and granting relief to the poor.

Here again we find the idea of equalizing fortunes by law, by force.

In Greece, there were two kinds of republics, One, Sparta, was military; the other, Athens, was commercial. In the former, it was desired that the citizens be idle; in the latter, love of labor was encouraged.

Note the marvelous genius of these legislators: By debasing all established customs — by mixing the usual concepts of all virtues — they knew in advance that the world would admire their wisdom.

Lycurgus gave stability to his city of Sparta by combining petty thievery with the soul of justice; by combining the most complete bondage with the most extreme liberty; by combining the most atrocious beliefs with the greatest moderation. He appeared to deprive his city of all its resources, arts, commerce, money, and defenses. In Sparta, ambition went without the hope of material reward. Natural affection found no outlet because a man was neither son, husband, nor father. Even chastity was no longer considered becoming. By this road, Lycurgus led Sparta on to greatness and glory. This boldness which was to be found in the institutions of Greece has been repeated in the midst of the degeneracy and corruption of our modern times. An occasional honest legislator has molded a people in whom integrity appears as natural as courage in the Spartans.

Mr. William Penn, for example, is a true Lycurgus. Even though Mr. Penn had peace as his objective — while Lycurgus had war as his objective — they resemble each other in that their moral prestige over free men allowed them to overcome prejudices, to subdue passions, and to lead their respective peoples into new paths.

The country of Paraguay furnishes us with another example [of a people who, for their own good, are molded by their legislators].*

*Translator's note: What was then known as Paraguay was a much larger area than it is today. It was colonized by the Jesuits who settled the Indians into villages, and generally saved them from further brutalities by the avid conquerors.

Now it is true that if one considers the sheer pleasure of commanding to be the greatest joy in life, he contemplates a crime against society; it will, however, always be a noble ideal to govern men in a manner that will make them happier.

Those who desire to establish similar institutions must do as follows: Establish common ownership of property as in the republic of Plato; revere the gods as Plato commanded; prevent foreigners from mingling with the people, in order to preserve the customs; let the state, instead of the citizens, establish commerce. The legislators should supply arts instead of luxuries; they should satisfy needs instead of desires.

A Frightful Idea

Those who are subject to vulgar infatuation may exclaim: "Montesquieu has said this! So it's magnificent! It's sublime!" As for me, I have the courage of my own opinion. I say: What! You have the nerve to call that fine? It is frightful! It is abominable! These random selections from the writings of Montesquieu show that he considers persons, liberties, property — mankind itself — to be nothing but materials for legislators to exercise their wisdom upon.

The Leader of the Democrats

Now let us examine Rousseau on this subject. This writer on public affairs is the supreme authority of the democrats. And although he bases the social structure upon the will of the people, he has, to a greater extent than anyone else, completely accepted the theory of the total inertness of mankind in the presence of the legislators:

> *"If it is true that a great prince is rare, then is it not true that a great legislator is even more rare? The prince has only to follow the pattern that the legislator creates. The legislator is the mechanic who invents the machine; the prince is merely the workman who sets it in motion.*
>
> *And what part do persons play in all this? They are merely the machine that is set in motion. In fact, are they not merely considered to be the raw material of which the machine is made?"*

Thus the same relationship exists between the legislator and the prince as exists between the agricultural expert and the farmer; and the relationship between the prince and his subjects is the same as that between the farmer and his land. How high above mankind, then, has this writer on public affairs been placed? Rousseau rules over legislators themselves, and teaches them their trade in these imperious terms:

> *"Would you give stability to the state? Then bring the extremes as closely together as possible. Tolerate neither wealthy persons nor beggars.*
>
> *If the soil is poor or barren, or the country too small for its inhabitants, then turn to industry and arts, and trade these products for the foods that you need.... On a fertile soil — if you are short of inhabitants — devote all your attention to agriculture, because this multiplies people; banish the arts, because they only serve to depopulate the nation....*

> *If you have extensive and accessible coast lines, then cover the sea with merchant ships; you will have a brilliant but short existence. If your seas wash only inaccessible cliffs, let the people be barbarous and eat fish; they will live more quietly — perhaps better — and, most certainly, they will live more happily.*
>
> *In short, and in addition to the maxims that are common to all, every people has its own particular circumstances. And this fact in itself will cause legislation appropriate to the circumstances. This is the reason why the Hebrews formerly — and, more recently, the Arabs — had religion as their principle objective. The objective of the Athenians was literature; of Carthage and Tyre, commerce; of Rhodes, naval affairs; of Sparta, war; and of Rome, virtue. The author of The Spirit of Laws has shown by what art the legislator should direct his institutions toward each of these objectives.... But suppose that the legislator mistakes his proper objective, and acts on a principle different from that indicated by the nature of things? Suppose that the selected principle sometimes creates slavery, and sometimes liberty; sometimes wealth, and sometimes population; sometimes peace, and sometimes conquest? This confusion of objective will slowly enfeeble the law and impair the constitution. The state will be subjected to ceaseless agitations until it is destroyed or changed, and invincible nature regains her empire."*

But if nature is sufficiently invincible to regain its empire, why does not Rousseau admit that it did not need the legislator to gain it in the first place? Why does he not see that men, by obeying their own instincts, would turn to farming on fertile soil, and to commerce on an extensive and easily accessible coast, without the interference of a Lycurgus or a Solon or a Rousseau who might easily be mistaken.

Socialists Want Forced Conformity

Be that as it may, Rousseau invests the creators, organizers, directors, legislators, and controllers of society with a terrible responsibility. He is, therefore, most exacting with them:

> *"He who would dare to undertake the political creation of a people ought to believe that he can, in a manner of speaking, transform human nature; transform each individual — who, by himself, is a solitary and perfect whole — into a mere part of a greater whole from which the individual will henceforth receive his life and being. Thus the person who would undertake the political creation of a people should believe in his ability to alter man's constitution; to strengthen it; to substitute for the physical and independent existence received from nature, an existence which is partial and moral.* In short, the would-be creator of political man must remove man's own forces and endow him with others that are naturally alien to him."*

Poor human nature! What would become of a person's dignity if it were entrusted to the followers of Rousseau?

*Translator's note: According to Rousseau, the existence of social man is partial in the sense that he is henceforth merely a part of society. Knowing himself as such — and thinking and feeling from the point of view of the whole - he thereby becomes moral.

Legislators Desire to Mold Mankind

Now let us examine Raynal on this subject of mankind being molded by the legislator:

> *"The legislator must first consider the climate, the air, and the soil. The resources at his disposal determine his duties. He must first consider his locality. A population living on maritime shores must have laws designed for navigation.... If it is an inland settlement, the legislator must make his plans according to the nature and fertility of the soil....*
>
> *It is especially in the distribution of property that the genius of the legislator will be found. As a general rule, when a new colony is established in any country, sufficient land should be given to each man to support his family.... On an uncultivated island that you are populating with children, you need do nothing but let the seeds of truth germinate along with the development of reason…*
>
> *But when you resettle a nation with a past into a new country, the skill of the legislator rests in the policy of permitting the people to retain no injurious opinions and customs which can possibly be cured and corrected. If you desire to prevent these opinions and customs from becoming permanent, you will secure the second generation by a general system of public education for the children. A prince or a legislator should never establish a colony without first arranging to send wise men along to instruct the youth...."*

In a new colony, ample opportunity is open to the careful legislator who desires to purify the customs and manners of the people. If he has virtue and genius, the land and the people at his disposal will inspire his soul with a plan for society. A writer can only vaguely trace the plan in advance because it is necessarily subject to the instability of all hypotheses; the problem has many forms, complications, and circumstances that are difficult to foresee and settle in detail.

Legislators Told How to Manage Men

Raynal's instructions to the legislators on how to manage people may be compared to a professor of agriculture lecturing his students: "The climate is the first rule for the farmer.

His resources determine his procedure. He must first consider his locality. If his soil is clay, he must do so and so. If his soil is sand, he must act in another manner. Every facility is open to the farmer who wishes to clear and improve his soil. If he is skillful enough, the manure at his disposal will suggest to him a plan of operation. A professor can only vaguely trace this plan in advance because it is necessarily subject to the instability of all hypotheses; the problem has many forms, complications, and circumstances that are difficult to foresee and settle in detail."

Oh, sublime writers! Please remember sometimes that this clay, this sand, and this manure which you so arbitrarily dispose of, are men! They are your equals! They are intelligent and free human beings like yourselves! As you have, they too have received from God the faculty to observe, to plan ahead, to think, and to judge for themselves!

A Temporary Dictatorship

Here is Mably on this subject of the law and the legislator. In the passages preceding the one here quoted, Mably has supposed the laws, due to a neglect of security, to be worn out. He continues to address the reader thusly: "Under these circumstances, it is obvious that the springs of government are slack. Give them a new tension, and the evil will be cured.... Think less of punishing faults, and more of rewarding that which you need. In this manner you will restore to your republic the vigor of youth. Because free people have been ignorant of this procedure, they have lost their liberty! But if the evil has made such headway that ordinary governmental procedures are unable to cure it, then resort to an extraordinary tribunal with considerable powers for a short time. The imagination of the citizens needs to be struck a hard blow."

In this manner, Mably continues through twenty volumes.

Under the influence of teaching like this — which stems from classical education — there came a time when everyone wished to place himself above mankind in order to arrange, organize, and regulate it in his own way.

Socialists Want Equality of Wealth

Next let us examine Condillac on this subject of the legislators and mankind:

"My Lord, assume the character of Lycurgus or of Solon. And before you finish reading this essay, amuse yourself by giving laws to some savages in America or Africa. Confine these nomads to fixed dwellings; teach them to tend flocks.... Attempt to develop the social consciousness that nature has planted in them.... Force them to begin to practice the duties of humanity.... Use punishment to cause sensual pleasures to become distasteful to them. Then you will see that every point of your legislation will cause these savages to lose a vice and gain a virtue.

All people have had laws. But few people have been happy. Why is this so? Because the legislators themselves have almost always been ignorant of the purpose of society, which is the uniting of families by a common interest.

Impartiality in law consists of two things: the establishing of equality in wealth and equality in dignity among the citizens.... As the laws establish greater equality, they become proportionately more precious to every citizen.... When all men are equal in wealth and dignity — and when the laws leave no hope of disturbing this equality — how can men then be agitated by greed, ambition, dissipation, idleness, sloth, envy, hatred, or jealousy?

What you have learned about the republic of Sparta should enlighten you on this question. No other state has ever had laws more in accord with the order of nature; of equality."

The Error of the Socialist Writers

Actually, it is not strange that during the seventeenth and eighteenth centuries the human race was regarded as inert matter, ready to receive everything — form, face, energy, movement, life — from a great prince or a great legislator or a great genius. These centuries were nourished on the study of antiquity. And antiquity presents everywhere — in Egypt, Persia, Greece, Rome — the spectacle of a few men molding mankind according to their whims, thanks to the prestige of force and of fraud. But this does not prove that this situation is desirable. It proves only that since men and society are capable of improvement, it is naturally to be expected that error, ignorance, despotism, slavery, and superstition should be greatest towards the origins of history. The writers quoted above were not in error when they found ancient institutions to be such, but they were in error when they offered them for the admiration and imitation of future generations. Uncritical and childish conformists, they took for granted the grandeur, dignity, morality, and happiness of the artificial societies of the ancient world. They did not understand that knowledge appears and grows with the passage of time; and that in proportion to this growth of knowledge, might takes the side of right, and society regains possession of itself.

What Is Liberty?

Actually, what is the political struggle that we witness? It is the instinctive struggle of all people toward liberty. And what is this liberty, whose very name makes the heart beat faster and shakes the world? Is it not the union of all liberties — liberty of conscience, of education, of association, of the press, of travel, of labor, of trade? In short, is not liberty the freedom of every person to make full use of his faculties, so long as he does not harm other persons while doing so? Is not liberty the destruction of all despotism — including, of course, legal despotism? Finally, is not liberty the restricting of the law only to its rational sphere of organizing the right of the individual to lawful self- defense; of punishing injustice?

It must be admitted that the tendency of the human race toward liberty is largely thwarted, especially in France. This is greatly due to a fatal desire — learned from the teachings of antiquity — that our writers on public affairs have in common: They desire to set themselves above mankind in order to arrange, organize, and regulate it according to their fancy.

Philanthropic Tyranny

While society is struggling toward liberty, these famous men who put themselves at its head are filled with the spirit of the seventeenth and eighteenth centuries. They think only of subjecting mankind to the philanthropic tyranny of their own social inventions. Like Rousseau, they desire to force mankind docilely to bear this yoke of the public welfare that they have dreamed up in their own imaginations.

This was especially true in 1789. No sooner was the old regime destroyed than society was subjected to still other artificial arrangements, always starting from the same point: the omnipotence of the law. Listen to the ideas of a few of the writers and politicians during that period:

> SAINT-JUST: "The legislator commands the future. It is for him to will the good of mankind. It is for him to make men what he wills them to be."

> ROBESPIERRE: "The function of government is to direct the physical and moral powers of the nation toward the end for which the commonwealth has come into being."

> BILLAUD-VARENNES: "A people who are to be returned to liberty must be formed anew. A strong force and vigorous action

are necessary to destroy old prejudices, to change old customs, to correct depraved affections, to restrict superfluous wants, and to destroy ingrained vices.... Citizens, the inexible austerity of Lycurgus created the firm foundation of the Spartan republic. The weak and trusting character of Solon plunged Athens into slavery. This parallel embraces the whole science of government."

LE PELLETIER: "Considering the extent of human degradation, I am convinced that it is necessary to effect a total regeneration and, if I may so express myself, of creating a new people."

The Socialists Want Dictatorship

Again, it is claimed that persons are nothing but raw material. It is not for them to will their own improvement; they are incapable of it. According to Saint-Just, only the legislator is capable of doing this. Persons are merely to be what the legislator wills them to be. According to Robespierre, who copies Rousseau literally, the legislator begins by decreeing the end for which the commonwealth has come into being. Once this is determined, the government has only to direct the physical and moral forces of the nation toward that end. Meanwhile, the inhabitants of the nation are to remain completely passive. And according to the teachings of Billaud-Varennes, the people should have no prejudices, no affections, and no desires except those authorized by the legislator. He even goes so far as to say that the inflexible austerity of one man is the foundation of a republic.

In cases where the alleged evil is so great that ordinary governmental procedures cannot cure it, Mably recommends a dictatorship to promote virtue: "Resort," he says, "to an extraordinary tribunal with considerable powers for a short time. The imagination of the citizens needs to be struck a hard blow." This doctrine has not been forgotten. Listen to Robespierre:

"The principle of the republican government is virtue, and the means required to establish virtue is terror. In our country we desire to substitute morality for selfishness, honesty for honor, principles for customs, duties for manners, the empire of reason for the tyranny of fashion, contempt of vice for contempt of poverty, pride for insolence, greatness of soul for vanity, love of glory for love of money, good people for good companions, merit for intrigue, genius for wit, truth for glitter, the charm of happiness for the boredom of pleasure, the greatness of man for the littleness of the great, a generous, strong, happy people for a good-natured, frivolous, degraded people; in short, we desire to substitute all the virtues and miracles of a republic for all the vices and absurdities of a monarchy."

Dictatorial Arrogance

At what a tremendous height above the rest of mankind does Robespierre here place himself! And note the arrogance with which he speaks. He is not content to pray for a great reawakening of the human spirit. Nor does he expect such a result from a well-ordered government. No, he himself will remake mankind, and by means of terror.

This mass of rotten and contradictory statements is extracted from a discourse by Robespierre in which he aims to explain the principles of morality which ought to guide a revolutionary government. Note that Robespierre's request for dictatorship is not made merely for the purpose of repelling a foreign invasion or putting down the opposing groups. Rather he wants a dictatorship in order that he may use terror to force upon the country his own principles of morality. He says that this act is only to be a temporary measure preceding a new constitution. But in reality, he desires nothing short of using terror to extinguish from France selfishness, honor, customs, manners, fashion, vanity, love of money, good companionship, intrigue, wit, sensuousness, and poverty. Not until he, Robespierre, shall have accomplished these miracles, as he so rightly calls them, will he permit the law to reign again.*

*At this point in the original French text, Mr. Bastiat pauses and speaks thusly to all do-gooders and would-be rulers of mankind: "Ah, you miserable creatures! You who think that you are so great! You who judge humanity to be so small! You who wish to reform everything! Why don't you reform yourselves? That task would be sufficient enough."

SPECIAL READING

The Indirect Approach to Despotism

Usually, however, these gentlemen — the reformers, the legislators, and the writers on public affairs — do not desire to impose direct despotism upon mankind. Oh no, they are too moderate and philanthropic for such direct action. Instead, they turn to the law for this despotism, this absolutism, this omnipotence. They desire only to make the laws.

To show the prevalence of this queer idea in France, I would need to copy not only the entire works of Mably, Raynal, Rousseau, and Fenelon — plus long extracts from Bossuet and Montesquieu — but also the entire proceedings of the Convention. I shall do no such thing; I merely refer the reader to them.

Napoleon Wanted Passive Mankind

It is, of course, not at all surprising that this same idea should have greatly appealed to Napoleon. He embraced it ardently and used it with vigor. Like a chemist, Napoleon considered all Europe to be material for his experiments. But, in due course, this material reacted against him.

At St. Helena, Napoleon — greatly disillusioned — seemed to recognize some initiative in mankind. Recognizing this, he became less hostile to liberty. Nevertheless, this did not prevent him from leaving this lesson to his son in his will: "To govern is to increase and spread morality, education, and happiness."

After all this, it is hardly necessary to quote the same opinions from Morelly, Babeuf, Owen, Saint-Simon, and Fourier. Here are, however, a few extracts from Louis Blanc's book on the organization of labor: "In our plan, society receives its momentum from power."

Now consider this: The impulse behind this momentum is to be supplied by the plan of Louis Blanc; his plan is to be forced upon society; the society referred to is the human race. Thus the human race is to receive its momentum from Louis Blanc.

Now it will be said that the people are free to accept or to reject this plan. Admittedly, people are free to accept or to reject advice from whomever they wish. But this is not the way in which Mr. Louis Blanc understands the matter. He expects that his plan will be legalized, and thus forcibly imposed upon the people by the power of the law:

> "In our plan, the state has only to pass labor laws (nothing else?) by means of which industrial progress can and must proceed in complete liberty. The state merely places society on an incline (that is all?). Then society will slide down this incline by the mere force of things, and by the natural workings of the established mechanism."

But what is this incline that is indicated by Mr. Louis Blanc? Does it not lead to an abyss? (No, it leads to happiness.) If this is true, then why does not society go there of its own choice? (Because society does not know what it wants; it must be propelled.) What is to propel it? (Power.) And who is to supply the impulse for this power? (Why, the inventor of the machine — in this instance, Mr. Louis Blanc.)

273

The Vicious Circle of Socialism

We shall never escape from this circle: the idea of passive mankind, and the power of the law being used by a great man to propel the people.

Once on this incline, will society enjoy some liberty? (Certainly.) And what is liberty, Mr. Louis Blanc?

Once and for all, liberty is not only a mere granted right; it is also the power granted to a person to use and to develop his faculties under a reign of justice and under the protection of the law.

And this is no pointless distinction; its meaning is deep and its consequences are difficult to estimate. For once it is agreed that a person, to be truly free, must have the power to use and develop his faculties, then it follows that every person has a claim on society for such education as will permit him to develop himself. It also follows that every person has a claim on society for tools of production, without which human activity cannot be fully effective. Now by what action can society give to every person the necessary education and the necessary tools of production, if not by the action of the state?

Thus, again, liberty is power. Of what does this power consist? (Of being educated and of being given the tools of production.) Who is to give the education and the tools of production? (Society, which owes them to everyone.) By what action is society to give tools of production to those who do not own them? (Why, by the action of the state.) And from whom will the state take them?

Let the reader answer that question. Let him also notice the direction in which this is taking us.

The Doctrine of the Democrats

The strange phenomenon of our times — one which will probably astound our descendants — is the doctrine based on this triple hypothesis: the total inertness of mankind, the omnipotence of the law, and the infallibility of the legislator. These three ideas form the sacred symbol of those who proclaim themselves totally democratic.

The advocates of this doctrine also profess to be social. So far as they are democratic, they place unlimited faith in mankind. But so far as they are social, they regard mankind as little better than mud. Let us examine this contrast in greater detail.

What is the attitude of the democrat when political rights are under discussion? How does he regard the people when a legislator is to be chosen? Ah, then it is claimed that the people have an instinctive wisdom; they are gifted with the finest perception; their will is always right; the general will cannot err; voting cannot be too universal.

When it is time to vote, apparently the voter is not to be asked for any guarantee of his wisdom. His will and capacity to choose wisely are taken for granted. Can the people be mistaken? Are we not living in an age of enlightenment? What! are the people always to be kept on leashes? Have they not won their rights by great effort and sacrifice? Have they not given ample proof of their intelligence and wisdom? Are they not adults? Are they not capable of judging for themselves? Do they not know what is best for themselves? Is there a class or a man who would be so bold as to set himself above the people, and judge and act for them? No, no, the people are and should be free.

They desire to manage their own affairs, and they shall do so.

But when the legislator is finally elected — ah! then indeed does the tone of his speech undergo a radical change. The people are returned to passiveness, inertness, and unconsciousness; the legislator enters into omnipotence. Now it is for him to initiate, to direct, to propel, and to organize. Mankind has only to submit; the hour of despotism has struck. We now observe this fatal idea: The people who, during the election, were so wise, so moral, and so perfect, now have no tendencies whatever; or if they have any, they are tendencies that lead downward into degradation.

The Socialist Concept of Liberty

But ought not the people be given a little liberty?

But Mr. Considerant has assured us that liberty leads inevitably to monopoly!

We understand that liberty means competition. But according to Mr. Louis Blanc, competition is a system that ruins the businessmen and exterminates the people. It is for this reason that free people are ruined and exterminated in proportion to their degree of freedom. (Possibly Mr. Louis Blanc should observe the results of competition in, for example, Switzerland, Holland, England, and the United States.)

Mr. Louis Blanc also tells us that competition leads to monopoly. And by the same reasoning, he thus informs us that low prices lead to high prices; that competition drives production to destructive activity; that competition drains away the sources of purchasing power; that competition forces an increase in production while, at the same time, it forces a decrease in consumption. From this, it follows that free people produce for the sake of not consuming; that liberty means oppression and madness among the people; and that Mr. Louis Blanc absolutely must attend to it.

Socialists Fear All Liberties

Well, what liberty should the legislators permit people to have? Liberty of conscience? (But if this were permitted, we would see the people taking this opportunity to become atheists.)

Then liberty of education? (But parents would pay professors to teach their children immorality and falsehoods; besides, according to Mr. Thiers, if education were left to national liberty, it would cease to be national, and we would be teaching our children the ideas of the Turks or Hindus; whereas, thanks to this legal despotism over education, our children now have the good fortune to be taught the noble ideas of the Romans.)

Then liberty of labor? (But that would mean competition which, in turn, leaves production unconsumed, ruins businessmen, and exterminates the people.)

Perhaps liberty of trade? (But everyone knows — and the advocates of protective tariffs have proved over and over again — that freedom of trade ruins every person who engages in it, and that it is necessary to suppress freedom of trade in order to prosper.)

Possibly then, liberty of association? (But, according to socialist doctrine, true liberty and voluntary association are in contradiction to each other, and the purpose of the socialists is to suppress liberty of association precisely in order to force people to associate together in true liberty.)

Clearly then, the conscience of the social democrats cannot permit persons to have any liberty because they believe that the nature of mankind tends always toward every kind of degradation and disaster. Thus, of course, the legislators must make plans for the people in order to save them from themselves.

This line of reasoning brings us to a challenging question: If people are as incapable, as immoral, and as ignorant as the politicians indicate, then why is the right of these same people to vote defended with such passionate insistence?

The Superman Idea

The claims of these organizers of humanity raise another question which I have often asked them and which, so far as I know, they have never answered: If the natural tendencies of mankind are so bad that it is not safe to permit people to be free, how is it that the tendencies of these organizers are always good? Do not the legislators and their appointed agents also belong to the human race? Or do they believe that they themselves are made of a finer clay than the rest of mankind? The organizers maintain that society, when left undirected, rushes headlong to its inevitable destruction because the instincts of the people are so perverse. The legislators claim to stop this suicidal course and to give it a saner direction. Apparently, then, the legislators and the organizers have received from Heaven an intelligence and virtue that place them beyond and above mankind; if so, let them show their titles to this superiority.

They would be the shepherds over us, their sheep. Certainly such an arrangement presupposes that they are naturally superior to the rest of us. And certainly we are fully justified in demanding from the legislators and organizers proof of this natural superiority.

The Socialists Reject Free Choice

Please understand that I do not dispute their right to invent social combinations, to advertise them, to advocate them, and to try them upon themselves, at their own expense and risk. But I do dispute their right to impose these plans upon us by law — by force — and to compel us to pay for them with our taxes.

I do not insist that the supporters of these various social schools of thought—the Proudhonists, the Cabetists, the Fourierists, the Universitarists, and the Protectionists — renounce their various ideas. I insist only that they renounce this one idea that they have in common: They need only to give up the idea of forcing us to acquiesce to their groups and series, their socialized projects, their free-credit banks, their Graeco-Roman concept of morality, and their commercial regulations. I ask only that we be permitted to decide upon these plans for ourselves; that we not be forced to accept them, directly or indirectly, if we find them to be contrary to our best interests or repugnant to our consciences.

But these organizers desire access to the tax funds and to the power of the law in order to carry out their plans. In addition to being oppressive and unjust, this desire also implies the fatal supposition that the organizer is infallible and mankind is incompetent. But, again, if persons are incompetent to judge for themselves, then why all this talk about universal suffrage?

The Cause of French Revolutions

This contradiction in ideas is, unfortunately but logically, reflected in events in France. For example, Frenchmen have led all other Europeans in obtaining their rights — or, more accurately, their political demands. Yet this fact has in no respect prevented us from becoming the most governed, the most regulated, the most imposed upon, the most harnessed, and the most exploited people in Europe. France also leads all other nations as the one where revolutions are constantly to be anticipated. And under the circumstances, it is quite natural that this should be the case.

And this will remain the case so long as our politicians continue to accept this idea that has been so well expressed by Mr. Louis Blanc: "Society receives its momentum from power." This will remain the case so long as human beings with feelings continue to remain passive; so long as they consider themselves incapable of bettering their prosperity and happiness by their own intelligence and their own energy; so long as they expect everything from the law; in short, so long as they imagine that their relationship to the state is the same as that of the sheep to the shepherd.

The Enormous Power of Government

As long as these ideas prevail, it is clear that the responsibility of government is enormous. Good fortune and bad fortune, wealth and destitution, equality and inequality, virtue and vice — all then depend upon political administration. It is burdened with everything, it undertakes everything, it does everything; therefore it is responsible for everything.

If we are fortunate, then government has a claim to our gratitude; but if we are unfortunate, then government must bear the blame. For are not our persons and property now at the disposal of government? Is not the law omnipotent?

In creating a monopoly of education, the government must answer to the hopes of the fathers of families who have thus been deprived of their liberty; and if these hopes are shattered, whose fault is it?

In regulating industry, the government has contracted to make it prosper; otherwise it is absurd to deprive industry of its liberty. And if industry now suffers, whose fault is it?

In meddling with the balance of trade by playing with tariffs, the government thereby contracts to make trade prosper; and if this results in destruction instead of prosperity, whose fault is it?

In giving protection instead of liberty to the industries for defense, the government has contracted to make them profitable; and if they become a burden to the taxpayers, whose fault is it?

Thus there is not a grievance in the nation for which the government does not voluntarily make itself responsible. Is it surprising, then, that every failure increases the threat of another revolution in France?

And what remedy is proposed for this? To extend indefinitely the domain of the law; that is, the responsibility of government.

But if the government undertakes to control and to raise wages, and cannot do it; if the government undertakes to care for all who may be in want, and cannot do it; if the government undertakes to support all unemployed workers, and cannot do it; if the government undertakes to lend interest- free money to all borrowers, and cannot do it; if, in these words that we regret to say escaped from the pen of Mr. de Lamartine, "The state considers that its purpose is to enlighten, to develop, to enlarge, to strengthen, to spiritualize, and to sanctify the soul of the people" — and if the government cannot do all of these things, what then? Is it not certain that after every government failure — which, alas! is more than probable — there will be an equally inevitable revolution?

Politics and Economics

[Now let us return to a subject that was briefly discussed in the opening pages of this thesis: the relationship of economics and of politics — political economy.*]

Translator's note: Mr. Bastiat has devoted three other books and several articles to the development of the ideas contained in the three sentences of the following paragraph.

A science of economics must be developed before a science of politics can be logically formulated. Essentially, economics is the science of determining whether the interests of human beings are harmonious or antagonistic. This must be known before a science of politics can be formulated to determine the proper functions of government.

Immediately following the development of a science of economics, and at the very beginning of the formulation of a science of politics, this all-important question must be answered: What is law? What ought it to be?

What is its scope; its limits? Logically, at what point do the just powers of the legislator stop?

I do not hesitate to answer: Law is the common force organized to act as an obstacle to injustice. In short, law is justice.

Proper Legislative Functions

It is not true that the legislator has absolute power over our persons and property. The existence of persons and property preceded the existence of the legislator, and his function is only to guarantee their safety. It is not true that the function of law is to regulate our consciences, our ideas, our wills, our education, our opinions, our work, our trade, our talents, or our pleasures. The function of law is to protect the free exercise of these rights, and to prevent any person from interfering with the free exercise of these same rights by any other person.

Since law necessarily requires the support of force, its lawful domain is only in the areas where the use of force is necessary. This is justice.

Every individual has the right to use force for lawful self- defense. It is for this reason that the collective force — which is only the organized combination of the individual forces — may lawfully be used for the same purpose; and it cannot be used legitimately for any other purpose.

Law is solely the organization of the individual right of self-defense which existed before law was formalized. Law is justice.

Law and Charity Are Not the Same

The mission of the law is not to oppress persons and plunder them of their property, even though the law may be acting in a philanthropic spirit. Its mission is to protect persons and property.

Furthermore, it must not be said that the law may be philanthropic if, in the process, it refrains from oppressing persons and plundering them of their property; this would be a contradiction. The law cannot avoid having an effect upon persons and property; and if the law acts in any manner except to protect them, its actions then necessarily violate the liberty of persons and their right to own property.

The law is justice — simple and clear, precise and bounded. Every eye can see it, and every mind can grasp it; for justice is measurable, immutable, and unchangeable. Justice is neither more than this nor less than this.

If you exceed this proper limit — if you attempt to make the law religious, fraternal, equalizing, philanthropic, industrial, literary, or artistic — you will then be lost in an uncharted territory, in vagueness and uncertainty, in a forced utopia or, even worse, in a multitude of utopias, each striving to seize the law and impose it upon you. This is true because fraternity and philanthropy, unlike justice, do not have precise limits. Once started, where will you stop? And where will the law stop itself?

The High Road to Communism

Mr. de Saint-Cricq would extend his philanthropy only to some of the industrial groups; he would demand that the law control

the consumers to benefit the producers.

Mr. Considerant would sponsor the cause of the labor groups; he would use the law to secure for them a guaranteed minimum of clothing, housing, food, and all other necessities of life.

Mr. Louis Blanc would say — and with reason — that these minimum guarantees are merely the beginning of complete fraternity; he would say that the law should give tools of production and free education to all working people. Another person would observe that this arrangement would still leave room for inequality; he would claim that the law should give to everyone — even in the most inaccessible hamlet—luxury, literature, and art.

All of these proposals are the high road to communism; legislation will then be — in fact, it already is — the battlefield for the fantasies and greed of everyone.

The Basis for Stable Government

Law is justice. In this proposition a simple and enduring government can be conceived. And I defy anyone to say how even the thought of revolution, of insurrection, of the slightest uprising could arise against a government whose organized force was confined only to suppressing injustice.

Under such a regime, there would be the most prosperity — and it would be the most equally distributed. As for the sufferings that are inseparable from humanity, no one would even think of accusing the government for them. This is true because, if the force of government were limited to suppressing injustice, then government would be as innocent of these sufferings as it is now innocent of changes in the temperature.

As proof of this statement, consider this question: Have the people ever been known to rise against the Court of Appeals, or mob a Justice of the Peace, in order to get higher wages, free credit, tools of production, favorable tariffs, or government-created jobs? Everyone knows perfectly well that such matters are not within the jurisdiction of the Court of Appeals or a Justice of the Peace. And if government were limited to its proper functions, everyone would soon learn that these matters are not within the jurisdiction of the law itself.

But make the laws upon the principle of fraternity — proclaim that all good, and all bad, stem from the law; that the law is responsible for all individual misfortunes and all social inequalities — then the door is open to an endless succession of complaints, irritations, troubles, and revolutions.

Justice Means Equal Rights

Law is justice. And it would indeed be strange if law could properly be anything else! Is not justice right? Are not rights equal? By what right does the law force me to conform to the social plans of Mr. Mimerel, Mr. de Melun, Mr. Thiers, or Mr. Louis Blanc? If the law has a moral right to do this, why does it not, then, force these gentlemen to submit to my plans? Is it logical to suppose that nature has not given me sufficient imagination to dream up a utopia also? Should the law choose one fantasy among many, and put the organized force of government at its service only?

Law is justice. And let it not be said — as it continually is said — that under this concept, the law would be atheistic, individualistic, and heartless; that it would make mankind in its own image. This is an absurd conclusion, worthy only of those worshippers of government who believe that the law is mankind.

Nonsense! Do those worshippers of government believe that free persons will cease to act? Does it follow that if we receive no energy from the law, we shall receive no energy at all? Does it follow that if the law is restricted to the function of protecting the

free use of our faculties, we will be unable to use our faculties? Suppose that the law does not force us to follow certain forms of religion, or systems of association, or methods of education, or regulations of labor, or regulations of trade, or plans for charity; does it then follow that we shall eagerly plunge into atheism, hermitary, ignorance, misery, and greed? If we are free, does it follow that we shall no longer recognize the power and goodness of God? Does it follow that we shall then cease to associate with each other, to help each other, to love and succor our unfortunate brothers, to study the secrets of nature, and to strive to improve ourselves to the best of our abilities?

The Path to Dignity and Progress

Law is justice. And it is under the law of justice — under the reign of right; under the influence of liberty, safety, stability, and responsibility — that every person will attain his real worth and the true dignity of his being. It is only under this law of justice that mankind will achieve — slowly, no doubt, but certainly — God's design for the orderly and peaceful progress of humanity.

It seems to me that this is theoretically right, for whatever the question under discussion — whether religious, philosophical, political, or economic; whether it concerns prosperity, morality, equality, right, justice, progress, responsibility, cooperation, property, labor, trade, capital, wages, taxes, population, finance, or government — at whatever point on the scientific horizon I begin my researches, I invariably reach this one conclusion: The solution to the problems of human relationships is to be found in liberty.

Proof of an Idea

And does not experience prove this? Look at the entire world. Which countries contain the most peaceful, the most moral, and the happiest people? Those people are found in the countries where the law least interferes with private affairs; where government is least felt; where the individual has the greatest scope, and free opinion the greatest influence; where administrative powers are fewest and simplest; where taxes are lightest and most nearly equal, and popular discontent the least excited and the least justifiable; where individuals and groups most actively assume their responsibilities, and, consequently, where the morals of admittedly imperfect human beings are constantly improving; where trade, assemblies, and associations are the least restricted; where labor, capital, and populations suffer the fewest forced displacements; where mankind most nearly follows its own natural inclinations; where the inventions of men are most nearly in harmony with the laws of God; in short, the happiest, most moral, and most peaceful people are those who most nearly follow this principle: Although mankind is not perfect, still, all hope rests upon the free and voluntary actions of persons within the limits of right; law or force is to be used for nothing except the administration of universal justice.

The Desire to Rule over Others

This must be said: There are too many "great" men in the world — legislators, organizers, do-gooders, leaders of the people, fathers of nations, and so on, and so on. Too many persons place themselves above mankind; they make a career of organizing it, patronizing it, and ruling it.

Now someone will say: "You yourself are doing this very thing."

True. But it must be admitted that I act in an entirely different sense; if I have joined the ranks of the reformers, it is solely for the purpose of persuading them to leave people alone. I do not look upon people as Vancauson looked upon his automaton. Rather, just as the physiologist accepts the human body as it is, so do I accept people as they are. I desire only to study and admire.

My attitude toward all other persons is well illustrated by this story from a celebrated traveler: He arrived one day in the midst of a tribe of savages, where a child had just been born. A crowd of soothsayers, magicians, and quacks — armed with rings, hooks, and cords — surrounded it. One said: "This child will never smell the perfume of a peace-pipe unless I stretch his nostrils." Another said: "He will never be able to hear unless I draw his ear-lobes down to his shoulders." A third said: "He will never see the sunshine unless I slant his eyes." Another said: "He will never stand upright unless I bend his legs." A fifth said: "He will never learn to think unless I flatten his skull."

"Stop," cried the traveler. "What God does is well done. Do not claim to know more than He. God has given organs to this frail creature; let them develop and grow strong by exercise, use, experience, and liberty."

Let Us Now Try Liberty

God has given to men all that is necessary for them to accomplish their destinies. He has provided a social form as well as a human form. And these social organs of persons are so constituted that they will develop themselves harmoniously in the clean air of liberty. Away, then, with quacks and organizers! Away with their rings, chains, hooks, and pincers! Away with their artificial systems! Away with the whims of governmental administrators, their socialized projects, their centralization, their tariffs, their government schools, their state religions, their free credit, their bank monopolies, their regulations, their restrictions, their equalization by taxation, and their pious moralizations!

And now that the legislators and do-gooders have so futilely inflicted so many systems upon society, may they finally end where they should have begun: May they reject all systems, and try liberty; for liberty is an acknowledgment of faith in God and His works.

SPECIAL READING

Made for "Real World" Homeschooling

FAITH-BUILDING

We ensure that a biblical worldview is integral to all of our curriculum. We start with the Bible as our standard and build our courses from there. We strive to demonstrate biblical teachings and truth in all subjects.

TRUSTED

We've been publishing quality Christian books for over 40 years. We publish best-selling Christian authors like Henry Morris, Ken Ham, and Ray Comfort.

EFFECTIVE

We use experienced educators to create our curriculum for real-world use. We don't just teach knowledge by itself. We also teach how to apply and use that knowledge.

ENGAGING

We make our curriculum fun and inspire a joy for learning. We go beyond rote memorization by emphasizing hands-on activities and real-world application.

PRACTICAL

We design our curriculum to be so easy that you can open the box and start homeschooling. We provide easy-to-use schedules and pre-planned lessons that make education easy for busy homeschooling families.

FLEXIBLE

We create our material to be readily adaptable to any homeschool program. We know that one size does not fit all and that homeschooling requires materials that can be customized for your family's wants and needs.

VISIT **MASTERBOOKS.COM** — *Where Faith Grows!* — TO SEE OUR FULL LINE OF FAITH-BUILDING CURRICULUM OR CALL 800-999-3777.

JACOBS' MATH

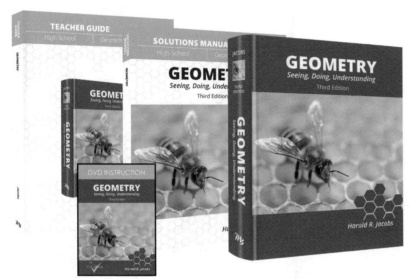

JACOBS' GEOMETRY

An authoritative standard for years, with nearly one million students having learned geometry principles through the text.

Jacobs' Geometry	978-1-68344-020-8
Solutions Manual	978-1-68344-021-5
Teacher Guide	978-1-68344-022-2
3-BOOK SET	**978-1-68344-036-9**
Geometry DVD	713438-10236-8
3-BOOK / 1-DVD SET	**978-1-68344-037-6**

JACOBS' ALGEBRA

This provides a full year of math in a clearly written format with guidance for teachers as well as for students who are self-directed.

Elementary Algebra	978-0-89051-985-1
Solutions Manual	978-0-89051-987-5
Teacher Guide	978-0-89051-986-8
3-BOOK SET	**978-0-89051-988-2**
Elementary Algebra DVD	713438-10237-5
3-BOOK / 1-DVD SET	**978-1-68344-038-3**